THE UNDEFEATED

ALSO BY JIM DENT

The Junction Boys

You're Out and You're Ugly, Too!
(with Durwood Merrill)

King of the Cowboys

THE UNDEFEATED

*The Oklahoma Sooners and the Greatest Winning
Streak in College Football*

JIM DENT

THOMAS DUNNE BOOKS / ST. MARTIN'S PRESS

NEW YORK

THOMAS DUNNE BOOKS.
An imprint of St. Martin's Press.

www.stmartins.com

Book design by Diane Hobbing of Snap-Haus Graphics

Library of Congress Cataloging-in-Publication Data

Dent, Jim.
The undefeated : the Oklahoma Sooners and the
greatest winning streak in college football / Jim Dent.—1st ed.
p.   cm.
ISBN 0-312-26656-1
1. Oklahoma Sooners (Football team)—History.   2. University of
Oklahoma—Football—History.   I. Title.

GV958.U585 D45 2001
796.332'63'0976637—dc21
2001034896

First Edition: September 2001

10   9   8   7   6   5   4   3   2   1

This book is dedicated to the resilient Oklahomans. Tough land. Tough times. *Tougher* people.

CONTENTS

One day I mentioned to Darrell Royal that I was writing a book about Oklahoma's fabled forty-seven-game winning streak. Royal, of course, won a slew of national championships as the coach of the Texas Longhorns and was an All-American quarterback for the Sooners in 1949. He reached for my notebook and entered this data on the back:

31-0
16-4-2
47-0

It didn't take a math major to interpret this information. Simply, from the second game of the 1948 season to the eighth game of the '57 season, the Oklahoma Sooners under Bud Wilkinson won ninety-four games, lost four, and tied two (94-4-2). The Sooners compiled winning streaks of thirty-one *and* forty-seven games. Are you listening Bob Stoops, Bobby Bowden, and Steve Spurrier? Is there anyone out there who can top *that*?

To eclipse the Division I record today for consecutive wins, a team would need to compile four straight undefeated seasons, along with four straight wins in both the conference and the national championship games.

What Wilkinson and the Sooners accomplished in winning forty-seven straight is the football equivalent of Joe DiMaggio's fifty-six-game hitting streak. In fact, it might be more difficult to break. Once you read about the tedious preparation, along with the fourth-quarter comebacks, you will understand the intense pressure that accompanied this feat.

The first person I would like to thank for making the book and this journey possible is Peter J. Wolverton, the associate publisher of Thomas Dunne Books, who once again saw the merit of the idea and seized it. A writer is extremely lucky to have two great editors—Wolverton and Jim Donovan, my literary agent. My twin gunslingers greatly improved this book.

The Undefeated owes much of its heart and soul to Charlie Rountree and Joe Rector (captain of the '58 team). They welcomed me to Oklahoma with open arms. They opened doors and even knocked down a few when I needed it. I called upon these two friends almost daily, and they never failed. They provided enough information for two books.

A big round of applause for Jerry Cross, Bob Burris, and Johnny Pellow, three of the most interesting characters of the Wilkinson era. I just wish that everyone could someday take a three-hour car trip with Rector, Rountree, Cross, and Burris to Muskogee. The ribs were never better and the laughs never louder at Mahlon's Barbeque.

A special thanks goes to Norman Lamb and Lanny Ross, two of the greatest guys in Oklahoma and men with special insight and great stories.

Though a bibliography is contained within these pages, the late Harold Keith receives a standing ovation for his great book titled *Forty-seven Straight*. The former OU sports information director was a great resource for anyone who ever crossed his path, including me. I would also like to acknowledge authors Jay Wilkinson *(Bud Wilkinson: An Intimate Portrait of an American Legend)*, Donald Worster *(Dust Bowl)*, Dr. George Cross *(Presidents Can't Punt)*, and Brent Clark *(Sooner Century)*.

Listed below are the people who either were interviewed or provided assistance in the writing and research of this book. I didn't mean for it to be a Who's Who in Oklahoma sports. But it certainly reads like one:

Claude Arnold, Emil Bayouth, Dr. Don Beck, John Herman Bell, George Brewer, Ken Brunsman, Buddy Burris, Lyle Burris, Lynn Burris, Gary Buxton, Gene Calame, Tom Carroll, Joe Castiglione, Dick Champlin, Brent Clark, Bob Cornell, Leon Cross, Carl Dodd, Isabel Dove, Jan Fikcs, Ronnie Fletcher, Jerry Furseth, Gray Fredrickson, Prentice Gautt, Buzz Goodwin, Merrill Green, Kenny Greer, Angie Harris, Billy Carr Harris, Jimmy Harris, Hoggy Harrison, Doc Hearon, Brewster Hobby, Danny Hodge, Steve Jennings, Wallace Johnson, Buddy Leake, Bob Loughridge, Doug Marcella, J. W. Mashburn, Paul Massad, Matt Mays, Tommy McDonald, Norman McNabb, Harry Moore, Jay O'Neal, Buddy Oujesky, Phil Perry, Sally Pricer, Port Robertson, Jakie Sandefer, Byron Searcy, David Shelton, Blackie Sherrod, Dr. Harry Singleton, Harry Singleton Jr., Lee Allan Smith, Dick Snider, Clendon Thomas, Jerry Tubbs, Marlene Tubbs, Billy Vessels, Leon Vineyard, Warren Weakland, Stan West, and John Wooten.

Last but not least, Rolly "Big Cat" Dent again provided moral support and kept my chair warm during the coffee breaks. Perhaps I should thank him for letting me use *his* chair.

Jim Dent
April 7, 2001

When I think about the fabulous Oklahoma football tradition, the first thing that comes to mind is Bud Wilkinson and his great teams of the fifties. The forty-seven-game winning streak was one for the ages, and I doubt that any big-time college team will ever break that record.

The game of college football was lucky that a man like Bud Wilkinson came along in 1947 to lead the Sooners. He created a legacy and raised the standard for all of us. I still remember thinking that I was stepping into some mighty big shoes back in 1973, when I took over the head coaching job at the University of Oklahoma. Talk about feeding the monster. My job was *not* to win games. My job was to win national championships.

Bud Wilkinson was one of the truly unique individuals to coach the college game. Here was a guy with a great amount of brain-power and savvy. He coached an offense that was far ahead of its time, and I like to think that in the seventies and eighties we were innovative, too. The Wilkinson years were marked by both great imagination and fine execution. The Sooner State came to love its football in that era. We are all still proud of Bud's three national championships and a winning streak that will never be broken.

I saw many game films from this era and let me tell you that I was shocked at the speed of those guys. I mean, I thought they would be three yards and a cloud of dust. No way. these guys were fast, agile, and ran the option just like some of the great ones two decades later. Jimmy Harris, Jerry Tubbs, Clendon Thomas, and Tommy McDonald were some of the great players of that time.

I'm not so sure that Oklahoma football would have won seven national championships if it wasn't for those great teams of the fifties. I wonder just how successful I would have been without that great tradition behind me. A few years ago, thanks to all of our success at Oklahoma, we were able to lure another outstanding coach to Norman by the name of Bob Stoops. He has returned the Sooners to their rightful place of glory. From Wilkinson to Stoops, Oklahomans have a lot to be proud of. I feel fortunate to be right in the middle of that group.

A lot of people might not remember that I was a college football player myself in the fifties. I was playing for the University of Arkansas during the time of the Oklahoma winning streak. In fact, I was on the team plane traveling from Dallas back to Fayetteville that fateful afternoon in November of 1957, reading a copy of *Sports Illustrated,* when the pilot came on the public address system and said, "Gentlemen, you might be interested to know about this score: Notre Dame 7, Oklahoma nothing." I almost fell out of my chair. Right there on the cover of *Sports Illustrated* was the headline "Why Oklahoma is Unbeatable." I found out that day that no one is really unbeatable.

That forty-seven-game winning streak meant so much to the people of Oklahoma. They were looking for something to hang their dreams on. The state was battered pretty badly during the Dust Bowl, and it was Bud Wilkinson and the Sooners who brought the morale back. You see, this event goes beyond football. It is a lesson about faith and resiliency. I think that people all over America could learn a lot about life itself from this great story.

Barry Switzer
Norman, Oklahoma

1

TIGHTWIRE

A football sailed high above the east grandstand of Owen Field, just a brown speck against a cloudless sky while Bud Wilkinson, the man in a gray flannel suit, paced the sideline, watched, and waited. A crowd of 50,878 braced itself for the absolute worst.

"Dangit, Bud, he's gonna screw it up!" assistant coach Gomer Jones yelled. "That boy ain't got the sense of a mullet."

Jimmy Harris, a tall, wiry sophomore, circled underneath the punt and sneaked a peek upfield at the band of TCU Horned Frogs charging toward him in a blur of purple and white. His heart ran faster than Citation. Every eye traced the flight of the football as it dived toward Harris. Wilkinson said a fast prayer for his Sooners, a team as untamed as the Oklahoma wind.

This September afternoon of 1954, the Oklahoma Sooners were walking a tightwire, having already lost four fumbles, along with starting quarterback Gene Dan Calame, one of the most dependable and durable players anyone could remember, who now lay in a painful knot on the bench, his torso so battered he could barely breathe. Gene Dan had prevailed through fifty-seven minutes of the '54 season opener a week earlier against California in spite of this disturbing prognosis from the attending physician: "His eleventh and twelfth ribs are loose, sort of bouncing together like two xylophone boards." Calame inured himself against the pain with a generous pregame injection of Novocain. Numb from neck to waist, he managed to lead the Sooners past the Cal Bears 27–13, and after the game the doctor who had prescribed the needle said, "He's quite a boy, isn't he?"

Doc didn't know Gene Dan had been shooting up with painkillers for various injuries since the ninth grade and could spell *Novocain* backward if he had to.

Harris took most of the snaps in the practices leading to the TCU game. Everyone already had an opinion about young Jimmy, some of them not so favorable. He had swaggered into Norman a year earlier with an ego the size of Texas, his native state, and an eye for every skirt that shimmied across campus.

Port Robertson, the team's czar of discipline, had approached Jimmy a few weeks earlier and said, "Peahead, I guess I'll have to get a little red wagon to cart your ego around." Robertson, an ex-army captain, struck fear into the heart of every Sooner. Players who broke Port's rules ran seventy-two stadium steps at five in the morning until they threw up. He addressed all of them as "peahead."

Since the fall of 1947, when Wilkinson became the head coach, the Oklahoma Sooners had been a machine churning up the south plains. They had compiled a thirty-one-game winning streak and won their first national championship in 1950. Billy Vessels, one of the best all-round players in the history of college football, won the Heisman Trophy in '52.

Wilkinson stood shoulder-to-shoulder with the best coaches in the college game—Frank Leahy, Paul "Bear" Bryant, Gen. Robert Neyland, and Biggie Munn. The sporting press believed Wilkinson was on the verge of greatness once more. His Sooners had won ten straight, dating to the third game of the 1953 season. Now if only he could put a harness on this wild bunch.

Wilkinson was trim and athletic at age thirty-eight and in better shape than some of his players. He worked out, jogged, played golf, and was deeply tanned most of the year. On the sideline, he wore a red tie, a gray suit, blue socks, deeply glossed dress shoes, and a fedora when the weather called for it. This was the era when most college coaches went days without shaving and chili stains on the shirt were a sign the man had enjoyed a good meal. Television had yet to train its prying eyepiece on the sport, and the better part of a coach's wardrobe was a gray sweatshirt and white socks. A few rare exceptions, like Wilkinson and Leahy, along with Paul Brown of the Cleveland Browns, even bothered to knot a necktie before kickoff. Leahy preferred bow ties.

Talk around the fraternity was that Bud Wilkinson was the product of his own vanity. Coaches were not supposed to dress like bankers and lawyers and Adlai Stevenson himself. But in Oklahoma, where folks were gratified with any symbol of success, you could hang any photograph of Wilkinson over the fireplace. *Life* magazine's photo spread on their dapper coach had been dazzling, and *Sports Illustrated* was planning a cover story. It truly felt like Oklahomans were raising a favorite son to become the next commander in chief.

So conservative was Wilkinson, at least on the surface, that he had been dubbed the "Great White Father." The Sooners feared him, but in a different way than Robertson. Wilkinson was distant from his players and rarely excused injuries or the tiniest mistakes. He didn't brutalize his players as Bear Bryant had for years. But he did cut to the quick with the cold blade of his calculating mind.

His number-one project at the moment was Jimmy Harris, who had replaced Calame at quarterback in the second quarter against TCU. Though Jimmy's arrogance had pissed off many Sooners, Wilkinson viewed him as a boy with a load of moxie. If the Sooners were to win another national championship, they would do it behind Harris, Wilkinson believed.

Wilkinson couldn't explain why he knew so much about football players, but after eating, drinking, and sleeping the game for twenty years, he had developed a sixth sense. Bud had a way of taking a flashlight to a boy's soul. He also knew how to motivate, though his manner seemed offbeat.

A year earlier, when the freshman class of '53 arrived on campus, he had called a meeting on the fourth floor of the Jefferson House, the jock dorm on the Oklahoma campus. The roomed was filled with such blue-chippers as Tommy McDonald, Jerry Tubbs, John Bell, Billy Pricer, Jay O'Neal, Edmon Gray, and Harris.

"If you will dedicate yourselves, you will win a national championship before you leave this campus," Wilkinson told the boys. "But it will require a commitment like you have never given before."

Now those boys were sophomores and on the verge of becoming the heart and soul of the Sooners. Naturally, some jealousy was developing among the upperclassmen who were now losing starting jobs to the new kids.

One player you didn't want to cross was senior center/linebacker Kurt Burris, a six-two, 220-pound package of muscle and grit. In the one-platoon era, when players played both offense and defense, Burris was hell on wheels and the meanest man in college football. He grew up on an eighty-acre farm in Muskogee, plowing behind a team of mules, and as a teenager could stand on a flatbed truck all afternoon and toss bales of hay fifteen feet into the barn's loft. He beat up at least one of his four younger brothers every day just for practice.

At the moment, the target of his ire was the cocky sophomore quarterback.

"If that Jimmy Harris don't stop struttin' so much, he's gonna dislocate a hip," Burris said to anyone who would listen, and they all did.

Burris was a bully. It had been an Oklahoma football ritual for years that any uppity underclassman would be broken like a wild mustang, and Burris gladly appointed himself as the cowboy in charge of this rodeo.

The week before the TCU game, Burris drew a mental bull's-eye on Jimmy's jaw as the mouthy boy lined up in the backfield on the punt protection team. Most upperclassmen had been tipped on what was coming and held their breath for the moment when Burris would unload. Bursting between the guard and the tackle, Burris drew back his right fist. Since there were no facemasks in college football, he had a clean shot at the target. With a loud pop, two front teeth were disengaged. His mission accomplished, Burris then peeled back and ran upfield, hunting for somebody else to abuse. He didn't know that Jimmy was right on his tail, spitting out pieces of broken teeth.

About twenty yards up the field, Jimmy jumped on Burris's back and began pounding the sides of his helmet with both fists. Blood from Jimmy's mouth poured onto Burris's white jersey. Teammates tore them apart before Burris could land another punch.

As the two were separated, Burris wheeled and said, "Remember what I'm tellin' you, boy. No sophomore oughta be startin' for this football team."

Harris smiled a gap-toothed smile and walked away.

Wilkinson grimaced at the sight of blood. But Jimmy, he knew, could talk a big game, and also back it up.

Wilkinson had several other options to replace Calame. He could have chosen steady senior Pat O'Neal or his brother, Jay, the most highly recruited quarterback from the state of Oklahoma two years earlier. Harris and Jay O'Neal were sophomores. Jay O'Neal was more low-key and seemed a better fit for Wilkinson's conservative formula, since the coach firmly believed in moving the chains and protecting the ball.

"Never depend on the big play," Wilkinson preached.

Harris was the antithesis of that sermon. The boy had lightning quickness and a flair for the dramatic. While Wilkinson worshiped his own system, he knew it was time for a change. The offense ached for a kick in the backside, and if the Sooners were to win another national championship, the chips would ride on the young stud from Texas.

• • •

Oklahoma–TCU was the matchup America lusted for—two great teams, two great coaches, and enough part-time roughnecks on both teams to bury six thousand feet of drilling pipe before sundown. The Sooners were ranked number three in the Associated Press poll and the Frogs number four.

On one sideline stood Wilkinson, tall and fluid, the portrait of the movie star as coach.

On the other sideline was Orthol "Abe" Martin, the good-ol' country boy from Jacksboro, Texas, who chomped an unlit cigar constantly. Some folks took him for a hick, but the perceptive ones knew him to be a nabob of the subtle psychological ploy. The vilest oath he ever uttered was "Shistol Pot," a spoonerism for "Pistol Shot." In practice, he liked to crawl on hands and knees into the huddle, peer up at the boys, and say, "Run Thirty-four."

About twenty minutes before kickoff, he had walked to the center of the TCU locker room, removed his hat, placed it over his heart, and stared at the floor for several seconds before speaking: "Laddies, hold tight to your left nut today, because we're playin' one of the best teams in America."

To keep this ten-game winning streak alive and remain a contender for the national title, Oklahoma would have to slow down one of the best offensive units in the country, led by quarterback Chuck Curtis and jitterbug halfback Jim Swink. TCU was one of the powerhouses of the Southwest Conference, having risen to glory in the midthirties on the arm of Slingin' Sammy Baugh, then capturing the

1938 national championship with Davey O'Brien at quarterback. O'Brien became the fourth player to win the Heisman Trophy.

Oklahoma trailed the Frogs 2–0 at halftime, and every Sooner expected to hear one of Wilkinson's patented halftime speeches. He had been known to quote Churchill, Byron, and Teddy Roosevelt in the same paragraph.

But Wilkinson traveled a rare road this day, preferring to stick to Xs and Os. The only inspirational words were, "Men, this is the toughest game we'll play all season. They're a great team, and they won't let up until the final gun. But win today and we'll keep winning for a long time."

It was early in the third quarter when Harris stationed himself beneath the punt that sliced through the south wind. Wilkinson was about to learn if Harris was the right choice to lead the Sooners. As he fielded the punt at the Oklahoma thirty-one, he was trapped by a gaggle of Frogs but angled toward the sideline and began picking up blocks. Fans in the north end zone spotted a running lane unfolding ahead of Harris, and the boy dimly heard a thunderous roll from behind him. Before the Frogs could blink, he split the first wall of defenders and was quickly at the fifty with only one TCU defender in his path. Out of the blue rumbled Jerry Tubbs, a Sooner lineman, who weighed 210 pounds but was faster than most of the backs. Tubbs's chin thrust forward and his gangly arms pumped wildly. He actually passed Harris and managed to chop down the last man at the forty. As Harris cruised alone toward the end zone, his teammates swore they saw the familiar swagger. The Sooners now led 7–2.

Oklahoma held the upper hand for all of about three minutes. The Frogs moved down the field eighty-one yards on ten running plays. At the five-yard line, from the spread formation, quarterback Chuck Curtis rolled right and, when he found no receiver open, hip-faked Sooner cornerback Bob Burris and sprinted into the end zone. The Frogs led 9–7.

This day, the Sooners would fumble ten times, losing five, a sign of their immaturity. Following Curtis's touchdown, Harris led the Sooners on a fifty-six-yard drive to the TCU two before halfback Bob Herndon fumbled into the end zone and linebacker Hugh Pitts recovered.

The game was slipping away from Oklahoma as the Frogs' offense grabbed control. They moved eighty yards for another touchdown, with Swink doing most of his damage on the ground. Curtis picked up good yardage on two end runs. Swink scored around right end from the three-yard line, and Wilkinson paced and wondered if his raw quarterback could lead them back.

Oklahoma trailed 16–7 with ten minutes to play when Harris trotted confidently into the huddle.

"Look, you guyths," he said, his tongue hampered by two missing teeth. "We're gonna run the theventy, I mean seventy series. Got it?"

Harris peered across the huddle at a grinning Burris.

"Got it," Burris said. Then he leveled his eyes on Jimmy and said, "We're gonna win this damn game. Just don't screw it up, meathead."

"Don't worry about me," Jimmy said. "Worry about yourthelf."

That was all that anyone needed to lisp. Harris moved the chains, just as Wilkinson had ordered. Eight yards, five yards, seven yards, five yards, eleven yards, five yards. He didn't call a single pass. From the twenty-eight-yard line, Herndon slanted through a huge hole opened by Burris and wasn't tackled until he reached the TCU seven. Running the Split-T option to the left, Harris kept the ball and scored standing up. Now the Sooners trailed by two points.

The defense held, and minutes later TCU's Ben Taylor drove a high spiral through the south wind to Buddy Leake, the only senior in the Sooners backfield and a young man who had grown up fast in

1951. That year, Leake was rushed into the lineup as a freshman when Billy Vessels tore knee ligaments in the Texas game. Leake would start six games at left halfback and lead the Big Seven Conference in scoring. It was the last year that freshmen were eligible for varsity play under NCAA rules.

The Sooner faithful were quite familiar with Leake's speed and versatility, and more than fifty thousand fans were on their feet when he fielded Taylor's punt and took off down the left sideline, his knees churning, his face glistening in the September sunlight. Leake was quickly behind the picket fence and picking up speed. Only one Horned Frog had a chance of stopping him, and that was TCU captain Johnny Crouch, who pulled him down at the ten-yard line. The return had covered fifty yards.

Herndon scored on the next play, taking the option pitch from Harris, and the Sooners led, 21–16.

Wilkinson had been so right about the Frogs. They just wouldn't give up. With Curtis now passing and Swink skittering between the tackles, TCU picked their way through the Sooners for another drive of eighty yards. Curtis hit Crouch with the winning touchdown pass in the right corner of the end zone. It covered twenty-one yards as the clock ticked toward triple zero. Owen Field fell deathly silent as an entire state lapsed into mourning. The ten-game winning streak had been sweet but far too short. Fans sat rigidly in their seats, some drawing deeply on cigarettes, and refused to go home. Defeat bored into their hearts. The philosophical ones were already telling themselves that the Sooners would simply have to regroup. Of course, the pollsters would drop OU out of the Top Ten, and everyone could just forget about the story planned for the cover of *Look* magazine.

Then, out of the blue, the fans witnessed a rare event that only Hollywood could have invented. Crouch sauntered toward field judge Don Rossi and held out the ball.

"Ref, I didn't catch it," he said. "I trapped it."

Back judge Don Looney ran from the other side of the field. He'd had a clear view of the play and wanted to discuss it with Rossi.

While the man in the gray flannel suit waited, watched, and paced, a crowd of 50,878 held its collective breath and prayed.

2

DUST BOWL

Long before the Oklahoma Sooners came to dominate the landscape, the land itself suffered through droughts, floods, and agrarian disasters. The thirties seemed to last forever. More than a million people migrated from Oklahoma in a decade when the soil dried up and blew away.

Oklahomans in 1930 suffered a double whammy as both the Great Depression and the drought arrived virtually on the same train. Ironically, two of the most brutal events of the twentieth century were born of a common thread. While farm operators of the Midwest were ignoring important environmental limits, Wall Street plowed ahead in spite of a top-heavy economy, thus helping to trigger the market crash of 1929.

Signs of doom were everywhere, and Oklahoma had become a metaphor for the Depression. In the eastern part of the state, banks and land companies were becoming increasingly impatient with the slow production of crops, mostly corn, and with the slow payment of loans by the landowners. America was moving rapidly into the era of the "factory farms," when lands were plowed and harvested by the tractor. For generations, fathers had taught their sons to plow behind a team of mules or horses. Now the farmers were falling behind in both production and payments. The motto of the times was "bigger farms and fewer men."

Entire families were literally tractored off their property as operators of the heavy machines steamrolled rickety shacks; a common sight was the shotgun-toting cropper standing tall and bull-chested on his front porch, staring a bullet hole through the goggle-eyed tractor man. Silently the farmer prayed. Two facts were self-evident: hell or high water couldn't stop a piece of machinery that big, and the first farmer to kill an operator would fry in the chair.

The upper eastern sector of the state was still a pale green, thanks to occasional rains, but a radical weather pattern was taking shape on the Oklahoma plains. Just west of Oklahoma City, the plains unfolded, and the horrific dust storms of the thirties roared all the way into the Panhandles of Oklahoma and Texas and the flatlands of eastern New Mexico.

Life had been glorious on the Great Plains in the 1920s in an area that included Oklahoma, Kansas, Nebraska, Missouri, and Iowa. The area was considered the new frontier of farming, and America watched with great curiosity as huge profits were pulled from the ground.

The huge Oklahoma land rushes of 1889 through 1895 had sent hundreds of thousands of people racing toward a dream of a promised land. They traveled on horseback, in wagons, on bicycles, and on trains, and after the final land rush of '95 most of the Indian Territory land had been swallowed up all the way to Oklahoma's western boundary.

Over hundreds of thousands of years Native Americans had come to recognize the delicate balance of nature. The plains were known for attracting too much rain or not enough. Floods followed by droughts were soon followed by dust storms that were followed by floods. The Indians valued land for the thickness of its native grama grasses that fed the prodigious bison. But the white man wasted no time putting a plow to a land regarded as a bottomless gold mine. The rains stopped and the winds came and, inch by inch, the topsoil was peeled away. Wheat to the north and cotton to the west shriveled and died as small towns like El Reno, Burns Flat, Dill City, Clinton, Kingfisher, Watonga, Woodward, Weatherford, Hydro, Cloud Chief, Cordell, Altus, and Hollis went bone dry. The winds grew stronger and carried away straw and old leaves and even the clods of broken earth. There was nothing to stop the wind, nothing to even slow it down, on a land both treeless and as flat as a skillet.

Dust collected everywhere—on fence posts and doorsills, inside the houses. At night, the dirt-soaked air muffled sound even more than a heavy ocean fog. All along the western boundary and up in the Oklahoma Panhandle and in southern Kansas and on the hardpan around Amarillo, the Dust Bowl was forming.

As the farms died, so did the ranches. With nothing left to eat, cattle turned to the tumbleweeds. With nothing to drink, they died, and their bones and skulls were scattered over thousands of miles in the blowing sand.

Silly rumors abounded in the Texas Panhandle about the crows spinning nests out of barbed wire. Natives snickered at this folly, but it didn't stop the eastern press from running with the story. At the height of this devastation came the black blizzards. They rolled in with tornadic force, darkening the horizon and turning day into night. The storms arrived with a rolling turbulence and rose like a wall of muddy water as high as eight thousand feet. Not only were they terrifying to watch; they also caused utter destruction to what remained of the area's fine, rich soil. The hell storms were much like the winter blizzards in that they were pushed along by the polar continental air mass. Electricity from the atmosphere lifted the dirt higher and higher as thunder and lightning accompanied the curtain of blackness, giving rise to predictions that the world was ending.

More than a powerful physical presence, the black blizzards battered man's psyche. Farmers and ranchers awoke each morning in a state of dread. Roosters were so confused during the Dust Bowl that they were tricked into roosting at midday. Dust was so thick that it derailed trains. An agronomist from Stillwater estimated there was enough dust in the air to cover 5 million acres a foot deep.

Men and women who depended on the land were soon looking for a way out. They were inundated with handbills that promised enough work in the California fields to last a lifetime. Prospects of a new life picking peaches, grapes, oranges, cauliflower, melons, prunes, apples, apricots, pears, beans, asparagus, and healthy cotton reenergized the families. They sold off plows, picks, shovels, rakes, wheelbarrows, and livestock for the money to invest in an old truck or car. They left the state by the hundreds and by the thousands each day. Most of the migrators followed a new trail—Route 66. Completed in 1926, the "Highway" was a symbol of a vibrant time in a flourishing America, when man grew obsessed with automobiles that could reach speeds of fifty miles per hour on a smooth surface. Route 66 was the American dream—a concrete-and-asphalt ribbon that linked the West to the center of America. It rose from the shores of Lake Michigan, rolled past the Mississippi River in Saint Louis, and seven states later rolled gracefully up to the Pacific Ocean at the Santa Monica pier. When word spread of its completion, every red-blooded American with a set of car keys dreamed of setting wheels to it.

Route 66 covered 850 miles. The longest section was 332 miles through Oklahoma. A mile didn't pass in the Sooner State in the thirties without another radiator boiling over or a tire blowing. People slept on the ground just a few feet from the highway known as the Mother Road, which was littered with junked cars and shattered dreams. Along Route 66 in Hydro, Oklahoma, a woman and her husband fought to keep their grocery store/filling station alive. Lucille Hamons would take a long pull from her Bel Air and brace herself for another sad story as the head of another wayward family would invariably pull his car to the gas pumps and enter the front door slowly, hat in hand.

"Ma'am, I was wondering, we're plumb broke, and—"

"I can afford to buy some stuff from ya," Lucille would say. "That'll give you money to get a piece down the road."

"Got nothin' to sell—"

"Then I'll buy your danged car."

Car parts were strewn for several hundred feet behind the store.

"Ma'am, honestly—"

"OK, I'll give you a little gas. Then you can putter on outta here. But I expect to see some money when y'alls gets to California." A trickle of envelopes, each with a California postmark, had been arriving with dimes, nickels, and quarters taped inside.

"Ma'am, my kids are starvin'. Could you spare a few pieces of baloney?"

As the old truck sputtered and wheezed and rocked slowly back onto the highway, Lucille would look up from the stove to see another charity case making his way toward the gas pumps.

Okies were not the only folks suffering. Lucille saw them coming from Kansas, Missouri, and Arkansas. She'd also heard the drought stories about New Mexico and Texas. It just seemed that the Oklahoma burnouts were more needy. Okies migrated westward from all parts of the state, but none more rapidly than from the western edge, where the sand dunes were piling up and hope was running out.

During the great drought, the red country to the west cracked beneath a sun that scorched the cotton fields and the knee-high buffalo grass. Anthills rose out of the wheel tracks.

Tucked into the southwest corner of the state, Hollis, Oklahoma, in the thirties was a place where a boy with a good arm could chuck a rock all the way to the Texas Panhandle. Situated an equal distance between Amarillo and Oklahoma City, the small town withered to a heap of dust. Weathermen kept predicting the cycle of drought would end, but it lasted into the next summer and into the next as heavy clouds that had boiled up from Texas and the Gulf of Mexico came no more and a once-fertile land died of thirst.

The shoeless young boy with red freckles had stood motionless in the shadows of his grandmother's front porch and watched as another family packed their belongings into the car and pulled onto the highway that headed west, then north, then west again. He waved to the folks, packed tight as cotton bolls into a burlap sack, and he could see his friend Buddy Milsted scrunched down in the backseat, tears streaking his face. Goodbye was just another part of the day, like wiping dust from the kitchen cabinet. Men barely had money to feed their families, so they took off in rattletrap cars with leaky radiators and tires about to pop.

Buddy would never see Hollis again. Folks left Oklahoma without closing the doors. They never looked back. They left behind broken windows covered by cardboard and a windmill creaking in a ghostly wind.

On a day that August, when the sun flared down and the mercury rose to 108 degrees, the eight-year-old boy leaped from the porch and suddenly remembered the law that had been laid down by his grandmother.

"Don't you go runnin' out of here, Darrell Royal!" she always shouted. "It's too danged hot. You go runnin' across town and your engine'll overheat."

Grandma Harmon was now out of sight, busy with a clothesline filled with wet laundry in the backyard, but Darrell could feel her presence, and the familiar words rang in his ears. So he reminded himself about the drill—walk until you're over the hill and out of her sight, then tear-ass down the dirt road. Darrell ran everywhere every day. His shoulders didn't feel the lash of the summer sun, and his bare feet rarely noticed the smoking hot road. He figured he could run thirty miles to Altus and back without breathing hard, and it always seemed he was running to something and away from something else. He spent much of his time alone, and his loneliness was as visible as his sunburned ears.

The boy was happy to see the burgundy Packard turn onto Cactus Street, kicking up dust as it rolled toward town. There were no paved roads in Hollis. A walking man could raise the dust knee-high; a wagon sent clouds over the fence line; an automobile, even at a low speed, stirred up dust tall enough to choke a walking man.

Darrell Royal got down into a three-point stance in the road, just like Earnest "Iron Mike" Massad, the famous fullback for the Oklahoma Sooners, and waited until the car was upon him. Then he bolted into a full sprint, arms driving and knees pumping.

The driver saw the specter of a boy . . . running.

"Need a ride, Darrell?" he shouted over the engine.

"Nah. I'm racin' ya."

"You're racin' what?"

"You."

The man laughed. "Why, Darrell, you're gonna tucker out."

"I'm gonna beat ya."

Darrell targeted the gate to the Smith farm as his imaginary finish line, and now it was coming up fast. His face was red and contorted. *Ten more yards.* He had sprinted almost the length of a football field and beaten the car by two feet.

"Touchdown, Sooners!" he yelled as he slowed and the car passed.

A woman on a nearby porch turned to her husband and said, "That Darrell sure needs somebody to play with."

Darrell was lucky to have three older brothers—Don, Ray, and Glen—but they were normally busy with work or with girlfriends. When they had time for football, the "ball" was a Clabber Girl baking can that had been plucked from Grandma Harmon's trash. It was six inches long and three inches in circumference, and, in time, the boys learned to throw tight spirals with the tin missiles. They would gather on Grandma Harmon's long front yard while listening to the Oklahoma football games blaring from a radio on the front porch. When the Oklahoma band played "Boomer Sooner," Darrell daydreamed they were playing it for him.

In spite of its abject poverty, Hollis did produce a handful of OU football players, who returned home during the Christmas holidays and walked the dusty streets of Hollis wearing letter jackets with a huge **O** sewn on the front.

"I want to be like those boys," Darrell said. He often followed them and listened to their voices.

Other times, he was racing against cars or daydreaming or saying good-bye to friends or attending funerals. In Hollis, it seemed that folks were always dying or going away. Katy Royal had passed away during Darrell's infancy. No one had taken the time to address the actual cause of death. But the boy suspected his mother had succumbed while giving birth to him on July 6, 1924. Her death plagued him night and day. He didn't know that *cancer* was an unspeakable word in that day and time, and that, out of sheer superstition no one would discuss Katy's horrible and painful death. Family members lived in constant fear that if they talked about it, the devil himself would come back to Hollis and strike them dead.

The young boy often dreamed about having a mother.

Originally a farmer, Burley Royal had bounced from job to job, working as a trucker and a bookkeeper and a jailer and a deputy sheriff. He was not unlike most men at that time in Oklahoma.

One day, Darrell Royal asked his daddy where the Dust Bowl actually started and where it ended.

"Just stand there," Burley said. "It'll find you."

Most of the Dust Bowl damage was in the Texas and Oklahoma Panhandles, southern Kansas, and a large part of the western Oklahoma plains. Its boundaries often shifted, like the boundaries of a sand dune in high winds.

Darrell Royal couldn't escape a creeping depression that haunted most people. At nights, folks of the Dust Bowl slept with damp washcloths covering their noses and mouths. Darrell would lie still, trying to believe this nightmare wasn't happening, and although the houses were shut tight, dust seeped through every crack and crevice as the wind howled. Grandma Harmon would awake in the morning to find that her dishes, left on the kitchen counter overnight, were indistinct shapes beneath the thick dust and sand. She could barely make out the outline of each one. Dishes had to be washed and rewashed, as did the clothes. Sounds were muffled at dawn, and Darrell didn't hear the roosters. The sun hung over the horizon like a copper ball. Standing on the porch at Grandma Harmon's, he silently watched the overloaded cars with trailers in tow roll past, leaving one after another, each one threatening to burst at the springs, and he waved good-bye to friends he would never see again. Then he walked into the kitchen, where his nose met the rich aroma of bacon frying and biscuits in the oven.

"Grandma, do you think we'll have to leave Oklahoma?"

"I certainly hope not. Not yet, anyway."

Darrell Royal prayed they would stay. Leaving meant he would never play for the Oklahoma Sooners.

3

THE CURSE

Another ball-and-chain exclusive to Oklahoma was John Steinbeck's *The Grapes of Wrath*. Published in 1939, it depicted Oklahomans as dirty, destitute, sullen, and dispossessed. Like restless ants, they traveled in caravans of rattling and smoking cars, crawling westward across New Mexico and Arizona, suffering through the desert before streaming over the mountains into California. Landowners and locals kept them down by paying a meager wage, about a dollar a day per family, and by setting fire to the pitiful camps, known as Hoovervilles and Little Oklahomas.

The wayworn travelers were arrested, pistol-whipped, kicked, and left to starve. Signs at movie theater entrances read: NIGGERS AND OKIES SIT IN THE BALCONY.

Steinbeck wrote: "And the men of the towns and of the soft suburban country gathered to defend themselves; and they reassured themselves that they were good and the invaders bad, as a man must do before he fights. They said, 'These goddamned Okies are dirty and ignorant. They're degenerate, sexual maniacs. These goddamned Okies are thieves. They bring disease, they're filthy. We can't have them in the schools. They're strangers. How would you like to have your sister go out with one of them?' "

The Grapes of Wrath was banned in several Oklahoma school districts, and Oklahomans screamed to the high heavens that Steinbeck's portrayal of them was faulty. But fifteen million copies of the book were sold nationwide. In 1940, shortly before Steinbeck won the Pulitzer Prize, the movie, starring Henry Fonda, was released to great reviews.

So in January of 1946, nine well-dressed men assembled in a paneled boardroom on the campus of the University of Oklahoma with the intention of fighting back. Members of the OU board of regents wanted to vanquish the stereotype set down by Steinbeck. They knew that America viewed Oklahoma as the land of battered and dirty pickup trucks, cream gravy for breakfast, and pigs on the porch.

At the head of the table was university president Dr. George Lynn Cross, a man with a wide forehead and bright, lively eyes.

"Gentlemen," he began. "I think that every man in this room knows why we are here. The war is over and our state's upside down. We must make sure that this does not translate into a downward spiral for this university."

Regent Lloyd Noble was quick to pick up the theme: "The problem is Steinbeck's damn book. Everyone in this room understands the impact the Okie image is having on our state. Our people need to stop being so gol-darn apologetic about where they live."

The OU board of regents comprised doctors, lawyers, oilmen, and business leaders—monied men whose lives were not derailed by the drought and its destruction or the Depression or the massive migration. For the most part, they were rich, famous, ambitious, and forward-thinking but hardly academic. Each one had an appreciation of football; each had an idea of how a winning team could jump-start not only the economy but the collective morale of the state as well. Cross took one look as these stout men and knew instantly he was preaching to the choir. One of the regents was Erl Deacon, who had played guard for the Sooners in the early twenties.

"Men," Cross said. "There is only one way to get this state back on track, and that's football, football, football."

Cross seemed an odd fit for the presidency of OU. He had

arrived in Norman in 1934, and his improbable rise from assistant professor of botany and microbiology to university president had taken only ten years. In 1943, university president Joseph A. Brandt resigned to become a publisher. Cross seized the interim job and a year later took root as the permanent president.

Cross was known for a friendly smile, a strong handshake, and a fierce appreciation of the common man. He also believed in getting straight to the heart of the matter—on all matters. Quoting dead poets or lecturing on van Gogh, Monet, Gauguin, or Toulouse-Lautrec just wasn't the man's style. He'd rather talk football and knew it was the language of the people, especially the people of the south plains.

He was about as athletic-looking as Harry Truman, but there was football on Cross's résumé. He'd attended South Dakota State on a football scholarship. The scholarship included washing dishes in a women's dining hall and wheeling concrete for a construction crew during the summer months.

Like Richard Nixon, an old tackle at Whittier College, Cross never lost his love for the game. Still, he never desired to coach or to rise through the ranks of the athletic department. Beyond professing plant life, his other passion was studying football. He learned straightaway that football and religion were about the same thing. From the countless small towns to the largest universities, football had become the spiritual rallying center of American life. The game stirred emotions that no one could define. People didn't come to the stadium so much to root for the home team as to live out their hopes and aspirations.

To fortify the university and boost self-confidence statewide, Oklahomans would need a kind of beacon to guide them, and it was Cross's hope that Memorial Stadium Field, home of the Oklahoma Sooners, would come to represent that light.

Cross stood and slowly walked around the large oaken table, his hands clasped behind his back, his mind formulating the sale.

"Men, just think of how they feel in South Bend, Indiana, every Saturday afternoon. Think about West Point in late September with the leaves changing. Think about Harvard and Yale on a frosty November afternoon. Think about Frank Leahy at Notre Dame and Red Blaik at Army and Bernie Bierman at Minnesota. Where can we get ourselves one of those *men?*"

Cross's number-one ally in the room was Noble, who also happened to be the most respected and possibly the most influential man in the entire state. Noble was a legend among the new breed of wildcatters that had been punching holes all over Oklahoma and one of the most successful independent oilmen anywhere.

In the 1920s and '30s, as the land diminished and the agrarian economy tumbled toward bankruptcy, Noble ran a double reverse on the state—he struck black gold. While millions were being lost on the parched and dying land, Noble drilled and drilled and struck Big Oil. He had a nose for the deep rivers that meandered through rock. The oil was often thousands and thousands of feet deep. Without technical training or wealth, Noble made his money the old-fashioned way—through sweat equity. He drilled all over Oklahoma, Texas, and parts of Canada. His success ratio was astonishing. Other wildcatters tracked him as an Indian would scout the cavalry, trying to learn where he was going and what he knew. He hit a home run in more than a hundred oil patches, and his success story stretched all the way to England's Sherwood Forest, where he struck oil during World War II.

Oil created an overnight aristocracy in Oklahoma. A handful of wildcatters became stinking rich, most of them buying expensive cars and airplanes and sending their sons to the Ivy League and their daughters to finishing schools back east. But Noble had simple tastes and lived by a personal philosophy that belied the others'. With his new wealth, he endowed a foundation to conduct soil research to help the farmers make a comeback. He also funded a foundation to seek cures for cancer and other diseases.

Cross would have laid a million-to-one that Noble would stand by him in this crusade to fix OU football—a cause that he truly loved. The football program had suffered a downturn beginning on January 3, 1939, when the Sooners lost 17–0 to Tennessee in the Orange Bowl. They hadn't been back there since. Coach Dewey "Snorter" Luster had compiled an 18-4-1 record over a period of five years and won two Big Six championships, but his teams never defeated the University of Texas and lost by lopsided scores to Oklahoma A&M in 1944 and '45. Oklahoma fans would rather see the black blizzards come tearing back down the plains than lose on a regular basis to those pissants.

Luster resigned after the '45 season, citing health reasons. Cross probably would have fired him anyway. Though Luster was a likable character and had played tackle for the Sooners decades earlier, he was an odd-looking bird with thick glasses—not the kind of *man* Cross had in mind.

The hope was to resurrect the era of Benjamin Gilbert Owen, which had lasted from 1905 through '26, a time when he put the Sooners on the map with a wide-open offense, his teams employing the forward pass more than any other outfit in America. Owen produced Oklahoma's first undefeated season in 1911 and compiled two more in '15 and '18. If that weren't enough, Owen was the visionary, the architect, and a chief supervisor in the construction of the new stadium—in spite of having only one arm.

Thanks to Owen's foresight and perseverance, Oklahomans poured their hearts into the Sooners. The first forty years of Sooner football were marked by long stretches of greatness and plenty of colorful characters.

The idea of a collegiate football team was born in 1895 at Bud Risinger's barbershop on Main Street in Norman. John A. Harts had come to the university to teach and study. He also brought with him tales of his own football past at Winfield College in Kansas.

Harts's ragtag players made their own uniforms and challenged a group of students from an Oklahoma City high school. They lost 35–0. When the team shut down after one game, Harts took off for the Arctic to do some prospecting, never realizing he had started a football program that someday would be recognized as among the best in America.

The first game against a team of collegians was played two years later. It received less publicity than the Territorial Intercollegiate Oratorical Contest that same weekend. The matchup against King-fisher College of Guthrie was interrupted in the second half by the sheriff of Logan County. He had never seen a football game and mistook it for a drunken brawl. The contest was allowed to continue after college officials explained what was going on. Oklahoma won 17–8.

The Oklahoma–Oklahoma A&M rivalry kicked off in 1904 with a game in Guthrie, the territorial capital. At the time, football still had rules that inspired some curious scenarios. For instance, a fumble could be recovered anywhere—even beyond the boundary lines. At one point in the contest, Oklahoma A&M punter B. O. Callahan set up in his team's end zone and was forced to hurry the kick. The football shot straight up and was blown backward by a gust of wind. It tumbled all the way to Cottonwood Creek and rolled into the icy water, bobbing like a cork on the surface. Several players from both teams made a mad dash for the creek and were followed by a group of fans huffing and puffing behind them.

Billy Baird of the Aggies was the first to reach the creek and, as he tried retrieving the ball with a stick, was shoved into the water. Several players dived in, including a few who suddenly realized they couldn't swim. But nothing could stop Oklahoma guard Ed Cook, who swam like Charles Daniels, the great American freestyler. Cook clutched the pigskin to his chest and swam to the edge of the creek, touching the ball down in the sand for an Oklahoma touchdown.

Oklahoma drowned the Aggies that day 75–0.

The Sooners lost a shoot-out in Fayetteville, Arkansas, in 1909 when a drunken Razorback fan stumbled onto the field wielding Colt revolvers in both hands. Firing two shots into the ground, he shouted, "That Oklahoma bunch won't cross this goal. I'll see to that!" The Sooners didn't and lost 21–5.

A photograph taken in the 1920s of a gathering on Main Street in Norman captured the affection that Oklahomans held for their football team. Hundreds of men, dressed in suits and ties and hats, milled about the square, smoking cigars and pipes and staring aimlessly at the ground. No one seemed to be speaking. They listened intently to a Western Union messenger standing on a stage behind a lectern. Oklahoma and Missouri were playing that day in Columbia, and the messenger slowly read the account of each play over the public-address system. Every so often, the men would gaze upon the brick wall behind the announcer, where a miniature football field was positioned. A tiny ball, moving up and down the field, tracked the movement of the offense.

Cross was moved to tears the first time he set eyes on the photograph. He knew the time was right to rekindle that flame of Oklahoma football.

Of course, the Sooners would need one hell of a man to lead them back to the championship years—a Rockne, Leahy, Neyland, Munn, Blaik, and Bierman rolled into one.

Noble stood and revealed his plan to the board: "We're going to need to recruit a lot of boys out of the military. The NCAA says it's open season on recruits. Military boys can change schools without losing eligibility. I suggest that we go after a man who's been coaching one of these military outfits. He'll know where the best players are."

• • •

Jim Tatum was a bearish man with a huge head and a jagged edge to his personality. He didn't seem happy until everyone was mad at him. But he qualified under the terms set down by the OU board of regents, having coached the offensive line in the Iowa Pre-Flight program under Don Faurot and later served as an assistant with the Navy team in Jacksonville, Florida. Oklahoma athletic director Jap Haskell had discovered Tatum during his wartime leave of absence at Iowa Pre-Flight, also known as the V-5, a program designed to improve the physical skills of prospective pilots. Haskell made a strong recommendation on Tatum's behalf to Cross and the board of regents.

In spite of his limited coaching experience and in spite of the lack of name recognition, Tatum certainly fit the OU profile. He was a walking, talking ball of fire. At North Carolina, during his only year as a head coach in 1942, he spent most of his time combing the mountains and the countryside and handing out cash to the biggest, strongest, and fastest football players he could find.

During the war, Tatum was lucky that his life had merged with that of Faurot, the father of the Split-T offense, who taught the greatest lessons of Tatum's Naval days. At first, the Split-T offense appeared to be a simple variation of the conservative T-formation when, in fact, it was a radical departure. And it just so happened that Faurot was the *master* of this new and stylish offense. He had won two Big Six Conference championships at Missouri in 1939 and '42.

Completing the triad of coaches at Iowa Pre-Flight was a tall, lanky man with wavy blond hair. He didn't talk much, but he listened intently to just about everything that Faurot and Tatum had to say. Bud Wilkinson was absorbing information that might be useful in the years to come, depending on the course of his life's journey.

Wilkinson had promised his father, C. P., that he would return to Minneapolis at the end of the war to work in the mortgage banking business, but the more time Bud spent around football, the more fascinated he became with the sport and all of its intricacies. When he was playing guard and quarterback for the University of Minnesota, the Golden Gophers won the national championship in 1934, '35, and '36. Bud often acted like a coach on the field, and

Bernie Bierman assigned him to call all of the plays, even when he was playing guard, knowing that Bud was the best offensive mind to pass through Minnesota in a long time.

Wilkinson, after graduation, led the College All-Stars to a first—they defeated the defending NFL champions, the Green Bay Packers, in the annual summer exhibition game 7–0.

• • •

Cross informed Tatum that he was scheduled to interview for the Oklahoma head coaching job on January 9, 1946.

"Doc," Tatum said over the phone, "there's somebody I'd like to bring along with me to the interview. I think you'll like this guy."

At precisely eight o'clock that morning, the two men made an impressive entrance at the university president's office near the center of campus. Both wore dark suits and white shirts and stood over six feet tall.

"Dr. Cross, I would like you to meet Bud Wilkinson," Tatum said. "Bud has one of the best coaching minds I've ever seen."

Football was the common thread that connected Tatum and Wilkinson; they had little to discuss after that. Wilkinson carried himself like a young law professor. If not for football, their paths never would have crossed and they wouldn't have been standing before the president of the University of Oklahoma at that very moment.

Though Tatum had total confidence in both his résumé and his coaching ability, boardrooms, big shots, and academicians made him nervous.

Tatum had brought Wilkinson to the interview for the purpose of entertaining these power brokers and to deflect much of the attention away from his rough edges. With Wilkinson along, Tatum would have to do far less talking, far less thinking.

Not surprisingly, many of the early questions were directed at Wilkinson, who seemed to relish the solemnity of the paneled boardroom and the furrowed brows of his inquisitors. Tatum took mental notes on Wilkinson's cool demeanor.

"Gentlemen," Tatum said confidently, "I am here to tell you one important thing about myself. I believe in high academic standards for my athletes. And I also believe in complete and one hundred percent cooperation between the athletic department and the rest of the university. No cheating. Period."

Cross sensed the coach was lying through his teeth but didn't interrupt. He could tell from the body language of each regent that they weren't buying Tatum's speech. After examining the men for over an hour, Cross excused Tatum and Wilkinson and, before adjourning the meeting, decided to poll the regents on their feelings.

"I think we've found our coach, but I don't think it's Tatum," Noble said. "I don't think I've ever been as impressed with a young coach as I am with that Bud Wilkinson fellow."

Cross quickly learned that most of the other regents felt the same way. Each man stressed his positive feeling for Wilkinson. But as a matter of ethics, Cross knew the board of regents would be violating an important code by passing over Tatum.

"Gentlemen, you know as well as I do that we can't invite Mr. Tatum for an interview and then offer the job to his friend," Cross said. "But here is what I suggest. We'll offer a three-year contract to Tatum with the stipulation that he has to bring Mr. Wilkinson with him."

Cross telephoned Tatum the next day and tendered the offer.

"You've got to be out of your goddamned mind," Tatum blared. "You can't force me to bring Wilkinson. Besides, the man says he's going back to Minnesota."

"All I can tell you," Cross said, "is that's the offer of the regents and I can't ask them to change it."

The next day, Wilkinson and Tatum started packing and making plans for Norman.

4

GROUND ZERO

They worked relentlessly around the clock, scouring the entire country for the best soldiers back from the war. Anyone who knew that a football was blown up and not stuffed with feathers became the target of their dragnet.

Tatum realized he was lucky to have Wilkinson. They had bonded while serving as assistant coaches on the Iowa Pre-Flight team that finished second in the final Associated Press poll behind Notre Dame in 1943. Wilkinson's fascination with the Split-T offense was the single greatest reason he had foreclosed on a promise to enter his father's business. Bud found it stimulating that he could apply his intellect to game strategy. He envisioned the day when he would study reels and reels of film and concoct game plans that would befuddle the best defensive minds. His head was filled with ideas, and those ideas drove him to work every morning.

Tatum and Wilkinson, in both disposition and appearance, were as different as Laurel and Hardy. Wilkinson was dignified and well groomed. Tatum went days without shaving. Wilkinson loved to quote poets and politicians. Tatum's salty language could wither a seasoned sailor.

Wilkinson had excelled both academically and athletically at Shattuck School and the University of Minnesota before pursuing his

Master's in English at Syracuse University. His life had been filled with structure from birth. At Shattuck, the discipline began at dawn and lasted throughout the day, and those four years at the all-military school left a lasting impression.

Shattuck was located on the frozen tundra of Faribault, some fifty miles south of Minneapolis.

Wilkinson dreaded the morning when his dormitory room felt like an icebox and he reached for his favorite pen, only to find the ink frozen. Then, as the first light streaked through the blinds, he could see goldfish stiff in the tank. Hours would pass before the ice thawed and they wiggled back to life.

With America sinking deeper into the Depression, Shattuck also struggled financially and, at night, electricity was either turned down or shut off. Fellow students compounded the problem by propping dorm windows open as proof of their machismo. It was no wonder that a young man's feet felt like frozen meat as temperatures plunged to a minus-thirty degrees in the night.

Though the campus was stately and elegant with its Gothic architecture, far-reaching tree lines, and green lawns, it turned gray and dour in the brutal months when the icy winds sliced down from Canada and Lake Superior, sending the student-soldiers scrambling underground, much like gophers. Tunnels connected many of the buildings.

The four-year military academy was as rigid as the school's founder himself, the Right Reverend Henry Benjamin Whipple, the first Episcopal bishop of Minnesota, who had been established to develop "manly bearing, precision in movement, and the spirit of leadership."

Bud's full name was Charles Burnham Wilkinson and, to most, he was simply Charles. But he had picked up a nickname as a kid playing football on the streets of Minneapolis—Burnie. That would be changed to Wilky at Shattuck.

Sons of the rich and famous were sent here. Troubled boys who had been in and out of jail were consigned to Shattuck. The place had its share of bright and dedicated students, but Shattuck was mostly about a hellish brand of discipline.

After shaking off the numbing predawn cold and climbing into uniforms, the soldiers assembled outside of their respective dorms, lining up in lockstep formation. They rigidly stood shoulder-to-shoulder, only inches apart, front and back. Knees and elbows swung in perfect unison. They moved as a single interlocked unit for several hundred yards, all the way to the mess hall. Most of the upperclass units traveled in perfect harmony, arriving in perfect formation. Inevitably, though, at least one of the freshman squads would collapse, the plebes tumbling into each other like dominoes.

Shattuck students were expected to follow a rigorous honor code, much like West Point. In fact, the military structure of Shattuck mirrored that of the Army. Step out of line and you were on the next train out of Faribault. The most important component of Shattuck was ROTC, taught by military officers assigned to active duty at the school and paid for by the U.S. Army. Representatives of the War Department arrived every spring for "government inspection."

A secretive hazing system existed that was patterned after the aggressive style of discipline at West Point. Freshmen were brutalized for their mistakes and lack of decorum as seniors were allowed free reign to dole out the most radical and inhuman forms of punishment.

For instance, for the crime of oversleeping, a freshman was tied with duct tape to a hot radiator, his body greased with analgesic balm and an old sock stuffed into his mouth. He was left there to sizzle and squirm until the others returned from breakfast. His burns would be treated the next two weeks at the campus infirmary.

Some offenders were wrapped in military coats and pushed down several flights of stairs. Bruises and broken bones took several weeks to heal. It wasn't uncommon for a plebe to disappear for a month while his body was on the mend.

A senior decided to punish a rowdy plebe one morning while they were lining up in lockstep. The freshman was struck several times on the foot with a saber, until blood spewed like a geyser from his boot. Several witnesses turned their heads and retched.

As they stood at attention, plebes were ordered to drop their trousers. Seniors would strike the backs of their legs with coat hangers, flaying layers of skin. New cadets became quite focused on not repeating their errors.

On the day that he arrived at Shattuck, Charles Wilkinson wrote a letter to his father, Charles Patterson Wilkinson, pleading for his speedy return to the family's warm and spacious home on a tree-lined street on the south side of Minneapolis. When C. P. wrote back and told his son to stick it out, the boy cried himself to sleep. C. P. Wilkinson had drawn up a rigorous blueprint for his son, and Shattuck was the foundation.

While Charles and his older brother, Bill, were growing up, disaster struck out of the blue on Saturday afternoon, August 12, 1922, as the Soo Line passenger train that carried the immediate family, along with an aunt, an uncle, and several cousins, struck an oil truck a few miles south of the small town of Annandale, Minnesota. The oil truck slammed into several passenger cars. A baggage car imploded and the smoker car burst into flames. Young Charles saw smoke and fire and heard the screams of passengers who were sliced apart by flying steel and glass. The boy heard the cries for help and believed he would be the next to die.

He stumbled through the darkness, seeking an exit passage, and was grabbed from behind and poked through a hole in the torn steel. He suddenly felt himself falling. Bracing for a collision with the ground, his heart pumping, the boy landed in the powerful hands of a man whose face was blackened by soot and smoke. That same nameless, faceless hero caught several others as they were lobbed from the burning wreckage.

Aside from bumps, scratches, and bruises, all members of the Wilkinson family were thought to be safe and sound. Edith Wilkinson, the mother of Charles and Bill, did spend two days in the hospital but was released in seemingly good health. As weeks and months passed, though, her strength waned and her vibrant spirit faded. She was in and out of the hospital, and a year later, after both her heart and liver failed, Edith Wilkinson died. Internal injuries from the train crash were eventually listed as the cause of death.

Seven-year-old Charles Wilkinson was motherless.

The trauma of the train wreck, accompanied by Edith's death, led to a fear of the dark. The young boy was afraid to go to sleep at night, and years would pass before his life became settled again.

The happiest times of his childhood were playing touch football. They chose up sides every day after school and played a loose game of sandlot football that often starred a female quarterback named Patty Berg. Though golf was her favorite sport, Patty loved mixing it up with the 50th Street Tigers and didn't mind the scrapes, bruises, and blackened eyes.

Like several boys of that era, young Charles was fascinated with the Minnesota Golden Gophers. Since there were no radio broadcasts at the time, fans would gather at several locations around Minneapolis and listen to the play-by-play accounts read by a representative of the Western Union telegraph. Fans were kept apprised of the down and distance of each play, and young Charles tried to guess what Bernie Bierman would do next.

Just as the youngest Wilkinson was starting to smile and laugh again, C. P. decided to send him away to Shattuck.

"That man is cold-blooded," said Florence, the sister of Charles's deceased mother. "How could he send a fine boy to a mean place like Shattuck?"

Thirteen-year-old Charles Wilkinson was not hard-wired for the fierce challenges that lay ahead. He thought about sneaking a train out of Faribault but realized his father would not accept him back in Minneapolis.

"I want to go," he told Robert Crabb, a childhood friend with whom he had played football. "But I really have no place to go."

Crabb nodded and said, "We'd better make the best of this."

In the privacy of his dorm room, Charles cried at the start of each semester. Charles was not like his brother, Bill, who had inherited a hot temper from C. P. and often clashed with him. Charles was reserved and cool and preferred to run when emotions erupted.

Every cadet was required to participate in at least one sport, and it was on the playing fields where Wilkinson began to exert himself. The boy who had shed buckets of tears was now terrorizing football practice. Somehow, the idea of physical contact—of bloody noses and bruised knuckles—appealed to him. It wasn't long before he was moved from guard to tackle, where, oddly enough, he called the offensive plays.

By the eleventh grade, fellow students were viewing Wilkinson in a new light. He had grown three inches to six-one, and he now weighed 216 pounds—more than any other player on the team. He had wavy brown hair and an expanding air of confidence. Sports and studies were starting to come easily. Though he had never given hockey a second thought, he tried out as the goalie and became the best in the conference. He hit a grand slam to defeat one of Shattuck's greatest rivals, Culver Military School of Indiana, in the bottom of the ninth inning, and soon he was the starting center and the school's best basketball player. Almost from the day he walked onto the golf course, he was shooting in the seventies.

Perhaps his most satisfying accomplishment was not only making the Crack Squad—the nationally known precision drill and rifle unit—but also excelling as its finest member. It was the Crack Squad that representatives from the War Department deemed the greatest unit from any military school in the country. Thanks to long hours of work and discipline, the Shattuck drill unit had never lost in competition. Ten hours of pracice usually equaled one minute of performance.

Outwardly, it appeared that Wilkinson was headed for a career in the military or one in sports. But professors at the academy discovered yet another side to the young man and were forming other opinions. Earle "Duke" Wagner, an English professor in his midthirties, with his pencil-thin mustache, bright neckties, and British tweeds, eptitomized everything that Shattuck was not. He lived in an apartment decorated with Oriental rugs, overstuffed leather chairs, bookshelves filled with leather-bound classics, and walls filled with eighteenth-century lithographs. He exuded class, and Wilkinson was drawn to him.

Wagner loved to quote Lord Byron, and Wilkinson loved to hear him do so. Soon Byron became Wilkinson's favorite poet and poetry his favorite subject. The young cadet was among the throng of students who would come to Wagner's apartment and sit on the floor while he read poetry; Wagner was also the head of the Dramatic Association, and he soon convinced Wilkinson to become a prominent member.

Day by day, it became evident that Wilkinson was an eclectic young man. His life was more than trap blocks, glove saves, lay-ups, grand slams, and birdie putts.

Wagner often drove his black Packard convertible out to the practice field with his scarves blowing in the wind and his English bulldog seated beside him. Students often called him a gay blade. Though Wilkinson adored the man as a teacher, he seemed embarrassed whenever Wagner showed up around the football team. But he had a definitive and lasting impact on Wilkinson's life, as he would have on a student passing through six years later—a boy named Marlon Brando.

Shattuck might have been one of the strictest military schools in

America. But a few students rolled the dice in matters like drinking beer in the ravine behind campus, firing off the school cannon during unscheduled times, and courting students at St. Mary's, an all-girl school adjacent to the academy.

Wilkinson avoided the cannon but not the beer and the girls. He was seen at St. Mary's at all hours and, according to several friends, had sex with more than one coed underneath the bleachers inside the field house. Of course, he was not completely alone in that regard. The padded floor beneath the bleachers was the equivalent of a secluded spot in the woods on a campus where students had cars. Wilkinson just seemed to make better and more frequent use of the space than others.

Upon graduation, he was the most decorated senior, earning cum laude honors along with the Harvard Cup for the highest excellence in combined sports and academics, and the Williams Cup for being the best all-round athlete.

The 1933 Shattuck yearbook, *the Shad,* noted that Wilkinson was a "triple-threat man, not only on the athletic field, but in the halls of St. Mary's as well."

Contradictory impulses were already at work. He seemed cold and aloof at times and warm at others. He was a self-disciplined young man, but one with a huge appetite for certain pleasures. Beneath the conservative veneer emerged a risk taker. That dichotomous nature would serve to produce a complex man who wasn't at all what he appeared to be.

• • •

On May 14, 1945, kamikazes had taken dead aim at the hangar deck of the USS *Enterprise,* and now they descended in formation through the heavy flak. As the *Enterprise* fired upon the kamikaze bases in Kyushu, the Japanese counterattacked. It was the third consecutive day of terror in the sky.

The Japanese planes had guns in the nose, tail, top, and bottom. But their mission today was not to kill with bombs or bullets but with the aircraft itself. A Kamikaze strayed off course and struck the deck. A bomb detonated under the forward elevator, launching it four hundred feet into the air. Fourteen men were killed instantly and thirty-four seriously injured. Standing behind a beam was Wilkinson, a hangar deck officer. Thanks to Wilkinson and his crew, the fire was controlled before it tore through the ship.

Wilkinson was the coolest hand on deck. He rarely changed expressions, even with death and destruction all around him. The ship's commanding officer would later commend him for organizing both the men and the fire-fighting equipment during the fire at Kyushu. Friends and fellow officers would remark for weeks just how calm he appeared through the intense fighting, not to mention the carnage at his feet.

The *Enterprise* was one of the deadliest carriers in the Pacific. It was responsible for almost a thousand Japanese aircraft shot down. But nothing was more horrific than the bloodiest battle at Okinawa, where Americans suffered their greatest casualties. Again, Wilkinson was the hangar-deck officer, and conducted himself with a workmanlike efficiency. He often seemed emotionally disconnected from the heavy fighting, from the bloodshed and the smell of death.

America's human toll at both land and sea was close to 20,000 men at Okinawa. The navy lost thirty-six ships. But it was the Japanese ferocity that frightened war leaders more than anything else. Okinawa was a key consideration in the decision to use the atomic bomb against Japan.

On August 14, after the second bomb was dropped on Nagasaki, the war in the South Pacific was all but over. And as the *Enterprise* floated into the port at Seattle weeks later and the sirens sounded and the confetti flew, Wilkinson's mates were still talking about the "icewater in Bud's veins."

. . .

During the football recruiting wars of 1946, Tatum almost wore himself out trying to get his hands on Paul "Buddy" Burris, an army staff sergeant who had fought the Germans across Europe and the Japanese in the Philippines and won two battle stars for his courage.

Burris had been a guard at Tulsa before the war, and the Hurricane finished the 1942 season as the fourth-ranked team in the nation. Now, in February of '46, he was back in Muskogee, plowing behind a team of mules, when he sighted a cloud of dust boiling up from the west. A black limousine crawled along the dirt road in front of the Burris farmhouse and stopped at the end of the furrows. "Whooa, mules!" Buddy yelled. "I gotta see what these folks want."

Stepping gracefully from the sleek automobile was Jewel Ditmars, the richest woman in several counties, wearing diamond rings on both hands and a long black dress and high heels. At forty, she was one of the most attractive women in Oklahoma. Her skin was unusually tanned for the winter months, and her hair was black and flowing. Thanks to direct strikes in both oil and the construction business, Jewel and her family were among the wealthiest in the state. When she wasn't counting her money, she was following her favorite football team—the Oklahoma Sooners.

Emerging from the other side of the car was a man with broad shoulders and a large head. He wore a dark suit and sunglasses.

Jewel had become acquainted with Buddy during his high school career with the Muskogee Roughers. Jewel's son, a high school teammate of Buddy's, was killed fighting as a marine during a battle at Iwo Jima.

"Buddy, come here," Jewel said. "I want you to meet my new friend."

Buddy's forearms were as thick as plow handles, his chest as round as a beer keg. Like Pop Burris and his five brothers, Buddy had a broad nose. As he lumbered toward the car, his large bare feet raising plumes of dust, Buddy wore the visage of a two-legged ox. His huge head was squarely shaped. His body was thick with slab muscle, and his legs could have supported a piano. Buddy had come to believe that plowing barefoot in the soft dirt would strengthen his calf muscles for football. A Green Bay Packer scout might have signed him on the spot.

"Buddy, I want you to meet the new coach of the Oklahoma Sooners," Jewel said. "This is Jim Tatum, the man who's gonna lead us to the national championship. Jim wants you in Norman. I think he has a few goodies you might be interested in."

Buddy was invited to the Oklahoma campus for a recruiting visit. At the time, the National Collegiate Athletic Association was in the process of assembling its first investigative staff, and the hounds had yet to sniff out the trail. Tatum peered across the desk at Buddy and said, "OK, King Kong, how much you need up front?"

"Jeez, Coach, how 'bout a thousand now and some more later?"

"You got it."

The next day, Buddy was invited to Tatum's house for Sunday lunch. When the big tackle started tearing through the southern fried chicken with his bare hands, Janice Tatum said, "Buddy, don't you like my chicken?"

"Yes, ma'am, I really do. But I just lost my false teeth in this big ol' breast, and I'm tryin' to find 'em."

• • •

As the Ford coupe eased into the city limits, Darrell Royal thought about the roads he had traveled to reach Norman.

Sitting in the middle of the front seat was his three-year-old daughter, Marian, and next to her was Edith, his wife. Though Darrell had only two hundred bucks in his pocket, this was the most exciting day of his life as he arrived at the University of Oklahoma.

Months earlier, Royal had been discharged from the Third Air Force, where he had played football in the same single-wing back-field with Charlie Trippi, the All-American from Georgia. A highly trained door-gunner, Royal was spared combat duty in Europe by the timely eruption of an acute abdominal infection. Thus the better part of his military career was spent refining his passing and punting skills.

Darrell felt lucky to be standing on the verdant lawn of OU, surrounded by the red brick buildings of both Gothic and Georgian architecture. It seemed he'd been to hell and back the last ten years.

In 1939, when Joe DiMaggio led the major leagues in hitting for the first time and the Nazis marched into Poland, Burley Royal had decided to pack the family into a broken-down Whippet and join the parade of harvest gypsies on Route 66 heading to California. Darrell hated leaving Oklahoma. Twenty blowouts later, the junker sputtered into Porterville, just north of Bakersfield, where Darrell's step-mother had relatives.

"Okies and niggers, go home," the locals often told them. "Get your asses back to Oklahoma."

Darrell learned to tame his southern accent, hoping the locals wouldn't peg him as an Okie. Instead of saying "fanger," he said "finger." Instead of "strait," he said "street." Days passed when he said nothing at all, hoping no one would notice him. The boy was quick to learn that Okies were not welcomed in the public schools and that he had a better chance of meeting cowboy movie star Johnny Mack Brown than he did of making the varsity football team.

"You're too damned small to play for me," the local coach had said. "Grow up and maybe you can play next year."

Darrell was running out of options when he received a letter from his high school back in Hollis that promised a starting job on the varsity football team and a real job at the local Ford dealership, sweeping up.

Burley Royal might have nixed the idea, but Darrell and his stepmother got along worse than Joe Louis and Max Schmeling. Thanks to a friend of a friend in Bakersfield, Burley arranged for his son to catch a ride back to Oklahoma. If Burley had taken the time to check the driver's credentials, though, Darrell wouldn't have been leaving with him that day—or any day, for that matter.

Along with some hard-earned cash, Darrell's only possessions were stuffed into a box that once had held a Victrola record player with a hand crank. He slowly approached the truck, now warming up for the long journey, and pulled a ten-dollar bill from his overalls. Sliding into the passenger seat, he placed the box close to his side but out of the way of the shifting rod that stuck up through the truck's floorboard. He had decided that he would never let the box out of his sight. Now, after only three months in California, he was on his way back to the south plains.

Darrell didn't notice at first that the man had only one arm or that a box resting on the floorboard was stuffed with pint bottles. Hours later, after the driver had slugged down enough whiskey to kill a mule, the car ascended into the mountains. The driver wasn't prepared for the blowout that caused the truck to swerve toward the edge of the cliff. Thanks to some timely luck, the truck stopped about two feet short of the edge. Otherwise, it would have tumbled over and plummeted several hundred feet.

Darrell peered at the old man with one arm and said, "Billy, do ya want me to drive?"

"Nah. But you can get out and fix the flat."

With the tire plugged and the car back on the highway, Darrell kept his eyes focused on the edge of the mountain. To his horror, there was no guardrail, and old Billy was drinking more and more as time passed and paying less attention to the road.

"How many times you made this trip?" Darrell said.

"Enough to know that it's scary'n hell."

Two hours later, the car descended into the desert and Darrell was able to sleep for a few hours. But he was haunted by a falling sensation—a nightmare that would plague him for several weeks.

Darrell decided to bail out at Amarillo, which was only about 150 miles from Hollis. He watched as the old truck swerved from one side of the highway to the other, old Billy driving southeast across the Texas Panhandle, headed into oblivion. The boy stuck out his thumb and prayed the next driver was drinking Coca-Cola.

• • •

Most folks would have thought that Darrell's world had gone to hell in a handbasket when, in fact, he was happy for the first time in years. He looked forward to living full-time at Grandma Harmon's house, a place that felt like home, anyway. Grandpa Harmon was long dead, so it would just be the two of them. He loved the way Grandma Harmon cooked and her thoughtful ways. On the frigid nights when he was off playing high school basketball in a bandbox down the highway, she would heat a flatiron on the wood-burning stove, wrap it in newspapers, and slide it into the covers of her favorite grandson's bed.

Darrell had spent the better part of an hour telling Mrs. Harmon about his hard road back to Oklahoma.

"Were you scared?" she asked.

"Nah."

"I guess you're either too young or too dumb."

They both laughed and sat down to a big dinner.

All of the predictions about Darrell's athletic future would come to pass. The twenty-five hundred residents of Hollis had known for years that he was destined to become their biggest star. Darrell quarterbacked the Tigers to an undefeated state championship season as a senior in 1942. Hollis beat Oklahoma City power Classen High, 27–14, in the state title game, as Darrell threw two touchdown passes and returned an interception sixty yards for another score.

Recruiters from several states were ready to offer scholarships to Darrell, along with a handful of others from Hollis. Just as soon as the war ended, Darrell planned to make a beeline to Norman.

5

RAW HIDE

The afternoon was like a cattle drive rumbling north from the Rio Grande Valley when the Oklahoma Sooners gathered for the first practice in the summer of 1946. For months Tatum and Wilkinson had coaxed and signed players at a frantic pace, and now they had enough meat on the hoof for a stampede.

Equipment manager Sarge Dempsey, a small and spirited Irishman, was exhausted after issuing 375 uniforms. He sprawled onto a stray blocking dummy, uncorked a bottle of Old Crow, and poured the amber liquid down his throat.

"Somethin' tells me that if you can walk and talk, they think you can play football round here," Buddy Burris said as he joined the herd. "We've got enough fart-knockers to start another war."

Homer Paine set eyes on Buddy, and his jaw dropped. "Dang, boy, I heard you got killed by the Japs. I never figured I'd ever see you again."

"Ain't no Jap mean enough to kill ol' Buddy."

Surveying the phalanx of players that stretched almost a quarter-mile, Dempsey cocked an eyebrow and took another long pull.

"We've got more players than all the goddamn NFL teams put together. Wonder where all them other schools plan to get theirs?"

Tatum knew the majority of these boys were not capable of playing big-time college football and pretty soon he would have to figure a way to cut the squad. But by bringing so many players to Norman for the *big* tryout, he was depriving other schools of some good hands.

War veterans really knew the value of M-O-N-E-Y. Most had returned from the service with empty pockets. Recruits who visited the campus were led into Tatum's office, where the coach was normally found sitting in his underwear, smoking a cigar. As the player took a seat across the desk, Tatum would open a deep desk drawer and say, "Feast your eyeballs on this, big fella."

Mountains of large bills caused eyes to pop. The slush fund, which amounted to $125,000, had been raised during the war years. Of course, most of the great players were at war and there was no need to pay the rinky-dinks, who were merely occupying uniforms until the studs got back. Of the thirty-three Sooners who suited up against Texas in '42, only two returned the following season.

When Snorter Luster resigned, the money was returned to the athletic department, and it was only a matter of days before Tatum got his sticky fingers on it. Tatum planned to pay big wads in advance to the best studs. During the season, players would receive twenty-five bucks for touchdowns, fifteen bucks for interceptions, and ten for fumble recoveries.

"I promise you," Tatum told each recruit, "there'll be plenty of dough to go around. But if you tell anybody, I'll personally cut your balls off."

Oklahoma possessed a wealthy elite that was by-god determined to return the Sooners to their former greatness. Not everyone had gone bankrupt during the hopeless thirties. Several doctors and real estate brokers flourished in both Oklahoma City and Tulsa. Wildcatters, in spite of falling oil prices, were turning black gold into great wealth.

"We might have just found ourselves a money machine," Tatum told Wilkinson. "Shit, the oilys, doctors, lawyers, and them real estate bubbas are buzzin' round here like a bunch of bees. We got thousands and thousands still comin'."

Among the leading OU power brokers were Bud Bowers, Harrison Smith, E. G. "Big Boy" Johnson, Carl Anderson, Dr. C. R. Rountree, and Eddie Chiles, a rich oilman from Abilene. Tatum also knew he could depend on a boost to his bankroll from Jewel Ditmars.

Like the fat cats with their thick wallets, Jewel started attending Tatum's practices from day one. While Tatum considered himself the main attraction, many eyes were tracking the new assistant coach with the wavy blond hair and the silky personality.

It didn't take Tatum and Wilkinson long to notice there was some fine-looking stock among the players they had recruited. The top blue-chippers included linebacker Myrle Greathouse, quarterback "General" Jack Mitchell, the brother tandem of Plato and Dee Andros, center John Rapacz, tackle Homer Paine, tackle Wade Walker, end Stan West, Buddy Burris, and a little tough by the name of Royal, who was a quarterback, halfback, punter, and possibly the most confident man on three fields.

Those practice fields were bursting at the seams with Sooners, and by the third day the grass was worn to a nub. Tatum knew it was time to start culling.

He told his assistants, "When you see a boy get the shit knocked out of him, take down his name. When you see a boy knock the shit out of another boy, get his name." It didn't take a genius to know that Tatum was placing a premium on hitting—that he would keep the hard guys and weed out the weaklings.

During the afternoon practice, Buddy steamrolled the tackle in front of him on three consecutive plays. One of the assistant coaches dashed across the field and breathlessly said, "Can I get your name?"

"Kiss my ass," Buddy growled. "If Tatum didn't want me, he wouldn't have paid me in advance."

One afternoon, a quitter stumbled into the locker room, bruised and bleeding. About the same time, Sarge Dempsey was upturning another bottle of Old Crow. The soon-to-be ex-player peered around the room and saw dozens of whiskey bottles. He uncorked one, threw back his head, and drank deeply.

"Now you're feelin' better, laddie," Sarge said. "Have another drink on me."

As the weeks passed, buses and trains carried more and more of the weakhearted away. The roster, now below 100 players, was almost manageable, and Tatum was ready to start prepping the team for the season opener at West Point.

But there was one more piece of important business. The boy's name was George Brewer, and he was about the only high school player that Tatum wanted on his squad. Adding to Brewer's value were the letters that Tatum had been receiving from a man he *really* wanted on his team—Eddie Chiles of Abilene.

Chiles's huge bankroll had been built in the oil well acidizing business and now was scaling tall mountains in the drilling industry. He was intelligent and sharply dressed and recently had been rubbing shoulders with oil baron H. L. Hunt himself. Chiles owned his own airplane, a fact that greatly impressed Tatum. More important, Chiles displayed an eagerness to play wallet whip-out.

The West Texas oilman had a lot to prove. He'd been a dirt-poor teenager when he arrived on the OU campus and, as a student, had lived in the basement of a sorority house where he washed dishes and took his meals in the kitchen. The sorority girls had paid little attention to Eddie and certainly had no intention of going out with him. He pledged to himself that he would never forget the humiliating experience.

Chiles now greatly admired Brewer, the fastest kid in Texas, so it became incumbent on Tatum to sign the boy.

During a coaches' meeting one afternoon, Tatum leaned toward

Wilkinson and said, "If I get Chiles on our side, we'll have a pot of cash."

Convincing Brewer to play for the Sooners would be another matter. Texas, SMU, Notre Dame, and several other powerhouses were recruiting him. Brewer had graduated from Lubbock High a semester early and spent the spring term at Texas Tech, where he won the 100-yard dash in the Border Conference track-and-field meet with a time of 9.7 seconds. Brewer's family preferred the University of Texas, but the speedy halfback had his heart set on SMU.

That's when Tatum and Chiles stepped in.

Wilkinson was wearing an OU T-shirt when he picked up young George at the airport.

"What position do you play?" George asked.

"Oh, I'm one of the coaches," Wilkinson said. George couldn't believe his ears. Wilkinson seemed no older than the students back at Texas Tech.

The next morning, Wilkinson took Brewer to Tatum's house for breakfast.

"We gotta have ya," Tatum said. "You're the best-looking running back that I've ever seen."

The boy thought he was going to choke on his ham and eggs. "Ah, Coach," he said. "I like it here. But I gotta talk to my parents first."

Tatum reached for the phone and said, "Operator, go ahead and place that call that I asked for."

Hearing his dad's voice on the other end, George said, "I think I fit pretty good here in Oklahoma. They say I can start as a freshman."

Charlie Brewer was reluctant to have his son leave Texas. Ma Brewer had the same reservations, but she knew of a certain petroleum engineer with his own airplane who would watch over her son. Both parents gave George their blessings.

After finishing his breakfast, George said good-bye to Tatum and

Wilkinson and headed for the door. A few steps down the sidewalk, he heard boisterous laughter and Tatum's booming voice.

"Looks like we just landed Eddie Chiles!" Tatum thundered.

"Shhhh. The boy might still be able to hear you."

They didn't need to whisper. George knew the whole story. He was just happy that he had a man like Chiles on his side.

• • •

Tatum, his shirttail flopping from his pants, was wrung out with stress as he prowled the sideline of Michie Stadium, where the famous Army Cadets had ruled college football for most of the 1940s. He wished for a stiff drink and a place to sit down. West Point was turning yellow-gold on a Saturday in late September when the wind rippled the Hudson River and a cardigan sweater would get you through the afternoon.

Unfolding before Tatum was a weird scene—the Army Cadets, proud holders of a nineteen-game winning streak, under siege from the Oklahoma Sooners. This was the Army of Blanchard and Davis, Mr. Inside and Mr. Outside. The Cadets had dismantled opponents by an average of almost three touchdowns the two last seasons. But America's top-ranked football team had registered but two first downs and the game was tied at seven at halftime.

Above the grandstand in a suite on the press level, George Cross was lost in thought. A balding man with wire-rimmed glasses rapped him on the arm with a fist hardened by a heavy ring.

"George," Pres. Harry Truman said. "You were right about one thing, by god. You boys have one helluva line."

Rapacz, Burris, West, Paine, Walker, and Andros were battering Army like Patton through Tunisia. Glenn Davis and Doc Blanchard had nowhere to run, and the Cadets were frustrated. For the first time in several seasons, they were facing a team with more scrap and muscle.

Stan West and Norman McNabb opened the scoring by stacking their bodies atop a loose football in the end zone. Punter Joe Green had botched the snap, and the two Sooners were upon him before he could put foot to the football. Army tied the score in the final minutes before halftime as the Cadets ditched their famous running game. Quarterback Arnold Tucker completed two straight passes to Blanchard and a third to Henry Foldberg for the eleven-yard touchdown.

Tatum's contorted face turned purple as the Sooners inched closer to the Army goal in the third quarter. From the eight-yard line, quarterback Dave Wallace attempted an option pitchout and was tractored under by two Cadets. The pitch fluttered like a wounded bird toward halfback Darrell Royal, who tipped the ball with his left hand but never controlled it. Tucker, who doubled as a defensive back, scooped the ball on one bounce and sprinted ninety-two yards for a touchdown.

A meltdown was under way on the sideline. Tatum's arms rotated like windmills, and his body shook as if an earthquake had struck the East Coast. He fell to his knees.

"Water!" he yelled. "Water! I am dying of thirst."

He wheeled and sprinted toward the bench, where halfback Charlie Sarratt was soaking a sprained ankle in a bucket of ice. Tatum yanked Sarratt's foot from the water and hoisted the large wooden container to his lips, drinking deeply. Players were so astounded at the sight that they stood frozen in their tracks.

"Why didn't he just drink out of one of the coolers?" George Brewer asked. Large water containers sat at both ends of the bench.

Rapacz didn't even smile. "Maybe he just likes the taste of Charlie's foot."

Tatum calmly dropped Charlie's foot back into the bucket and sauntered back to the sideline as if nothing out of the ordinary had happened.

If not for eight fumbles by the Sooners and Army's return of a botched pitch for one touchdown and a blocked punt for yet another, Oklahoma would have been poised to win in the final quarter. In spite of the 21–7 loss, the eastern press dispatched glowing reports on Oklahoma, praising Tatum for the rebirth of a languishing program. Indeed, the Sooners were back.

But they were also in a foul mood on leaving West Point.

"Dammit, Darrell, why'd you have to fumble?" Buddy Burris growled loud enough for the entire team bus to hear.

"Go to hell, you big ape," Royal shot back.

This would have been the trip of a lifetime for the Sooners, who had arrived two nights earlier at LaGuardia Airport in New York and turned the city upside down before being bussed seventy miles to West Point Saturday morning.

Thirty-seven players were paraded onto the stage of the St. James Theatre Friday night just minutes before the curtain went up on the musical *Oklahoma!* The packed house roared its approval. *Oklahoma!* had enjoyed an overwhelming success since opening on Broadway on March 31, 1943. The first collaboration between Richard Rodgers and Oscar Hammerstein had turned the New York theater scene on its ear, inspiring long waiting-lines for tickets. Folks in Oklahoma were experiencing a spiritual renewal, thanks to the positive light now shining on their state. Not since the onset of the Depression, the drought, the Dust Bowl, and World War II had Oklahomans felt so good about themselves. They were beginning to think of themselves as "the people of the golden haze."

Observing the well-groomed and affluent crowd from stage level, Buddy Burris said, "Hell, these people think we're gods. I'll bet they'll all be at the game tomorrow, just to see me."

After the disappointing loss to Army, the Oklahoma Sooners were exhausted and ready to go home. But Burris, Rapacz, Andros, and Walker had a little surprise planned for Jim Tatum on the eight-hour flight back to Oklahoma.

The Sooners were traveling on two DC-3 twin-engine airplanes used during the war and recently purchased by newly formed Braniff Airlines. The planes crawled through the air at speeds that approached 160 miles per hour. It was the first time that an Oklahoma squad had used air transportation—but it barely felt like flying.

Tatum had made the decision to charter two planes. "By god," he told Wilkinson, "if one of these suckers goes down, we'll still have enough players to play the game." Tatum's limited view made it impossible for him to anticipate that a fatal crash of either airplane would surely precipitate the cancellation of the game.

Now, as the aircraft was about to level off, Tatum knew in his heart they were going to crash.

Rapacz, Burris, Walker, and Andros gathered at the rear of the plane, near the kitchen, and discussed their strategy. They had imbibed a case of beer and now wanted to show their coach an old war trick. They ran together from the back of the plane to the front, then ran back.

The DC-3's nose and tail began to bob up and down in the air, much like a dolphin frolicking at sea.

Tatum leaned over and grabbed his ankles. "Goddammit! Make it stop!" he yelled. "I'm going to be siiick!"

Rapacz, Burris, Andros, and Walker had grown calloused to life-threatening situations. Now, with several beers under their belt, they certainly weren't afraid of a roller-coaster ride in the sky. They thundered up and down the aisle as fast as their feet would carry them.

Fortunately, the pilot also was unfazed. As the nose of the plane dipped the first time, he figured the boys were having some fun in the back. So he began to manipulate the trim tab—an instrument situated next to his right leg that resembled a small steering wheel. While several passengers, including the stewardesses, thought they were going to die, the pilot was confident he could keep this flying beer party in the air.

One of the stewardesses locked her arms around Rapacz's waist, trying to stop the big center. But he merely swept the small woman off her feet and carried her to the back of the plane. Three more players joined the parade up and down the aisle, and now the DC-3 was bucking like a bronco through the clouds.

The pilot opened his microphone and said in an unusually calm voice, "Gentlemen, it appears that we are experiencing some turbulence. Please take your seats or I'm going to *crash* this sonofabitch!"

Tatum lost his breakfast in a barf bag. Burris looked at Rapacz, who looked at Walker, who looked at Andros. They laughed and plopped into their seats. The flight was smooth sailing the rest of the way to Oklahoma City.

But the bumpy ride known as Oklahoma football was just beginning.

. . .

By anyone's standards, the first season under Tatum and Wilkinson would have been considered a success—a 7–3 record that included a bone-crushing 72–13 defeat of Oklahoma A&M in the season finale. Tatum pulled the starters at halftime, and A&M fans were so incensed that they waved car keys and threw pennies on the field, accusing the Sooners of being bought and paid for.

Word began to circulate that OU would be invited to its first bowl game since 1939 and the opponent would be North Carolina State in the Gator Bowl. Then some really interesting rumors started to spread.

A rift had developed at Maryland between the school president and the head coach, a man named Paul "Bear" Bryant. Curly Byrd couldn't get along with Bryant, who moved on to Kentucky. Now Curly wanted Tatum, who wasn't running from the rumors or the opportunity.

On December 29, two days before the Gator Bowl, Cross received a call at his office from Lloyd Noble.

"I'm hearing that he's going to Maryland and I say let's let him go!" Noble said. "Get Wilkinson's name on a contract." The president received a similar call from E. G. "Big Boy" Johnson.

Cross was known for doing everything by the book, and he wasn't quite ready to act. "I could fly down to Jacksonville and talk to Bud," he said. "But I'm sure all of the flights are booked up for the holiday."

"Sit tight," Noble said. "I'm sending my plane."

Down in Jacksonville, Wilkinson and Cross huddled in a small hotel room.

"Bud, this is going to sound a little odd," Cross began, "but I'm offering you the head coaching job even before Tatum resigns. If he changes his mind, we'll have to figure something out."

Wilkinson said he would have to analyze the situation, that he was still considering entering the business world, perhaps working for his father in Minnesota. After the Sooners' 34–14 victory over North Carolina State, Wilkinson sat down for drinks with Curt Gowdy, the play-by-play voice of the Sooners and his best friend.

"Curt, what you would think of me as the next coach of the Oklahoma Sooners?"

"Ah, Bud, you'd never make it. You're too nice."

"That's too bad, Curt. They just offered me the job."

For days upon days back in Norman, Tatum walked the halls, mumbling to himself and pounding his fists into the walls. He resigned twice and changed his mind both times. He demanded that publicist Harold Keith be fired. Tatum obviously didn't know that Keith was a great friend of Cross and that he was the most respected sports information director in college football.

At three o'clock one morning, Tatum banged on the front door of Big Boy Johnson's house on Main Street in Norman. His eyes were filled with rage. "By god," he said. "I know you're the one who's tryin' to get me run off. You boys want Bud. Well, I can tell you one thing, mister. Bud Wilkinson ain't gonna coach here. If I leave, he's goin' with me."

Big Boy was not one to be pushed around but decided to take the high road and offer the coach a stiff drink. An hour later, the two men hugged as Tatum left the house. Big Boy felt in his heart that he'd seen the last of the big man.

On January 17, Cross was working behind his oaken desk when he spotted a note that someone had slid beneath his office door.

It stated that Tatum had left Norman that day for another coaching job. The anonymous author also informed Cross that Tatum had kept a large stash of cash in the bottom drawer of his desk, and it might be worth checking to see if the money was still there.

Cross hurried out of his office and ran down the sidewalk toward the fieldhouse, where the coaches' offices were located. He marched into Tatum's dark and empty office and yanked open the right bottom drawer.

The drawer was empty.

6

GREAT WHITE FATHER

Bud Wilkinson sat rigidly behind the oaken desk in the room where dust refused to gather. His life was in perfect order in the fall of 1953—and so was his office. His hair was now the color of harvested cotton. The knot of his necktie bumped against the bottom of his Adam's apple. Four other offices adjoined this one, but voices were not audible. People whispered, knowing that Bud could hear them through the thin walls and that he heard *everything* they said about him.

"Shhhh," said Gomer Jones. "You know Bud's got the rabbit ears. Shush if you don't want him to hear ya."

Port Robertson, now standing in Jones's office, might have been the only person on earth more organized than Wilkinson. Robertson's life was like a passenger train ten minutes fast. He slept only four hours a night—every night—because the Oklahoma Sooners commanded the other twenty. Wilkinson found new jobs for Robertson the same way that Joe McCarthy found Communists.

It had begun a few years earlier when Port gained national attention as the Oklahoma wrestling coach. Bud so admired his work ethic that he assigned him to oversee academic counseling and then added another title—the czar of *everything*. Port's day ended with the eleven o'clock curfew, and it began at five in the morning when the laggards, the rogues, and the misfits ran seventy-two stadium steps until they dry-heaved.

"Port, if you ever quit," Gomer once said, "it'll take eight dang men to replace ya."

Port had become mystified at his own power. Wilkinson had recently named him the head freshman football coach, a job that hardly fit his résumé. Though Port was a rock-hard forty-six-year-old ex-marine, the notion of actually coaching football was discombobulating. He had been a great college wrestler and knew deep inside that he was born to teach the sport. But football?

"Sometimes I wonder if I'm doing my job right," Port half-whispered to Gomer. "I never get much direction from Bud."

"Well, if you're so dang worried, why don't you march yourself right up to *the Man's* office. I know he's up there."

Port took a deep breath and headed up the stairs to the office, where he found Wilkinson signing letters at his desk. For the next five minutes Port poured out his heart. He listed several concerns, including his lack of familiarity with the intricacies of football. Port confirmed that he could handle all of these jobs and the long workdays were no problem. But some advice would be nice. Then, waiting for a response, he suffered through a long silence while the coach continued to sign letters. Finally, without looking up, Wilkinson said, "Port, if there's anything I can do for you, just let me know."

That morning, Wilkinson never heard the door close, never heard footsteps down the stairway. His mind was traveling into the zone. He placed the ink pen on the desk and now his eyes were fixated on a place on a wall across the room. His mind settled into a meditative state. This was a time when Wilkinson planned everything, from the strategy sessions with the coaches, to the skull sessions with players, to the afternoon practice, to cocktails before dinner. Everything would be scheduled to the precise minute.

But things were going to change this day. Wilkinson desperately needed to solve a riddle that was driving him crazy. He hoped to unravel the enigma by going back in time.

Wilkinson didn't need anyone to tell him of his successes the last six seasons or his profound impact on the OU football program or that he had raised the bar for every college coach. He was moving rapidly into the company of the legendary coaches like Frank Leahy. The trappings included a national championship in 1950, a thirty-one-game winning, streak, and a Heisman Trophy won by halfback Billy Vessels.

Nothing was more satisfying to Wilkinson than the success enjoyed by Vessels. The coach had never seen a running back with a better combination of speed and power than Vessels, who might run over two defenders and outrun three more the distance of fifty yards to the end zone. He was a natural. Not only was he the most dominant offensive college player in '52, but also few tackled with a greater fury than Vessels. Two of his victims had to be carried unconscious from the field the year he won the Heisman Trophy, and one required brain surgery to survive the hit.

Adding to Wilkinson's list of impressive credentials was the fact that the Sooners had never lost in conference play during his tenure as the head coach. Also, the 1948 and '49 seasons were culminated with victories over North Carolina and LSU in the Sugar Bowl, and it had taken a wise strategist like Paul "Bear" Bryant to shatter America's longest winning streak. Kentucky beat the Sooners 13–7 in the 1951 Sugar Bowl.

Wilkinson grieved over losses, the acid boiling in his stomach for days, but he was quickly over the Kentucky defeat. Bryant was a drinking buddy and a close friend and Wilkinson deeply admired him. But Bryant was not an ally when the two were coaching against each other and knew how to attack Wilkinson's team better than anyone else. Bryant would set nine men within three yards of the line of scrimmage and dare the Sooners to pass.

Claude Arnold, who quarterbacked the Sooners to the 1950

national title, passing for a school-record fifteen touchdowns, over-threw open receivers time and again against Kentucky, greatly frustrating the Sooner fans.

After the team returned from New Orleans, Billy Vessels and five other players shuffled into a bar on the south side of Oklahoma City. As they ordered drinks, an inebriated customer blurted, "Arnold *threw* the game!"

It took the other four Sooner players almost five minutes to pull the hot-tempered Vessels off the battered and bleeding man.

. . .

After seven seasons of coaching, the pictures were on the wall for all to see: All-Americans Darrell Royal, Buddy Burris, Tom Catlin, Eddie Crowder, Buck McPhail, Jim Weatherall, Leon Heath, Buddy Jones, Frankie Anderson, Wade Walker, Stan West, Jim Owens, George Thomas, and Billy Vessels.

This amazing run had begun in 1947, when Wilkinson, at age thirty-one, became the game's youngest coach. Tatum, who left Norman with a loaded satchel, landed at the University of Maryland, ironically replacing Bryant as the head coach. Wilkinson already was considered one of the leading strategists and recruiters in America, with a sideline aura even larger than Leahy's. According to the *New York Times,* Wilkinson "was the most handsome man in all of college football." Hands down, he was the best dressed.

But gradual changes had taken place. Year by year, the thick blond hair had turned whiter and whiter, giving rise to his christening as the "Great White Father." The moniker was born from the lips of guard Joe Henderson, part–Cherokee Indian from East Texas. Because the early U.S. presidents were photographed in white wigs, Indians dubbed them "Great White Father." Though Wilkinson's hair was not powdery white, he certainly maintained an air that was presidential.

No one called him the Great White Father to his face. But word did weave its way to him one day that players were calling him something other than *Coach*. His reaction? "I certainly hope that I don't look that old."

So why, after such a great run of success, was the "Great White Father" so depressed? After all, the man had recruited most of the great players and created the blueprint for success. After Tatum skedaddled, Wilkinson took charge of the runaway train and molded the war veterans into sober soldiers. The lion's share of the thirty-one-game winning streak had been produced by ex–military men like Royal and Burris and Jack Mitchell, John Rapacz, Stan West, and a twenty-nine-year-old center named Harry Moore.

• • •

Notre Dame was the source of Wilkinson's consternation as the Sooners prepared to open the 1953 season. Wilkinson couldn't figure out Frank Leahy. Now, the Irish were coming to Norman as the top-ranked team in the preseason polls.

A year earlier, the Irish and the Sooners had staged one of college football's greatest games ever in South Bend. At the time, Leahy, who had succeeded Knute Rockne, had won 88 percent of his games. Remarkably, Wilkinson's winning percentage was 90 percent. Tickets to the '52 game were sold out for months in advance.

Billy Vessels tore through the Irish for 195 yards and three touchdowns, one that covered 62 yards. Though he averaged 11.5 yards per carry, the Sooners managed to lose 27–21. Years later, in his memoirs for *Look* magazine, Leahy would write: "The best team that our lads faced—and I didn't see the great Army aggregations of '44 and '45 because I was in the service—was Oklahoma of '52. Upsetting them was my greatest coaching thrill."

As he pondered the Irish coming to Norman that very weekend in 1953, Wilkinson remained in deep meditation. The stare became almost laserlike. This would be his last shot at Leahy, who was planning to retire at the end of the season, preferably with his fifth national championship tucked away.

The third Saturday of September was what you would expect in Norman—temperatures pushing 100 degrees and heavy humidity rolling up from Texas. Wilkinson's team had reported in the best overall shape of his coaching career, but he still worried about the size of his players. They would be outweighed twenty pounds per man in the line. Even more worrisome, the Sooners had graduated four All-Americans—halfbacks Billy Vessels and Buck McPhail, center Tom Catlin, and quarterback Eddie Crowder. The only member of the 1952 backfield not voted to the All-American team was Buddy Leake, and he was shifting from right halfback to quarterback, a move that inspired restless sleep. Though Leake was one of the best all-round players, the boy had never taken a snap from a center during a game—not in grade school, junior high, or high school. Playing quarterback in the Split-T offense was often like performing magic. The quarterback often audibled at the line of scrimmage. It became incumbent on him to read the movement of tackles, ends, and linebackers before pitching or keeping the ball.

To balance out their rawness, the Sooners prayed the suffocating heat and humidity would help. By the second quarter, concession stands had run dry of soft drinks and fans at Owen Field were leaning over the rails and asking the players to hand over the Cokes that were swimming in ice barrels at the end of the bench. The Sooners thought better about sharing the precious liquid. Dehydration and muscle cramps might be just around the corner. As the day progressed, fans fell out from heat exhaustion and were carried out of the stadium on stretchers manned by Boy Scouts. Some of the younger boys were not strong enough for the task, and a few fans were spilled.

The smaller Sooners unleashed a bottled aggression in the early minutes as guards Bo Bolinger and J. D. Roberts slammed into fullback Neil Worden and he fumbled into the arms of Bill Bowman. Leake ran the option in the same cool fashion as Crowder and pitched to halfback Larry Grigg, who cut inside and sprinted twenty-three yards to the goal.

It didn't take the Irish long to live up to their national reputation. Quarterback Ralph Guglielmi completed an eight-yard touchdown pass to Henry Heap, tying the score.

Little Jack Ging tore into the end zone from the eighteen-yard line minutes later with such force that Art Gleason, broadcasting the game for the Mutual Network, told his audience, "If the south stands hadn't been there, the little guy would have been in Paul's Valley by now." Paul's Valley is a farming town about sixty miles south of Norman.

The Sooners should have led 14–7 at halftime. But Doc Hearon and Roberts missed blocking assignments on a punt, allowing the linebacker a free lane through the middle of the line. He smothered Max Boydston's kick—the ball bounding to the Oklahoma nine. Guglielmi faked the pitch and ducked inside and reached the end zone untouched. The game was tied at fourteen. Roberts slung his helmet more than thirty yards when he got to the sideline.

Wilkinson worried that the blocked punt would cost his team momentum, and it did. Fumbles and interceptions didn't help. In all, the Sooners would turn the ball over seven times. Notre Dame scored two touchdowns in the third quarter, wearing down the Sooners with their bulk.

Half-jokingly Merrill Green often told the coaches, "Don't put me in unless you want a touchdown." Wilkinson rarely took him seriously, and the senior had spent the better part of his career on the second and third teams. He stood all of five-foot-seven and weighed about 145 pounds. In spite of these shortcomings, Wilkinson decided to send Green out for a spin in the fourth quarter.

Fielding a punt at the Sooner forty, Green juked and pulled himself free of three tacklers. Ging picked off a Notre Dame defender with a cross-body block, and Green saw wide-open spaces ahead. He hip-faked the punter at the ten and sprinted into the end zone, his sixty-yard return for a touchdown, taking some of the edge off the 28–21 loss.

Head down, Wilkinson paced for several minutes before addressing the team after the game: "One of these days . . . one of these *days* we will beat this team. I promise you that as I am standing here before you." Sooner players had never seen a more determined expression on the man's face.

The Great White Father felt a similar kind of frustration the following week after Pittsburgh and the Sooners played to a 7–7 tie, the Panthers holding the offense to sixty-three rushing yards, an all-time low for a Wilkinson team. The Sooners had to prevail four times on goal line stands just to tie the game. Wholesale changes were overdue. Only twice in Bud's seven seasons had the Sooners gone two straight weeks without a victory.

Monday, Wilkinson called Gomer Jones into his office. His chief assistant coach for the last six years didn't need a crystal ball to know what would be discussed.

"We must take the offense apart," Wilkinson said. "I know you probably don't think the time is right for this. But I want Gene Dan Calame to play quarterback."

It did rankle Jones to lose a fine defensive end like Calame, one of the brightest and toughest boys on the squad.

"You know, they'll be laughing up at Notre Dame," Bud said. "It does look pretty bad that we're moving a defensive end to quarterback."

Calame was not a particularly great athlete but possessed both guts and a tough outer shell. He was born to two deaf parents. As a child, he had accidentally set himself on fire while getting dressed for his early-morning newspaper delivery in the small town of Sulphur, located in south central Oklahoma. Wearing three layers of clothes to combat the cold, Gene's right leg brushed against a gas heater, igniting the cotton pants. He rolled on the bathroom's linoleum floor but couldn't snuff the fire. His screams went unheard. Finally, his mother, Lillian, saw flames shooting from underneath the door and doused her blazing son with a bucket of water.

A local doctor diagnosed the burns as first-degree. Then, when the skin began to shrivel and the knee to lock up, the doctor suggested to the family that knee ligaments be severed. Fortunately, Guy Calame sensed the doctor didn't know what the hell he was talking about. So he transported his son to the children's hospital in Oklahoma, where the burns were diagnosed as third-degree. Doctors at the hospital tied a rope around Gene Dan's right foot and attached weights to the other end. The weights were left to dangle over the footboard of the bed and, day by day, the leg straightened a little. The boy coped with a pain that felt like daggers piercing his skin. Six weeks later, after a series of skin grafts, Gene left the hospital, and three days later he was back on the streets, pitching newspapers.

The Sooners' backfield was now Calame at quarterback, Bob Burris at fullback, Tom Carroll at right halfback, and Larry Grigg at left halfback.

Fullback Max Boydston was moved from fullback to tight end. Roger Nelson replaced Doc Hearon at right tackle, and both Don and Melvin Brown received promotions into the offensive line.

Wilkinson knew it would take a gambler's guts to beat Texas, coming up next in Dallas.

As Jones stood to leave, Wilkinson said, "Gomer, I want you to get ready to coach. This might be my last season. You might have to take over next year."

Those words were not shocking. Wilkinson had threatened to quit after the 1950 season, informing university president George Cross that he had accepted a job in the West Texas oil firm of Eddie Chiles. It took Cross less than a day to talk Wilkinson out of it.

Before departing Wilkinson's office, Gomer peered through the window at the seventy or so freshmen practicing in the distance on the three fields south of the stadium. Gomer thought that Port Robertson couldn't possibly calculate the star power among those players. Never in the history of OU football had so many blue-chippers come to Oklahoma. Among the leading studs were Jerry Tubbs, Jimmy Harris, John Bell, Tommy McDonald, Jay O'Neal, Billy Pricer, and Ed Gray. Normally, a coach would be happy with a recruiting class that had two future All-Americans. This freshman class had *six,* possibly more.

As Gomer reached the door, he mumbled, "Frank Leahy would give his left nut for that bunch."

"What?" Wilkinson said.

"I didn't say anything."

"Oh."

Oklahoma's game with Texas is the biggest each year for both teams, bar none. An OU coach could lose half of his games and still keep his job by beating Texas. Ask Dewey "Snorter" Luster. He did just the opposite and found himself out the door.

Wilkinson had started beating Texas in 1948 and lost only once in a five-year span. One reason for his success, he believed, was a strategy to spend the night before the game in Fort Worth, some thirty miles from the bright lights and drunken brawls of Dallas. For decades, Oklahoma and Texas fans had met in the epicenter of downtown Dallas at sundown Friday and proceeded to drink and fight until two in the morning, when the cops washed them down with street cleaners. Many landed in the drunk tank of the city jail. But the savvy ones kept enough cash on hand for bail and would be back on the streets before kickoff the next afternoon.

The Worth Hotel in downtown Fort Worth was a laid-back dinosaur that promised nothing livelier on the jukebox than Perry Como. They rolled up the downtown streets about eleven o'clock, and Port Robertson could be sure that his boys were drinking Coke and reading nothing stronger than *Playboy.* But there was an undercurrent of excitement on this trip to cowtown. Her name was Shelia

Ann and her job was pushing buttons on the hotel elevator. Dressed in a black skirt and low-cut red sweater, she crossed her legs as she sat on the wooden stool, proudly revealing her long, shapely legs and alluring portions of her ample breasts. The little flirt was nineteen years old.

"That girl makes my pecker harder than Chinese arithmetic," guard Jerry Cross said.

Shelia Ann was having the same effect on all of the players and most of the coaches, and loving every minute of it. About twenty scraps of paper were tucked away in her purse with names and room numbers, and she had promised at least half of the boys that she'd be in their room by midnight. It seemed that her elevator was full most of the day.

The players were in their rooms by eleven, but few were asleep. The smart ones had placed their bets on Jack Ging, who, in spite of his size, looked like a young movie star. Ging, in fact, often dreamed of Hollywood. He had one more advantage over the other boys in that a shoulder injury would sideline him from the Texas game. While the others were stuck in team meetings, he was riding up and down the elevator with Shelia Ann.

Each room in the Worth Hotel had a transom window. By standing on your roommate's shoulders, you had a view in both directions down the long hallway. Every time the elevator reached the eighth floor, the bell dinged and a half-dozen players were boosted onto broad shoulders for a sneak peek. They couldn't wait to see where the jiggling Sheila Ann was going.

For years and years, players had heard stories and rumors about the Great White Father's courtship of other women. Bud was known to run with a crowd of fast and rich oilmen during the off-season; tales of drinking and hanky-panky were widespread. Of course, Wilkinson kept most of his affairs quiet. Most folks knew he liked to drink, but unless you were a member of the Oklahoma City Golf and Country Club, you rarely saw him down one. Bud liked to chase women but was discreet and did most of his womanizing out of town.

On the sideline, Wilkinson appeared upright and as pure as the wheat fields. In truth, here was a man of desires. During a road trip years earlier, Harry Moore had posed the question: "Do you wonder why the flight attendants won't have anything to do with us players?"

When none of the players answered, Harry said, "Because they're sending all the poontang Bud's way."

"Amen, brother," guard Norman McNabb said.

Braniff Airlines had provided all of the charters since Wilkinson and Tatum came to Norman in 1946. The pilots and the crew of stewardesses had remained almost intact those seven seasons.

At midnight, an hour past the players' bedtime, the elevator bell dinged on the eighth floor. A half-dozen players were lifted into the voyeur pose. But they didn't see Sheila Ann. Instead, they saw two Braniff stewardesses dressed in tight skirts, black stockings, and high heels, strolling down the hallway. Six sets of eyeballs traced the women's firm backsides. What happened next left the players speechless.

The women knocked and, when Bud Wilkinson swung open that door, they eagerly entered.

• • •

This time, the Great White Father pushed all of the right buttons. Wilkinson glanced at the scoreboard in the south end zone midway into the fourth quarter to see "Oklahoma 19—Texas 0" shining brightly. After riding around Korea for three years in an army jeep, halfback Tom Carroll had strengthened his legs by working out with the OU track team, and the Longhorns had trouble catching him all day. Gene Dan Calame was exactly what Wilkinson had ordered. His steady hands alleviated the turnover problem, and his play calling was superb. Merrill Green, the touchdown maker, did it again.

"Get out the kicking tee," Green chirped as he swept past the Sooner bench moments after returning a punt eighty yards for a touchdown.

What befuddled and eventually derailed Texas was the new defense that Wilkinson and Gomer had concocted. J. D. Roberts, Bob Burris, and Kurt Burris lined up in what amounted to the defensive equivalent of a three-man I-formation. Roberts dropped into a three-point stance over the center, and Bob Burris tucked in behind him. On the snap, the two piled into the line, one going right and the other left. Kurt Burris, lined up directly behind his brother, was free to pursue the ball carrier from sideline to sideline, and the Texas option was shut down all day.

On obvious passing downs, Kurt didn't mind calling his own blitz. He had returned to the huddle after making yet another tackle when a shocking event occurred. He was socked in the jaw by his brother Bob. This, of course, was *not* what the other Sooners expected to see. Kurt was the bully. Bob, however, was one of the nicest guys you could ever meet.

During a duck-hunting trip into Guymon, way up in the Oklahoma Panhandle, Kurt became irritated one night when he couldn't sleep, thanks to a light streaming into his hotel room. So he pulled out his twelve-gauge shotgun, threw open the window, and blew the offending street lamp into smithereens.

Bob was about as mild-mannered as Clark Kent.

"Why'd you do that, little brother?" Kurt snapped, wiping blood from his lip.

"Because you won't call any of my blitzes."

"Well, it's my defense."

"Then play it by yourself."

Kurt called Bob's blitz on the next play.

Trailing by three scores, the Longhorns marched seventy-eight yards for a touchdown late in the game. Then, in the final minute, with the Sooners backed up to their goal, Wilkinson opted for a safety and a 19–9 lead. That would allow the Sooners to have a free kick up from the twenty-yard line instead of a risky punt from their own end zone.

But the crowd of 76,109 couldn't believe their eyes. Calame tucked the ball and ran out of the end zone and headfirst into a bevy of Longhorns at the one-yard line. Calame couldn't believe his eyes, either, as he lay on the floor of the Cotton Bowl, watching more than a hundred five-by-seven cards sailing into the air. Gomer Jones had become so frustrated with Calame's blunder that he flung all of his play cards into the wind.

"Don't worry about it," Wilkinson told Calame as he trotted to the bench. "And don't talk to the writers after the game."

Texas scored on the next play, and the lead was now 19–14. Texas would recover the onsides kick. But luckily for Calame, the gun sounded before they could score again.

Of course, the press came in droves to the Oklahoma locker room armed with questions about the botched safety. *"What in the world was Calame thinking, Coach?"*

"It's more than you think," Wilkinson said. "One of our linemen told him to go for it if he saw an opening."

Which was the farthest thing from the truth. What happened to Calame was the equivalent of a brain fart. Plain and simple, the boy had blown it.

The real surprise was that Wilkinson had created a subterfuge for the sporting press. The Great White Father was known for sticking his neck out for nobody. Wilkinson often seemed as warm and caring as a snowball. But it was clear from this cover-up that he respected Calame, a boy who had overcome huge obstacles as a kid.

As the writers turned to go, Wilkinson said, "Fellas, one more thing. Winning *one* in a row sure feels good."

The next week, the Kansas Jayhawks thought another black blizzard had thundered across the plains. They were smothered 45–0 by an Oklahoma team now gaining momentum. Then came Colorado, the newest member of the Big Seven Conference and an aching thorn in the Sooners' backside. Boulder fans had torn down the goalposts the previous season when Colorado tied the third-ranked Sooners 21–21.

History was repeating itself once again in mid-October of 1953. More than 40,000 fans stood and began their exodus from Owen Field with a minute to play and Oklahoma and Colorado tied at twenty.

The Sooners' first string was pooped. So Wilkinson dispatched the alternate offensive line consisting of Joe Mobra, Dick Bowman, Bo Bolinger, Gene Mears, Cecil Morris, Doc Hearon, and Kay Keller. In delicious irony, the little TD man himself got the call with thirty-one seconds left on the clock.

Merrill Green couldn't have been traveling any faster if he had been shot from a circus cannon. He slashed to the outside, where Don Brown wiped out a linebacker. Carl Allison bagged the safety. In the blink of an eye, the little halfback was gone, seventy-two yards to the end zone: Oklahoma 27, Colorado 20.

Jerry Cross bear-hugged the little man. "You ain't nothin' but a second-string All-American," he said.

Rich Oklahoma alumni flooded the OU dressing room after the game. Green set his helmet on a chair next to his locker and it soon was brimming with tens, twenties, fifties, and a couple of Ben Franklins. Doc Rountree was, as usual, the biggest contributor. The stash became so large that Green worried that someone would steal it. He didn't shower until the locker room had cleared out, almost ninety minutes later.

Green, the son of a Nazarene minister, led the nation in punt returns that season by an average of *forty-five* yards per attempt. Oklahoma's final five opponents that season scored only twenty-one points; two were held scoreless. The combined score of those final five games was 182–21. A record of 8-1-1 that included eight straight victories was certain to attract a bowl invitation.

When the Sooners held off Oklahoma A&M in the season finale by the score of 42–7, all of college football was suddenly abuzz. It would be Bud Wilkinson versus Jim Tatum in the Orange Bowl. The hype didn't stop there. The Maryland Terrapins were the number-one-ranked team in the country, and Oklahoma was weighing in at number four.

In the weeks leading to the Orange Bowl, Tatum told the sporting press, "This is the greatest team that I've ever coached."

Tatum should have mentioned he was facing the greatest coach he had ever coached—the man who had saved Oklahoma's season by shuffling the lineup against Texas. Tatum apparently forgot at least one of the tricks he had taught Wilkinson back in 1946.

As the Sooners prepared for the Orange Bowl against North Carolina, Tatum had dispatched his chief assistant to the opposing team's hotel to do some snooping around. It was Wilkinson's job to scour the hotel—mostly the hotel lobby—for North Carolina playbooks left lying around. Wilkinson did happen to retrieve one of the playbooks, and the Sooners exploited the stolen material in their 34–13 defeat of the Tar Heels.

Though Wilkinson had the face of a choir director, his cards were not always on the table. He knew that Tatum would be sending his cons to the Fontainebleau Hotel, where the Sooners were staying for the '54 Orange Bowl. So on the flight to Miami, he drew up several fake playbooks. According to these diagrams, the Sooners would be scrapping the Split-T formation for a more wide-open passing offense. That first day in Miami, Wilkinson littered his team's hotel lobby with the counterfeits.

Then, to make sure Tatum had the *wrong* playbook in his hot little hands, Wilkinson dispatched a man wearing a disguise to the Maryland hotel. His assignment was to locate a Maryland assistant coach, approach the man, and hand off the phony material.

"Sir, I believe one of your players lost this playbook."

"Oh, yes, this looks like ours."

"I'm sure you'll return it to the proper owner."

"Why, yes. Right away."

On game day at the Orange Bowl, it didn't take Tatum long to realize he had been duped. The Sooners were sticking with the Split-T, and Calame's instructions were to throw the ball only when the situation demanded it. With Calame, Grigg, Ging, and Bob Burris doing the damage on the ground, the Sooners marched to the Maryland twenty-five-yard line late in the second quarter. In a whirlwind of precision blocking that typified the Oklahoma offense, Burris nailed the linebacker, J. D. Roberts cross-body blocked the end, and Ging knocked down the safety. If that weren't enough, Calame laid the clearing block around left end himself. Grigg dragged the last Maryland defender into the end zone, and Leake's kick made it 7–0.

Calame spent the second half on the bench after separating his shoulder, but the Sooners managed to survive with Jack Van Pool making a limited number of mistakes at quarterback. The Sooners won seven–zip and Tatum faced the harsh reality of having to shake hands with his former pupil at midfield. The Sooners hoisted Wilkinson onto their shoulders and carried him to Tatum.

"Bud, you sure fooled us with your game plan," the old grouch said.

The Sooners had won nine straight. Harold Keith, college football's finest sports information director, knew it was foolish to hype such a streak. Besides, the Sooners had won thirty-one straight a few years earlier.

It would be laughable to think OU could win another twenty-two in a row.

7

YOUNG GUN

Nothing in the history of college football could compare to the wild finish of the TCU–Oklahoma game of 1954 on a warm afternoon in Norman when the wind stiffened the stadium flags and two men in striped shirts held a conference at the ten-yard line that seemed longer than the Kefauver hearings.

The 50,878 fans at Memorial Stadium were now library-quiet as field judge Don Rossi and back judge Don Looney discussed the most controversial play that anyone could remember.

"I can't believe the boy admitted he didn't catch it," Rossi said. "I called it a touchdown."

"Well, he didn't catch it," Looney flatly stated.

What were they to do? Fortunately, Looney knew the answer. The ball had skipped into the arms of TCU tight end Johnny Crouch—that much was obvious. Rossi had signaled touchdown, but it was the wrong call. Of course, officials hated to overrule each other, but Looney knew there was really no choice. Besides, Crouch himself had confessed to trapping the ball, even though it was the dangdest display of sportsmanship that either man had ever witnessed in several years of calling college ball.

Crouch had actually walked up to Rossi, handed him the football, and said, "Ref, I didn't catch it."

This happened with Oklahoma leading 21–16 and time running out in the game.

Wilkinson was worried sick as he paced the sideline, not so much about the boy's honesty but about Looney's allegiance to TCU. Looney had been an All-American end on the Frogs' 1938 national championship team. Collegiate rules still allowed officials to work games involving their alma maters in spite of the controversy that was certain to arise. Wilkinson thought the rule outrageous until Rossi walked toward the middle of the field and waved his arms vigorously—nullifying the touchdown.

As the stadium erupted into a wild celebration, Abe Martin, the wise old sage from TCU, dropped to his knees and held his chest. He pulled off his hat and slammed it to the ground. He looked like a man who had just set eyes on the devil.

"Laddie, you succumbed to the pressure!" old Abe hollered at Rossi.

"No sir, Coach. Actually, I succumbed to your own boy. He's the most honest lad I've ever seen."

The victory over TCU, combined with the win over California the previous week, meant the Sooners were certain to climb even higher in the wire service polls. The winning streak now stood at eleven games. How amazing. The blue-chip recruiting class of '53 was already in high gear—Jimmy Harris running the offense, Tommy McDonald toting the football, and Jerry Tubbs knocking the stuffing out of everything that moved.

As Oklahoma prepared to play Texas, the Sooners' only call for anxiety was Harris's two front teeth. The sophomore quarterback, who had scored twice against TCU, once on a long and snaky punt return, was now the Sooners' future at quarterback. But he was still lisping the plays, thanks to a haymaker delivered during practice by Kurt Burris.

No matter how Burris felt about the situation, Jimmy was now the starting quarterback, and Wilkinson wasn't about to send him back to to the bench. Still, Jimmy fretted over his teeth and believed the team dentist was dragging his feet.

"By God, a senior would have been fixed up by now," he lisped.

"Don't worry, Jimmy," Tubbs said. "You'll be just fine when you get your store-bought teeth. And you'll sound a lot better, too."

Jimmy was now spending more time with Bud and the little men. Carved out of wood and standing about two inches tall, the little men wore little football uniforms that included helmets and shoulder pads. The little men wore red uniforms on offense and blue on defense. They even made regular appearances on *The Bud Wilkinson Show,* launched a year earlier by TV producer Howard Neumann, who also served as co-host. It was the first college coaches' show in America.

The little men were set up on a grid that resembled a real football field. Little wooden goalposts were situated at both ends. For hours, Jimmy and the coach would play make-believe games. Jimmy was uneasy with the little men, thinking of them as a kid's toy. Jimmy didn't have money for toys growing up.

Where Harris was reared, the Rock Island trains rumbled across the black land of East Texas, rattling windows and terrorizing fowl and livestock. The backyard of the Harris home on Pecan Street in Terrell was filled with chickens. The unpainted house, built at the turn of the century, required a mortgage payment of eighteen dollars. Pockets and purses were emptied most months to keep the collectors away.

A boy really had to pull his weight in those trying times, and Jimmy Harris began milking cows when he was five years old and throwing a paper route at age eight. He was driving the family's Chevrolet at a time when his left foot barely reached the clutch and he craned his neck to see over the steering wheel.

When the bell rang at four each morning, the boy's mind was already taking care of business. But his heart was with the Terrell Tigers football team. As the old army jeep eased into the gravel driveway, Jimmy and Joe Harris would slide into the backseat, news-papers already folded and bound by rubber bands and ready to fly. The jeep would crawl through the darkness of the town's streets as the boys hurled papers to daily subscribers. Before the sun popped over the hills of the Piney Woods, a hundred miles to the east, Jimmy and Joe would throw three thousand *Terrell Tribunes;* Jimmy pretended each one was a football and he was the star quarterback.

This was more than just a couple of boys having fun and making a few bucks on the side. Bedford Larry Harris had died months ear-lier at Veterans Hospital. The head of the Harris family had been in constant pain since being shot in the back by a German foot soldier. This occurred in France during World War I; the wound never healed and was often infected. His sad condition was compounded by the chain-smoking of nonfilter Camel cigarettes, along with rheumatoid arthritis, and at the time of his death Larry Harris looked seventy-five but was only fifty-two. Blood that oozed like corn syrup through his arteries caused his heart to pop.

His sons barely knew him.

Luckily, the boys were solid hands at milking cows, tending the garden, and wringing the heads off chickens. It took Jimmy about two seconds to break one off. The cotton fields around Terrell were planted on the rich, black soil that resembled the Mississippi Delta. H. L. Hunt owned most of the land, and he was often spotted driv-ing a dirty Chevrolet through the fields of waist-high cotton, sipping on a bottle of amber liquid. Black folks who lived on the south side of Terrell—the other side of the tracks from the whites—did most of the pulling and picking.

Hearing that work was plentiful in the cotton fields, Jimmy and Joe decided to tackle yet another project. The first order of business was buying a nine-foot burlap sack that cost four bucks and held a hundred pounds. Their pay would be fifty cents per hundred. The boys were well into their second day of pulling when they finally made enough money to break even for the sack. They dropped it right where they stood.

Chunking newspapers was not the most lucrative job in East Texas, paying each boy three-fifty a month, with five bucks as a Christmas bonus. Thankfully, Annie Harris had steady full-time employment, working six days a week. But making the mortgage payments and keeping food on the table was the work of many prayers. Annie had never learned to drive, so she depended on Jimmy's savvy to keep the car between the lines while he strained to see over the wheel.

Annie Harris stood six-foot and weighed almost two hundred pounds, and she was able to carry much of the family burden on her wide, strong shoulders by working at the Ranger Boot Factory. Her sons were so involved with milking cows, catching chickens, and playing sports that she rarely had to worry about discipline prob-lems. As a 4H project, Joe Harris was raising a calf in the backyard; the boys had brought the critter home in the backseat of a '48 Chevy.

Nothing about Terrell seemed prosperous, other than the high school football team run by a former army captain named Leon Vineyard, a large and barrel-chested man who worked the boys on a gravel lot sprinkled with grass where the goat heads were as sharp as razors. This was a flatland tailored for the raising of fire ants and goat heads—gnarly little grass stickers with thorns that resembled goat horns. During conditioning drills, Coach Vineyard made the boys run on their hands and feet, like a bunch of circus bears. He wasn't happy until there was blood all over their fingers.

Driving into Terrell, seeing the black dirt and the gray clouds, you would expect to find a town of smokestacks. But only one factory operated here—the Terrell football factory. Little else mattered. The high school's basketball gymnasium had burned down, and no one had raised a finger to rebuild it.

In December of 1952, Harris threw for four touchdowns and

rushed for two others as Terrell whipped Yoakum 63–0 for the class AA state championship. The Tigers were unbeaten, and it was a fact that Jimmy had never lost a game as the starting quarterback. A week later, the run of college recruiters began on Pecan Street, where Jimmy greeted, among others, Ray George of Texas A&M and Matty Bell of SMU. Jimmy signed a Southwest Conference letter of intent with Texas A&M but dreaded the thought of playing for a man as dull as George. He often dreamed of SMU, where Doak Walker and Kyle Rote had run wild in the late 1940s.

Not only were the recruiters impressed with his passing and running, but Jimmy also had a drawer filled with blue ribbons from track and field. He was among the state's leaders in the high jump and broad jump and was running the 100-yard dash in ten seconds flat.

On Jimmy's mind at the time was the only college football game he had ever set eyes on—the 1952 clash between Notre Dame and Oklahoma. Jimmy had watched the game on a small television at the home of Reeve Holmes. Only two or three TV sets could be found in the entire county at that time. Jimmy couldn't get the lightning-quick Sooners and the hard running of Billy Vessels off his mind. Holmes was an OU alumnus and avid booster and took it upon himself to send Jimmy's high school game films to Norman.

One afternoon, a gentleman with wavy white hair knocked on the Harris front door. He was wearing a gray flannel suit. Never before had Annie Harris been so captivated with any human. Bud Wilkinson sauntered into the house and charmed the entire family. Still, the man didn't fit Jimmy's vision of a college coach, and he certainly didn't talk like one.

"If you come up to Norman and play for us, you will be playing with the best," Wilkinson said. "And if you happen to start, your name will be nationally known. Regardless of what happens, you will earn a great education."

Jimmy had never met a coach who didn't dip snuff, chew tobacco, or cuss a blue streak. In spite of this confusion, Jimmy knew from the look in Annie's eyes that he was going to the University of Oklahoma—nothing else needed to be discussed.

Two years later, Jimmy found himself in Wilkinson's office almost every day, running make-believe plays with the little men or listening to lectures on the Split-T.

Rules of the time didn't allow coaches to call plays, even with hand signals from the sideline. So Wilkinson's job was to drill his principles of the Split-T offense into the head of every quarterback. Jimmy spent a lot of time fidgeting.

"Now, Jimmy, it's third-and-five at our fifteen-yard line and they are running the six-two gap defense with the cornerbacks pinching down. What should we call?"

Then Wilkinson would line up the little men in the Oklahoma offense and the Texas defense.

"Twenty-eight option."

"Not a bad call."

The Sooners' offense in a nutshell was four running plays left, four to the right, and two option passes. There were no straight drop-back passes like in the pros. The Sooner quarterback was always throwing on the run, and if there were open spaces ahead, his first priority was to tuck the ball and take off: *"Forget the open receiver if you have room to run."*

What made the Split-T offense both complex and artistic was the quarterback's maneuvers with the football. Previous OU quarterback Eddie Crowder possessed a sleight of hand, his fakes so smooth that the defense often couldn't find the ball.

Harris already possessed Crowder's field intelligence but was a superior athlete. Jimmy, with his long stride and fluid speed, was like having another halfback on the field.

"Jimmy has the quickest hands and feet I've ever seen for a quarterback," Bud told Gomer. That was saying a lot considering the talent that had come through Norman.

It was true that Wilkinson stressed defense over offense, telling his players, "If the other team never scores, we never lose." But his offensive teams ranked in the top ten of every category virtually every season, and Vessels won the Heisman Trophy as a running back, not as a defensive back. No team in America made better use of their thirteen or so possessions each Saturday, the Sooners scoring over forty points in ten of their last twenty-two games.

Wilkinson's fascination with Jimmy extended far beyond those offensive skills. On defense, he packed a wallop and was among the hardest-hitting cornerbacks anywhere. Jimmy Harris was the total package, even if he was still a little wild.

One more piece of business had to be taken care of before the Texas game, and it involved Jerry Tubbs, the hard-hitting line-backer from Breckenridge, Texas, a boy who made the coaches smile every day.

At the moment, Tubbs was lining up at the center and linebacker with the second string, also known as the alternates. Wilkinson viewed him as one of the best all-round prospects to ever set foot on the OU campus. But the coach wasn't about to replace senior Kurt Burris. So the decision was to move Tubbs to fullback on offense so he could play with the first team.

The switch would not be that complicated. Bob Burris would move from fullback to halfback on offense and from linebacker to cornerback on defense. Bob was tall and lean and possessed natural speed. He really didn't resemble his bulked-up older brother at all. Shifting Bob Burris to halfback and cornerback would be like loosening the bit on a thoroughbred racehorse.

Wilkinson could not imagine a better pair of linebackers in college football than Kurt Burris and Jerry Tubbs.

Wilkinson summoned Tubbs into his office and broke the news. He was shocked to see the boy with the fresh flattop drop his head in disappointment.

"Jerry, this is a *promotion.* You will be back at center next season when Kurt graduates."

Tubbs spoke in a thick and high-pitched West Texas drawl. When he said, "Well, Coach, I thought you were trying to run me off," it sounded like, *"Wail, Coach, I thawt yew were tryin' to run me ouff."*

Wilkinson laughed. "No, Jerry, I honestly believe you are going to be an Oklahoma Sooner for quite some time."

The Sooners trailed Texas 7–0 in the third quarter when Jimmy Harris had to make the first tough decision of his collegiate career. The ball was at the Texas thirty-six, fourth-and-one. The voice in his head told the quarterback to punt. Jimmy leaned into the huddle and said, "Boys, this might be my nuts, but we ain't punting. Forty-three dive on two." Halfback Bob Herndon dived off left tackle, and after he bowled over three Texas defenders on a fourteen-yard run, Jimmy could have kissed him.

Jimmy could also thank his lucky stars that Buddy Leake was an accomplished shortstop—he had almost signed a pro baseball contract out of high school. Jimmy's next pitchout was wild, but Leake scooped it on one hop and sprinted forty-nine yards to the one. Leake scored on the next play.

Thanks to Jimmy's clever play calling, the Sooners moved sixty yards on a fourth-quarter drive. With the ball at the one, he called his own number and danced into the end zone as the Oklahoma cannon exploded and a tide of Oklahoma crimson rolled across the Cotton Bowl.

Oklahoma won 14–7. It was Wilkinson's fifth win in the last six years over Texas, and the sporting press was talking about another national championship. Blackie Sherrod of the *Fort Worth Press* wrote: "You hear vocalisms about this being Oklahoma's greatest team in years. This is so much ripe balderdash. The acid test of a good football team is whether it can conquer its own mistakes. Oklahoma has managed to do just that."

The next two weeks, Oklahoma manhandled Kansas 65–0 and Kansas State 21–0. Then came the Colorado Buffaloes, and Wilkinson was experiencing stomach pains once more. The Buffaloes finished near the bottom of the Big Seven every year but played like the Cleveland Browns when OU came to town.

To complicate matters, Wilkinson detected a cockiness swirling about a team with a fourteen-game winning streak. He called captain Kurt Burris into his office to discuss the matter. Burris, for the moment, had made his peace with Harris but was growing more agitated by the day with McDonald, whose legs and mouth ran about the same speed.

Most of the Texas and Oklahoma boys arrived in Norman wearing a thick coat of humility. Tommy, however, was a loud little prankster. His arrogance grew as he got more playing time.

Burris and Boydston, known as the "Muskogee Duo," were getting dressed after practice one day when the subject of McDonald came up.

"I'm gonna stomp that pissant," Burris said.

Hearing the remark, Harris brightened. "I know of a good dentist."

That night, Burris made an announcement at the Jeff House that he planned to study until curfew. That, of course, meant that everyone else would study, too. Thirty minutes later, though, Burris was interrupted by loud chatter coming from Tommy's room.

"This is your last warning!" Burris yelled down the hall. "One more peep and your ass is grass!" Returning to his study table, Burris couldn't believe his ears. McDonald was still carrying on. *Did the boy have no common sense?*

Burris kicked open the door and grabbed McDonald by the throat. But the quick little halfback was suddenly around him and out into the hallway. Burris gave chase. The two thundered down the long hallway. A dozen Sooners cheered wildly.

"Catch that sonofabitch, Kurt! Kick his ass!"

Burris was only two strides behind his prey—not bad considering that Tommy was the fastest Sooner in full pads. This footrace was almost over. Burris would squash him like a bug. To Kurt's surprise, though, Tommy was still gaining steam with the dead end fast approaching.

Then he vanished . . . through an open window . . . gone. There was silence. Burris leaned through the window, his eyes searching the darkness, scanning the ground. "Oh, my god, I've killed the little peckerhead."

A stampede of Sooners players reached the stairway and rumbled down to the first floor, sounding like the German army. Kurt led the charge. They burst through the door and poured out into the courtyard, where they expected to find a broken body. But the night was still, and the full moon revealed no trace of McDonald. Then Tommy, perched high on the limb of a magnolia tree, yelled, "Hey, Kurt, I'll be your little monkey. But you gotta catch me first!" Kurt laughed as loud as the other boys—mostly out of relief. At least he hadn't killed little Bonzo.

Three days later, on a cold Saturday afternoon in Boulder, the Sooners prepared to reach a crossroads in their season. To maintain their number-three ranking behind Ohio State and UCLA, they would have to halt the Buffs, now an amazing 6–1. Colorado had throttled the first three opponents by a combined score of 132–0.

For the last year and a half, Wilkinson had been working to circumvent the rules of the one platoon, which basically required that players go both ways. One-platoon rules were complicated and changed each year.

If a player was removed from the game, and he hadn't participated in the first play of that particular quarter, he couldn't return until the next quarter. So instead of substituting one player, Wilkinson inserted an entire unit into the game. The second string became known as "the alternates."

The first team would play for the first seven or eight minutes, and Wilkinson would sub the alternates. Harris would lead the first stringers back onto the field early on the first play of the second quarter, and the alternates would replace them minutes before half-time. OU's first team was always rested in the third and fourth quarters.

But the Sooners were thin at quarterback against Colorado with Harris suffering from the flu. After riding the bench most of his career, feisty quarterback Pat O'Neal was about to get his chance. He had been bugging Bud about more playing time. Replacing Harris in the first half, though, O'Neal didn't play like a senior. On fourth-and-four from the Sooners' forty-four-yard line, he brought the offensive to the line of scrimmage, forgoing the punt.

Wilkinson was going nuts on the sideline. "Calame! Calame! Get in there and stop him!" At worst, the Sooners would be flagged for having twelve men on the field. But officials didn't notice that Calame had come tearing onto the field. O'Neal was stopped two yards shy of the first down.

Four plays later, the Buffs were on the scoreboard with the first touchdown of the day, Carroll Hardy flipping the screen pass to Frank Bernardi. The only good news was that Colorado blew the extra point.

In the third quarter, Calame led the Sooners to a quick twenty-six-yard scoring drive, pitching to Leake for the one-yard touchdown. Leake's kick was now the difference in a 7–6 game, a game that was still on the line with more than a quarter to play.

With Calame still sore from a variety of injuries, and Harris dry-heaving on the sideline, Wilkinson didn't have much choice. So back into the game trotted O'Neal with instructions to follow the code of the little men. "As you know," Wilkinson told O'Neal, "the little men would have punted on fourth-and-four."

This time, it was O'Neal's bright and shining moment as he directed the Sooners on a fifty-two-yard drive that provided some breathing room. O'Neal himself scored on a sneak at left guard, and although fullback Billy Pricer missed the kick, Oklahoma had a seven-point lead with four minutes to play, and it would stand up.

The Sooners had no trouble the next week with Missouri and coach Don Faurot, the father of the Split-T, winning 31–13.

The second half against Nebraska the following Saturday was embarrassing for the Cornhuskers, as both the OU first string and the alternates were in high gear the entire afternoon. The Sooners won 55–7.

Though Oklahoma A&M was the aggressor in the finale and out-hit Oklahoma, the Sooners won 14–0. The Aggies simply couldn't move the ball against one of the best defensive units in the country. The story of the 1954 season had been a defense that finished second nationally against the rush and fourth against the pass. No one, however, overlooked an offense that was seventh in total yards and punted only thirty-one times all season—an all-time low for a Wilkinson team.

The Sooners finished the season as the third-ranked team and a member of the Top Ten for the seventh straight year. But SID Harold Keith smelled a slight coming. Heisman voters were much more likely to vote for a quarterback or running back for the award, but the Sooners believed Kurt Burris was the best football player in the land.

So Keith went to work in his inimitable style. He wrote a short personal letter to every sports editor in America—or, at least, the 3,500 who were listed in the *Editor and Publisher Yearbook*. Since IBM had yet to invent the office copier, Keith enlisted a classroom full of aspiring secretaries to type 3,500 copies. He signed them and mailed them out from the U.S. Post Office on Gray Street. Then the Sooners waited and hoped.

This was the onset of a grand era in Oklahoma. The team with the longest winning streak in America—nineteen games—was making music you could dance to. A nation had turned its eyes to the Great Plains, believing a national championship loomed on the horizon.

In New York, Joe DiMaggio was gone and yet another superstar had emerged onto the World Series machine known as the Bronx Bombers. His name was Mickey Mantle, and he hailed from a small town in eastern Oklahoma, where his father had labored for decades in the dangerous mines.

The mines operated in every hole and corner of northeastern Oklahoma, stretching all the way to Joplin, Missouri. You could walk below the earth's surface from Commerce to Joplin, a distance of twenty miles, through the veins. Mutt Mantle, who worked underground twelve hours a day, coughed up globs of phlegm but never saw a doctor. But he did teach his son how to play baseball. One afternoon in the mid-1940s, Mutt took fifteen-year-old Mickey to an adults-only game several miles into the country. His first time up, the boy whanged a home run over the John Deere tractor that represented the left-field fence. He did it again next time up. Then, in the fifth inning, he turned around and with the same swing smashed one more than four hundred feet into the cattails beyond right field. Mickey slammed five that day, and folks were still talking about it when he took off for New York in 1951.

Mantle and Wilkinson now headed the growing list of heroes that Oklahomans had to cheer. An important message written into Rodgers and Hammerstein's musical masterpiece *Oklahoma!* was coming to pass. They were no longer the dusted-out Okies, full of despair. They were now the "people of the golden haze."

8

PIPELINE

The red earth of Oklahoma and the sands of West Texas produced oil, scrubby crops, dust storms, and football players—not in any order. Big Oil was a dream. But football was religion.

Bud Wilkinson's ascension to the head of the collegiate coaching class, and nineteen-game winning streak, was no mystery. His ability to recruit and develop talent from his own backyard was at the root of his success, his boys mostly coming from blue-collar communities where the work ethic was burned into their genes. Many grew up poor, and few enjoyed either the wealth or the privileges that Wilkinson had inherited at birth.

The Great White Father was from another part of America and, for all intents and purposes, another side of the world, where the upper-class neighborhoods of Minneapolis were tree-lined and trimmed in the color of money. His wealthy upbringing allowed him to develop his loves for both classical music and the poets of past centuries. Few could have predicted that Wilkinson would have adjusted so quickly to the Wild Western ways of Oklahoma—to the blowing dust, the sodbuster mentality, and the lust for punching holes all over the state. Of course, it didn't take a genius to recognize that boys from the southwest were hard-wired for football with their lean, hard bodies and, and more important, their tough minds.

Wilkinson wasted little time finding his way to Muskogee, situated in the rolling hills and rocky bluffs of eastern Oklahoma where three rivers converged. The Muskogee High Roughers would come to make huge contributions to the makeup of the Oklahoma Sooners. This grand era of prodigious winning would have been virtually impossible without Muskogee.

The Burris farm, south of town, was eighty acres of hell and frustration. Six boys and Paul "Pop" Burris had labored for years to keep the place alive. Back in the thirties and early forties, when the corn and the wheat shriveled and dust piled up between the furrows, they were lucky Pop Burris had a second job—buying and selling hogs.

Pop was a diversified man for this time in Muskogee County. He owned several grassy acres in Wagoner County, along with a half-dozen milk cows that provided sustenance for the large family and money for shoes and clothes. If not for the Ford tractor and the outside income, the Burrises would have been long gone down Route 66 with the other Okies fleeing to California.

Pop had already sent three boys to the University of Oklahoma to play football, and two more were ready for harvesting. Don was the only Burris boy who would never wear the crimson and cream, thanks to a knee injury that had crippled him to the point that he was lucky to walk.

Buddy was selected All-American three times, Kurt once, and Bob, the most underrated Burris of all, was about to become one of Wilkinson's most valued returning starters for the 1955 season. In fact, Harold Keith's public relations machine was already promoting Bob as OU's next All-American, along with Muskogee guard Bo Bolinger.

Kurt finished second in the 1954 Heisman race by 220 votes to Alan "The Horse" Ameche, the great running back from Wisconsin. But it was a fine consolation prize that Burris had received the most votes ever for a lineman—838. The previous high belonged to Chuck Bednarik of Pennsylvania with 336.

Max Boydston, the long, tall end from Muskogee, also won All-American honors as a senior. Now this little town in the hard country of eastern Oklahoma could count six All-Americans, five having starred for the Sooners. Halfback Preston Carpenter was the only defector to make All-American, playing at the University of Arkansas.

End Pete Smith was the first Muskogee All-American in 1937, followed by Buddy Burris in 1946-47-48, quarterback Eddie Crowder in 1952, and Kurt Burris and Max Boydston in 1954.

Located about eighty miles west of the Arkansas line, Muskogee was a quiet town where news rarely made the state wire. Until the day Deputy Sheriff Rennie Rector cracked a case that had everybody talking. Deputy Rector had been warily watching a Mexican man pushing a tamale cart through downtown Muskogee during the lunch hour. The Mexican fare was tasty but seemed underpriced to Deputy Rector. He couldn't figure how a man was feeding and clothing a large family on five cents a tamale. Deputy Rector decided to investigate one afternoon. He drove his pickup down a dusty, rutted road and discovered a tall crop of marijuana growing on two acres south of town. The tamale man, who owned the land, was arrested. But because local laws on the growing and harvesting of cannabis were hard to interpret, a local judge threw the case out. The next day, tamale man was back on the streets.

A stalk of the marijuana was kept around the Rector house several weeks so the curious townsfolk could see what the devil weed really looked like. Decades would pass before Muskogee became famous again for the mind-altering drug.

The Burrises lived just a mile from the Midland Valley railroad tracks, and it was a common sight to see broken and starving men wandering up from Hobo Jungle. Myrtle Ann often met them in the yard with a smile and a plate of food. She figured the hoboes would never steal anything with so many kids and dogs around to witness the act. There were three bedrooms—one for Myrtle and Pop, one for the boys, and one for the five girls. Another bunk bed was added each time a child was born. Like most folks at this time and place, the Burrises tolerated an outhouse.

Pop Burris was barrel-chested, with forearms the size of shoats. He was quick to laugh, quick to enjoy the moonshine brewed by local stills, and the first man in the county to rise each morning with his mind set on hard labor. By 4:00 A.M., Myrtle Ann Burris was pan-frying pork chops, baking biscuits, and beating eggs. She was legendary for her cooking, and the Burrises, in spite of their shriveling bank account, never turned away a friend, or a stranger for that matter.

A boy who spent a lot of time around the Burris farm was Joe Rector, the son Depupty Rector. Joe was a talented end and linebacker for the Muskogee Roughers and a close friend of all the Burris boys. At age six he had lost his mother to cancer, and he didn't have much of a family life. One summer day, between the morning and afternoon football practices at the high school, he spotted Pop Burris's truck pulling into the parking lot next to the team's practice field. Pop had come to pick up Lynn and Lyle, the twin boys and the youngest of the Burris clan. Joe decided to jump into the cab of the truck. He hoped to grab a free lunch at the Burris farm, where Mrs. Burris probably had the steaks battered and ready to fry. Nothing satisfied a hungry boy better than a chicken-fried steak with cream gravy spilling over the sides. Joe Rector could taste it already. The afternoon practice would be far easier to endure on a full stomach.

After the pickup traveled a few miles down the road, Joe was devastated to realize that Pop Burris had turned north and was driving the boys up to Wagoner County, where the grasses were growing again now that the rain had returned. Instead of eating a big lunch, the boys spent hours baling hay. By the time they finished sweating, grunting, and scratching every inch of their skin, they barely had time to eat baloney sandwiches before hitting the field for the afternoon practice. Joe Rector promised himself that he would avoid Pop Burris for the rest of that summer.

Year-round, the Burris farm was a beehive; no one was ever sure who was bunking in the boys' room until breakfast was served the next morning. Raymond Ford, a local boy and close friend, jumped at the chance to occupy Lynn's lower bunk one Saturday night when Lynn was sleeping over at a friend's house. At four the next morning, Pop Burris could be heard thundering down the hallway.

"Get up and milk them cows," he rumbled. "Time to milk them cows!"

When nothing stirred beneath Lynn's blanket, Pop kicked the bed and bellowed, "Get up *now* and milk them cows!" Finally, he yanked off the covers. "Raymond Ford, what the hell are you doin' here?"

With terror in his eyes and his voice rising to a girlish pitch, Raymond said, "Don't worry, Pop. I'll milk. I'll milk."

Raymond labored for two hours before the sun popped over the hills. But he was compensated in pork chops, scrambled eggs, and enough biscuits with gravy to choke a hog.

A normal day around the Burris farmhouse began with orders that revealed the chain of command:

Pop: "Kurt, milk them cows."

Kurt: "Don, milk them cows."

Don: "Bobby, milk them cows."

Bobby: "Lynn, milk them cows."

Lynn: "Lyle, milk them cows."

Lyle: "Patsy, milk them cows."

That's when Pop came unglued: "I told you boys, dammit, I don't want them girls milkin' them cows!"

Fishing trips were the happiest of times. Myrtle Ann would spend the better part of the morning filling baskets with meat and potatoes and jugs of water. Then they all piled into the cattle trailer that could handle about fifteen people, the casting rods, and enough food for an army. Kids from the neighboring farms like Crowder, Olen Treadway, Bolinger, Boydston, Carpenter, and Rector rarely missed one of these adventures. A game of football was almost certain to break out along the riverbank.

Pop drove the truck about five miles to a spot where three rivers converged—the Arkansas, the Grand, and the Verdigris. Thanks to the confluence, Muskogee was known as River City. Myrtle Ann loved nothing more than wading chest-deep into the water and hooking a ten-inch sand bass. After the brothers cleaned the fish, Myrtle Ann fired up the fryer and cooked until the Burrises and their friends and neighbors could not stuff another crumb into their mouths.

There was always time for football. "Football'll make you tough," said Pop, who had played sandlot as a kid in Idaho. "And my boys gotta be tough when they go off to play for that Wilkinson feller."

The boys practiced football every afternoon from August until January and played before ten thousand fans every Friday night at Indian Bowl, rarely leaving the field losers. During one three-year stretch, the Roughers were 38-1-1, winning consecutive state championships. The Muskogee players lived up to their nickname, Roughers, a tag placed on the team decades earlier when a visiting fan lamented, "God, those Muskogee boys are *rough.*"

Coach Paul Young was to Oklahoma high school football what Pop Burris was to farm labor. A disciple of Bear Bryant, Young drove the boys until their tongues hung out, never allowed them water breaks, and ran perhaps the most innovative high school offense in the nation, featuring an audible system that would put most college systems to shame. Having played center for the Sooners in 1930 and '31, Young was proud of the 160-mile pipeline he had built between Muskogee and Norman.

College recruiters from several states showed up at Rougher practices and the games on Friday night at Indian Bowl. But if they really wanted to see action, they needed to be at Pop Burris's farm on Sunday afternoons.

The field adjacent to the farmhouse was eighty yards long, and with the exception of the end zones, not a blade of grass was standing. The boys played so long and tackled so hard on Sundays that they wore the pasture to a brown nub. The bootleggers who lived in the white shotgun house down the dirt road set up their business on the sideline. After several swigs of white lightning, some of the customers turned rowdy. Large bets were placed on both teams. Fights broke out among the fans and Pop Burris was forced to control the crowd with a heavy hand.

With the departure of Buddy Burris to Norman, it became Kurt's job to choose the players for both teams and make up most of the rules. Like Buddy, Kurt had a mean streak and didn't smile much. In contests of heaving hay bales, Kurt always won. He could stand on the back of a flatbed truck and flip a bale fifteen feet into the barn's upper loft without grunting or breaking a sweat.

Like Pop, each of the Burris boys was born with a thick jaw and a broad nose. Slabs of muscle were added from the farmwork, including the hay baling and the cow milking. As the years passed, Kurt grew wider and stronger while Bobby developed lean muscle and speed. For years, Kurt had rubbed his younger brother's face in the dirt, but by the time they reached junior high school, Kurt couldn't catch him.

One afternoon, Bobby and and Mahlon Greer started throwing dirt clods at Kurt as he plowed a field on the Ford tractor. In a fit of anger, Kurt leaped from the tractor and started chasing the boys. Bobby sprinted to safety, but Mahlon's heavy feet became tangled in a gaggle of weeds. He was stomped into the hard ground by a boy who saw no humor in clod throwing.

When folks in Muskogee gathered at the barbershop, the courthouse, or the lobby of the fashionable Severs Hotel, a ten-story brick structure completed in 1911, they talked about the Muskogee Roughers. But there was another game, and another team, in town—Manual Training School, on the other side of the tracks.

Manual Training, the all-black school, rarely lost a game, and they barnstormed from Kansas to southeast Texas. It was state law that all-black teams couldn't compete against the all-white teams. So the Manual kids traveled great distances in old buses called yellow dogs. They were often followed by a caravan of fans chugging along in broken-down jalopies that required much attention in areas of both tire repair and radiator cooling.

Manual Training High was named for an obvious reason. Little emphasis was placed on academics. Instead, the Negroes learned much about manual labor—plowing, building fences, and fixing cars. They were hardly being prepared for athletic scholarships handed out by the big-time universities. They wore socks, jerseys, shoes, pads, and football pants that were handed down from the Muskogee Roughers.

Manual might have been the best team and the best-kept secret in eastern Oklahoma, but not in the eyes of Paul Young, who secretly scouted them. Young would tell anyone who listened, "Right now they're wearing our hand-me-downs. But the day of the black athlete is coming. You just mark my words."

Young, of course, was careful not to make such proclamations to members of the local Ku Klux Klan, a large and thriving order since well before the turn of the century. In Muskogee County, Jim Crow laws were strictly enforced, especially when it came to separate water fountains and rest rooms. Negroes rode in separate railroad cars and didn't come downtown after dark.

But the black and white kids didn't seem to care about the prevailing environment of separatism. They swam together in Coody Creek, next to the Midway Valley railroad tracks and Hobo Jungle, and they played baseball against each other in the summer. Nothing, however, caused more whispering and winking around town than when the Negro kids from the South Muskogee farms walked up through the trees behind the Burris place and joined the Sunday football games.

Pop Burris would groan and say, "I just hope the Klanners never hear about this." Then he relaxed and enjoyed the games, like everyone else.

No longer did Kurt have to pick the sides. It was black versus white, and the teams were both perfectly and evenly matched. They played until their clothes were in tatters and their skin was scraped and bleeding. They played into the golden light of dusk, often trying to break a tie. A touchdown by the white boys normally followed one from the colored black boys and vice versa. Few words were spoken during the games, as players from both teams were deeply focused on the work at hand. As much pride was poured into these games as the Friday night contests played in local stadia.

It was usually dark when Pop Burris called off the games, but the kids wanted to keep on playing. Neither side was ever able to claim a clear victory. The Negro kids would silently walk home through the woods, and there would be no contact with the white boys until the next game. But you could always be sure that there would be a next game.

• • •

Like most coaches of the time, Bud Wilkinson often skirted NCAA rules regarding practice time. Teams were allowed to hold organized workouts for twenty-one days in the spring and seventeen more during preseason camp, which consisted mostly of two-a-days. But Bud had the boys working overtime whenever he could.

Way up in the North Country existed a place called Camp Lincoln, a resort and summer camp for kids near Brainerd, Minnesota. C. P. Wilkinson held mortgage papers on the place. The camp was flooded every summer with rich kids from across the Midwest, and the cash register never stopped ringing, now that the Sooners were again the darlings of college football. Bud, of course, was the main attraction for the young campgoers, but Camp Lincoln served yet another function that was out-of-bounds according to NCAA rules. It was the perfect hideaway for some of the leading high school recruits with their eye on the Sooners and a learning center for players already at OU.

The camp was mostly about pimple-faced boys. But away from the canoe trips, the sack races, and the ghost stories, the larger boys were flexing their muscles on the manicured football field. Six years earlier, one of Wilkinson's most prized recruits arrived in Camp Lincoln the summer after graduating from high school, and it was here that Wilkinson had hidden out Billy Vessels. Every recruiter across the state of Texas and at Oklahoma A&M was hunting the stud halfback. But they all lost the scent, thanks to Camp Lincoln.

Vessels had befriended a thirteen-year-old named Charlie Rountree, from the rich neighborhood of Nichols Hills in Oklahoma City. "My gosh, you throw the football great," Charlie said. They played catch every evening until Vessels told the boy, "I'll be goin' back to Oklahoma City tomorrow. Gotta play in the high school all-star game."

Rountree's eyes almost popped. "When you get down there, I want you to call my parents," he said, handing Billy the number. "They're really nice folks. I bet they've heard of you."

It was almost two months later when Charlie regretfully boarded the train out of Minneapolis back to Oklahoma. He had been the happiest camper of them all and hated leaving the hiking, the boating, and the girls over at Camp Hubert. When Charlie stepped off at the Oklahoma City station, he quickly spotted his black nanny, Lee Rowland, standing on the platform with tears streaming down her face.

"Mister Charlie, I have missed you so," she said. "Don't ever go away that long again."

Charlie looked around and said, "I bet my dad's waiting with the Cadillac." Lee didn't know how to drive.

"Oh no, sir. Billy drove me."

"Billy who?"

"Billy Vessels—the big Oklahoma football star."

"Yeah, and Wyatt Earp is ridin' shotgun."

Then it hit Charlie. He couldn't believe his eyes. Hiding behind a post, grinning like a goose, was Billy Vessels. Grabbing his large, meaty hand, Charlie said, "How's my mom?"

"Oh, Kitty is doing great."

"How's my dad?"

"Oh, Doc's doing great, too."

Billy had telephoned the Rountrees the day after the all-star game. Predictably, they had been in the stadium the previous night to see him run all over the West team, scoring three touchdowns. They invited him over for dinner and then invited him to move in. Years earlier, Billy had been deserted at a young age by his dirt-poor parents from Cleveland, located in the backwoods of eastern Oklahoma. The Rountrees were obliged to help Billy. They also happened to be two of OU's greatest fans, and Doc Rountree was Gomer Jones's best drinking buddy.

Billy was clearly a changed man as he stood on the platform wearing starched white shorts, a starched button-down oxford shirt, and Italian loafers with no socks.

Lee laughed and said, "This here Billy sleeps till eleven in the morning. He eats like a horse. And I've already made him four lemon meringue pies this week."

Kitty Rountree had started tutoring Billy the day he moved in. Billy might have been the most highly recruited player in ten states, but his grades and board scores were fourth-string. For hours each day, Billy hit the books under Kitty's watchful eye.

Doc Rountree had offered up everything from the use of his Cadillac to an account at Connolly's, one of the most expensive clothiers in town. When Charlie opened his closet at home, he found enough oxford shirts and sports coats to clothe an entire team. He also discovered that Billy was now sleeping in his twin bed—but never said a word about it. He simply slid over to the other bed.

Years later, Gomer would tell Wilkinson, "If not for the Rountrees, and all of Kitty's tutoring, Billy Vessels would've been out on his ass." He was right. Though Billy's official home was the athletic dorm, he ate Lee's special recipe for fried chicken about every other day at the Rountrees' and even learned to throw the halfback rollout pass in the backyard under Kitty's tutelage. Charlie was his primary receiver.

Kitty and Doc Rountree were two of the most generous people in Oklahoma City. A well-known orthopedic surgeon, Doc Rountree often provided free services for those who couldn't afford expensive medical services. Years earlier, a man from Commerce had brought his nine-year-old son to the children's hospital with the hope that he could be saved from a crippling conditioning called osteomyelitis, an inflammation of the bone marrow in his right ankle. Doctors had informed the family that the boy would not be able to walk in two years if the sophisticated surgery was not performed. Not long after the operation, young Mickey Mantle was back on the baseball diamond, swatting home runs both right- and left-handed.

Now the Rountrees had come to the aid of one of the poorest kids in Oklahoma now driving a Cadillac on the weekends and wearing the best clothes on campus. Not only did Kitty tutor Billy Vessels for four years, she demanded that he study every night and the result was a passing grade in every subject.

After Billy won won the Heisman Trophy in 1952, Camp Lincoln became a magnet for every high school kid with a dream of playing college football. It was also a great place for Wilkinson to tutor his current players, who were hired as counselors but worked on their football skills every day.

In the summer of 1955, three months before his junior season began at OU, Jimmy Harris grabbed the train out of Norman for the two-day trip to Minnesota. When Jimmy set eyes on the place, he knew Camp Lincoln was a far cry from Terrell, Texas. There were rolling hills adorned with massive oaks and elms, along with Lake Hubert, a clear and natural body of water right in the middle of the camp. The temperature had soared past ninety degrees when Jimmy stepped onto the train in Oklahoma. Now a thermometer nailed to an oak tree and carved out like a grizzly bear revealed it was seventy-two in the shade.

On a football field stretching into the distance and lined with stout oaks, Jimmy could see three high school boys, their shirtless bodies glistening in the sunlight. They were running wind sprints. Little did he know that Gomer Jones was down at the other end, hidden in some trees, timing them with a stopwatch.

Far from the prying eyes of the NCAA, Wilkinson was able to spend several weeks honing the option skills of Harris, prepping him for the '55 season. He worked on the blind hand-offs and option pitches about two hours a day. His teammates were the high school kids who had come to Camp Lincoln to learn football from the Master. At the same time, Wilkinson was timing, testing, and evaluating these boys, trying to determine if they had the talent to play for OU.

Wilkinson seemed more impressed with Harris by the day, knowing that no better athlete was playing college quarterback in America. As a paid camp counselor, Jimmy started his day at dawn by running a mile with the kids—right past the all-girl camp. One morning he saw something that left him breathless—the smallest bikini he had ever set eyes on. Even more impressive was the body it was barely covering. Without even slowing down, Jimmy hollered in his resonant baritone, "I'll pick you up at seven. Be ready!"

The girl smiled and nodded her approval. Her name was Kathy Ann Pollard and, along with being a camp counselor, she was a sophomore at the University of Nebraska. Practically every girl at the camp was waiting at the front gate to catch a glimpse of Jimmy as he eased the Ford coupe into Camp Hubert that evening.

He would spend several nights with Kathy Ann that summer, parking in the deep woods of Minnesota or on a blanket beneath the stars. They promised to meet at least once each fall when Nebraska played Oklahoma.

• • •

On a hot September afternoon in 1955, a few weeks before the start of the season, Jerry Tubbs took one look at the boys bent over puking and said, "Y'all are a bunch of sissies. This practicin' ain't that hard." It seemed the boys were always on the run during two-a-day practices that were abnormally short according to major college standards. But there was little downtime, and the boys were rarely allowed to catch their breath. When they weren't running gassers, they were sprinting from one drill to the next. Unlike most coaches of that era, Wilkinson was not a monster who craved the sight of broken bones and blood. The Oklahoma boys did far more heavy breathing than hitting, although some days you could hear helmets cracking and bodies colliding all the way across campus.

Coach Paul "Bear" Bryant of Texas A&M would have laughed at the Wilkinson routine. The previous summer, he had run off seventy-six players during a ten-day hell camp down in Junction, Texas. A Bryant disciple by the name of Joe Kerbel had coached Tubbs in high school in West Texas.

"Jiminy Christmas, we practiced six hours a day, every day, without water breaks back in Breckenridge," Tubbs told the boys.

One year, Kerbel rounded up the Buckaroos three weeks before Texas high school preseason practices were scheduled to begin and had them scrimmaging beneath a searing July sun in a field cleared off by local ranchers. If the czars of the University Interscholastic

League down in Austin had gotten wind of these illegal practices, the Bucks would have been forfeiting games all the way back to the Depression.

Kerbel was short, overweight, and known for his ill temper. A Breckenridge Buck limped into the trainer's room one afternoon with welts and large bruises on his calves.

"What happened?" the trainer asked.

"Oh, Coach Kerbel was trying to kick me in the ass. And he couldn't get his leg up that high."

Wilkinson didn't curse players, didn't hit or kick players, and rarely raised his voice. He did imitate one of Bryant's drills, called bull-in-the-ring. Bear would have barely recognized it. In the original version, a player would stand in a ring encircled by twenty others. The coach would call a name, and that boy would plow into his teammate standing in the middle of the ring. Then the coach would call another, and another, and another. Helmets were driven into the boys' back, ribs, arms, legs, and even feet. If the coach didn't like the boy, he might yell, "All!" That meant *dogpile!*

Wilkinson was more concerned with technique in his updated version of bull-in-the-ring: "Step with your right foot and take on the man with your right shoulder." There wasn't enough hitting to break an egg.

Each morning, a five-deep roster was posted in the Sooners' dressing room. The Great White Father didn't tolerate even minor mistakes, and the offender might have to search for his name on the roster the next day. Boys plummeted from first to fourth string by virtue of one bad play. Starters from the previous season often languished as backups the entire length of two-a-days. But there was no use arguing with the coach. When he wasn't tutoring the boys on fundamentals, he stood and watched practice from a distance—a cold distance. Wilkinson didn't beat up the boys like Bear Bryant, but the damage inflicted to the psyche could seem as cruel.

Then, in a strange twist, Wilkinson would call the demoted boy into his office and pump him full of oxygen.

"Shoot, I was all ready to quit the team," said end Billy Carr Harris, no relation to Jimmy, "and I came out of Coach Wilkinson's office whistling 'Boomer Sooner.' "

All-American center Tom Catlin knew all about Wilkinson's emotional roller coaster. Catlin had advised his teammates back in 1951, "Just don't go into Bud's office. Go on to class. What Bud tells you ain't always going to be the way it is. He'll promote ya and demote ya before you walk out the door."

Typical of the rawboned and leather-toughened boys of the time, Billy Carr Harris weighed all of 160 pounds but played in the line. Two years earlier, Sooner assistant coach Bill Jennings had visited Ardmore High School and asked Harris, "Have you got any chance of going to college without a football scholarship?"

"No, sir."

"Well, then I'll give you one. But it's gotta be renewed on a year-to-year basis." Billy Carr survived because Wilkinson made an emotional connection with the rail-thin boy, and it would last a lifetime.

The coach had absolutely no tolerance for injuries. If a player went down, the practice wouldn't stop for even thirty seconds for the boy to be carried off the field. Instead, the scrimmage was moved over a few feet and the team played on. A year earlier, Wilkinson had almost run off one of the best recruits from Fort Worth, Byron Searcy, who eventually needed surgery on his lower back to repair a herniated disk. When Byron didn't practice, the coaches wouldn't even speak to him. Wilkinson strolled into the locker room one day and coldly strolled past Searcy, shaking hands instead with Buddy Oujesky.

"Buddy, you played a great game last Saturday."

With Wilkinson out of earshot, Oujesky turned to Searcy and said, "That's funny. I didn't even step foot on the field Saturday."

Billy Carr had been the victim of a brutal and bloody accident a few days before preseason practice started. He was working on a Phillips oil rig down by the Red River when his hand became tangled in a chain and four fingers were sliced off. Three fingers hung on by the thinnest layer of skin, and the fourth was completely severed. But Billy Carr, who didn't even yelp, folded up the remainder of his hand and carried the four fingers to the hospital, where they were sewed back on.

The stitches were still in his fingers when the Sooners gathered in Norman three days later for preseason practice. Trainer Ken Rawlinson wrapped each one in thin layers of steel so Billy Carr could practice.

"Are you sure you want to do this?" Rawlinson said, wincing at the sight of the fingers.

"Yep."

Rawlinson felt sick to his stomach as he watched Billy Carr holding the damaged hand above his head but ramming his head and shoulders into everything that moved. Harris participated in every practice that summer and earned every ounce of respect that Wilkinson could muster. Though Billy Carr wasn't going to play a lot during the '55 season, he definitely could count on a scholarship.

Three days before the season opener against North Carolina, Wilkinson posted the starting lineup:

End—Don Stiller
Tackle—Hugh Ballard
Guard—Bo Bolinger
Center—Jerry Tubbs
Guard—Ed Gray
Tackle—Tom Emerson
End—John Bell
Halfback—Bob Burris

Halfback—Tommy McDonald
Fullback—Billy Pricer
Quarterback—Jimmy Harris

The Sooners were greeted with a scene straight out of a Hitchcock film when they stepped onto the field in Chapel Hill, where the sun shone brightly, but it was raining buckets. The combination of ninety-degree heat and humidity had transformed North Carolina into the Congo.

"This is a day when the alternate unit will win the game for us," Wilkinson told the team minutes before kickoff. "You will soon see why I place so much emphasis on the depth of our team."

Bud and Gomer liked to say the Sooners had "two first strings." Back in '53, when Doc Hearon was demoted to the alternate team, Jones provided the standard explanation: "Doc, look at it this way: we really have two first strings." Doc then looked the coach squarely in the eye: "If it's all the same to you, Gomer, I'd rather be on that *other* first string."

The nightmare in North Carolina unfolded quickly. The Sooners fumbled the ball away twice in the first quarter. Sensing that the starting offensive line was already running out of gas, Wilkinson sent in the alternate line but kept the first-string backfield of Harris, Burris, Pricer, and McDonald on the field.

Not once in two seasons of receiving snaps from Burris and Tubbs had one exchange gone awry. Now, Harris was sticking his hands beneath the tail of Ken Northcutt, who had worked up a nervous lather. Jimmy felt bad vibes and almost called time-out. Northcutt snapped the ball straight through Jimmy's legs and it rolled into the end zone, where it was recovered for a Tar Heel touchdown. After missing the extra point, North Carolina led 6–0.

With Harris pitching to Burris and McDonald on the option and Pricer chewing up chunks of ground, the Sooners promptly moved the length of the field and were poised to overtake the Tar Heels when McDonald fumbled into the end zone. On three straight drives, the OU offense was stopped at the North Carolina thirty-one-, thirteen-, and one-yard lines. Wilkinson, like most coaches of the day, could care less about kicking field goals. Heck, the Sooners didn't decide who was going to kick the extra point until the touchdown had already been scored.

Oklahoma finally broke through in the third quarter with Burris rumbling around right end and scoring from the eight-yard line behind a crushing block delivered by Pricer. Harris kicked the extra point for the 7–6 lead. After a short punt by North Carolina, the Sooners had to traverse only thirty-nine yards in five plays, with McDonald sweeping right end for the touchdown. Pricer missed the PAT kick and the Sooners held on for a 13–6 win.

Oklahoma outgained North Carolina 482 yards to 145, but fumbles, missed opportunities, and general sloppiness kept the Tar Heels clinging to hope until the final gun. The streak had reached twenty games.

The second game of the '55 season was against the Pitt Panthers at Owen Field, and McDonald tore up the turf, averaging 11.5 yards every time he touched the ball. He scored two touchdowns, one on a pedal-to-the-medal forty-three-yard reverse following not one but two de-cleating blocks by guard Bo Bolinger. The Sooners raced to a 19–0 lead, thanks to a third touchdown by Burris. Then they ran out of gas.

The Sooners hadn't allowed a rushing touchdown in thirty-eight straight quarters, but in the second half they allowed two. But OU held off a talented Pitt team 19–14. Bullets had been dodged in the first two weeks. Some soul-searching would have to be done if the winning streak was to continue.

9

BUCKAROO

The University of Oklahoma moved to the new beat of Elvis Presley and Buddy Holly. Jocks mixed with the regular students, swilling the bootleg whiskey and pledging the same fraternities. A twenty-one-game winning streak provided more than an ample reason to celebrate.

The OU campus, a mélange of redbrick buildings, had a thriving Greek system—twenty-five fraternities and fourteen sororities. Most of the houses were filled to the brim. Jimmy Harris had instructed his teammates on the use of the fire escape at the Kappa Kappa Gamma house, and it seemed that every time he climbed the ladder, Jimmy was bumping into somebody he knew.

Jimmy was going through the Kappa house faster than free perfume.

Jerry Tubbs, however, was living proof that you could pack a fat bankroll and still be boring. Jerry could care less about gallivanting about campus with a blond, blue-eyed Kappa or Pi Phi or Theta on his arm. His teammates were forever trawling the tree-lined streets, returning with carloads of the bobby socks set. But Jerry wasn't interested, because his money was for saving. Besides, he had little use for the hard-drinking crowd and promised himself that he would practice abstinence for the rest of his life.

His nest egg was the result of a thriving ticket business. Each time the telephone rang in the Jeff House, Jerry grabbed it on the first ring, hoping a buyer was on the line. Mostly, he unloaded his tickets to Texas oilman and OU sugar daddy Eddie Chiles, who paid with Ben Franklins.

Every day, Jerry wore blue jeans rolled up at the bottom, and he walked straight to class and directly back to the Jeff House. He said "yessir" and "no, ma'am." His only indulgence was large second and third helpings that he devoured at the training table. "God put people here on earth for a lot of different reasons, and the best thing I do is eat," Jerry said. It seemed that every morsel he digested was converted to energy, and there wasn't a linebacker or center in America who could deliver a heavier blow. Here was Rocky Marciano in cleats. In five days, Tubbs would be the center of attention down in Dallas during the Red River War against the Texas Longhorns.

By most accounts, Tubbs was the best high school player ever to come out of Texas. Recruiters arrived by plane, train, bus, and automobile. They would have come by boat to Breckenridge if not for the sands of West Texas. Years earlier, Sam Boyd, a coach and recruiter from Baylor University, had riveted his eyes on the senior linebacker and said, "By god, son, if you're goin' to Oklahoma, they must be payin' you a ton."

"No, sir. If I'd wanted money, I'd have gone down to Texas A&M. They offered me a bundle. I'm goin' to Oklahoma because of the great Bud Wilkinson. Besides, they got the best football team in the country, and I'm used to winnin' a lot."

Boyd shoved his cap back on his head. He squatted and began to doodle in the dirt. Another man, Frank Jones, spoke up. He was tall and wiry, with skin like a salamander.

"Jerry, son, if you play football at Oklahoma, they ain't gonna let you back in Texas."

"I've heard that. Yessir, I have. But I can tell ya. I'll be back in

Breckenridge every Thanksgivin' and Christmas. I got my folks here. I got lots of friends. No, sir. I'll be back to Texas."

The men studied the rawboned boy with the pinkish skin for the umpteenth time and still couldn't figure him out. Here was a seventeen-year-old who didn't drink, smoke, chew, dip, cuss, or talk in class. He was polite beyond the point of good manners. He spoke in a cheery high-pitched West Texas twang. But on Friday nights, playing linebacker and center for the Buckaroos, he turned meaner than a rattlesnake. Tubbs was the fastest player on the team in spite of being twenty to thirty pounds heavier than the backs and the ends. West Point had offered an appointment. Wilkinson had to swoop down from Oklahoma, moving behind enemy lines, to snatch Tubbs from the grasp of the Southwest Conference.

Boyd rose from his catcher's stance and now stood eyeball to eyeball with the blue-chipper.

"Jerry, we'll match whatever the University of Oklahoma offered you. In fact, we'll up the ante."

"Coach Boyd, it's not the money. I just want to play for Bud Wilkinson."

"Jerry, you know this'll sully your reputation."

"Coach, I know you're mad. I signed a conference letter of intent with you. But it wasn't binding. I told you I was leanin' toward Oklahoma."

Agreeing to a conference letter of intent merely limited a player from signing with another school from the same conference. The national letter of intent had yet to be introduced, so Tubbs was technically free to sign with Oklahoma, a member of the Big Seven Conference. Trouble was that folks down in Waco believed he was already wedded to the Baylor Bears. The news of his signing had been trumpeted in two-inch headlines across the top of the *Waco Tribune*. Naturally, Boyd was not looking forward to telling Baylor head coach George Sauer about the boy's change of heart.

Boyd yanked off his cap and slapped it across his thigh. "Dammit, Jerry, Breckenridge is the cheatin'est dang town in Texas. Turn your back on Baylor, son, and the wrath of the NC-double-A will come down on ya like stink from a stockyard."

Word around Texas was that Oklahoma had offered Tubbs twelve grand. It was widely accepted that Breckenridge boys would jump at any cash offer because it was a way of life in their little town. Many had been recruited from other towns just to play *high school* ball. Truth be known, the unofficial offer from Oklahoma was closer to two grand. Oilman Eddie Chiles, known as a free spender around the Jeff House, also promised to buy Jerry's tickets. To Tubbs, that was a down payment on a deal that had gusher written all over it. The founder and president of the Western Company of Fort Worth had arrived in Breckenridge a week earlier on a fourteen-seat twin-engine Dove aircraft. One of the richest men in Texas, Chiles was more than obliged to help out his alma mater, his favorite coach, and his beloved Sooners.

What was important to Tubbs was the sight of Wilkinson stepping off the airplane at the Breckenridge airport. The man with the pressed suit, starched shirt, red tie, and prescient eyes was the ultimate symbol of success. Oh, there had been oil-rich men around Breckenridge for years and years, wearing fine clothes and dining at the Birch Hotel, the home of West Texas's only chandelier. But they hadn't won thirty-one straight games, as Wilkinson had in the late forties, or a national championship.

Tubbs would take a ride on that aircraft to Norman, where he pledged his services to Wilkinson and the Oklahoma Sooners. A few days later, another tall headline appeared in the *Waco Tribune*: **"Tubbs Takes Money and Runs Across the Red River."** He figured Sam Boyd had to be the unnamed source in the story.

• • •

Most of the tall tales about Breckenridge were true. As with most wide-open Wild West towns, a margin for exaggeration did exist. By the early 1920s, oil was the magnet that attracted the dreamers, schemers, tool pushers, roustabouts, hole cutters, and promoters. But folks worshiped football. What rose up out of the desert was a blind faith in any man or boy who drilled the earth by day, the rival team by night.

It had started when the town was nothing more than whorehouses, tent encampments, and gambling halls. Walker Street, the main artery through Breckenridge, was the world's largest mud puddle. The place looked and smelled like a carnival. Mule teams toted tons of drilling equipment straight through town. There was barely space for an automobile to pass. Oil derricks decorated the landscape like tall pine trees.

One night, a blue fireball rumbled several hundred feet down Walker Street, killing five people. Witnesses watched in horror as a man dripped fire for several frantic steps before falling dead. It was later explained that the human flame had been driving a truck that stalled. As he cranked the engine, the truck backfired, igniting gas that had gathered in a draw. There were no regulations about either cleaning up or sealing off gas that oozed from the earth during drilling. Men were too busy with profits to bother with concerns about life and limb, and it seemed that somebody died every day in Breckenridge—killed either by gunfire or by fire itself.

Dice danced and cards were dealt at all hours and moonshiners produced "Stephens County Corn." The boomtown boasted a 90 percent male population, so a need arose for female company. Bordellos sprang up on nearly every street corner. Texas Rangers, who were summoned to clean up the boomtown, often found themselves outgunned, despite their "one riot, one Ranger" reputation.

It was said that the oil boom was the blood brother to the gold rush, but the seekers of black gold seemed more . . . American. They flaunted their greed and operated with a greater sense of it. Drills never stopped drilling; wheels never stopped rolling; men never stopped thinking or drinking; deal makers never stopped dealing. As oil gushed and the money flowed, wildcatters danced in the streets. An eleven-story hotel and a bank fit for Dallas were opened in downtown Breckenridge.

Jake Sandefer Jr. was one of the new arrivals, and he didn't mix well at first with the rough-and-tumble crowd. He had been educated at Hardin Simmons, a Baptist college just up the road in Abilene, where his father, Jake Sandefer Sr., was the founder and president. His father had been christened Jefferson Davis Sandefer after the president of the Confederate states. Both father and son were conservative men of the South, but as they grew older, both developed a sense of humor, a sense of adventure, and a sense of fun. Both loved football, and their affection would spawn a win-at-all-costs attitude in the little West Texas boomtown.

Breckenridge wasn't the only wide spot in West Texas that possessed a mother lode of oil and talented football stock. Rivalries evolved within a chain of towns strung together tighter than a pearl necklace. It would become known as the Oil Belt League. By the 1930s, paved highways drew places like Cisco, Eastland, Abilene, Ranger, and Breckenridge closer together.

It wasn't long before Jake Sandefer, who always had a new cigar and a shiny car, was scouring the countryside for talent. If an oil field worker had a son with football potential, the man was offered a better, higher-paying job working in Breckenridge. One afternoon, Jake traveled far into the countryside to scout a big lineman by the name of Magness. As he talked to the boy's mother, he noticed the lineman's twelve-year-old brother flipping a cigarette off the porch. Jake was naturally interested in both of the Magness boys. His sales pitch worked, and the next day Jake sent out a flatbed truck to bring the entire family—cows, chickens, dogs, everything—into the Breckenridge school district.

A few years later, Breckenridge was preparing for one of the biggest games of the season against Waco High when Jake's drilling partner, Charley Atkinson, wandered into the Birch Hotel, where the lobby was filled with out-of-towners. Then he headed back to the office to discuss the game with Jake. A native of western Pennsylvania, Charley had fallen head over heels for whiskey, gambling, black gold, Florsheim shoes, and the Buckaroos.

"I've found a better way to make money," Charley announced.

"What is it?" Jake asked.

"Well, I bet on Breckenridge today, and all I had to do was give those people from Waco seven points."

"What do you mean, you gave them seven points?"

"Hell, I don't know what it means."

The amount that Charley had wagered was $1,400—a substantial sum for the time, when hamburgers were a nickel and movies a dime. A loss would be a major financial setback for the Atkinson-Sandefer team. Jake was known as a nickel hugger, and the mere suggestion of a four-figure wager roiled his stomach.

Since Charley had never heard of a point spread, he didn't realize that he was actually losing his bet when Breckenridge led Waco 7–6 late in the game. Fortunately, Breckenridge had a great quarterback named Boone Magness—the chain-smoker—and he led the Bucks to a late touchdown. Ironically, there was yet another Magness brother who would figure into the seven-point spread. Aubrey Magness kicked the extra point that provided the one-point cushion (14–6) to Charley's wager. Jake Sandefer had never been more relieved. Thanks to his discovery of the Magnesses, the company's drilling stake was still safe.

As time passed and Mother Nature belched more oil, betting became big business in Breckenridge. Bookies came from Fort Worth, about ninety miles to the east, and all wagers were placed at the Birch Hotel, where the money was held in the safe. On any given Friday night, there might be $50,000 locked up.

A quarterback from the tiny town of Moran had become the target of the Bucks boosters. As a freshman, he had led his Class B team to a state high school championship. He possessed not only a great passing arm but also tremendous speed, having won the hundred-yard dash at the state track meet.

The quarterback's father, however, balked at all efforts to move the family into Breckenridge. So when the family left town for a week's vacation, the Breckenridge supporters had the house moved off the foundation and into their school district. On his return, the father was told, "It's OK if you want to move the house back to the old spot, but you'll have to pay for it." The house stayed, and Jim Ed Plum became the Buckaroos' starting quarterback that fall.

Moran, in spite of being the defending state champion, wasn't able to field a team that season since the school lacked enough males to complete a starting lineup. Recruiters from the Oil Belt had cleaned them out.

Jerry Tubbs didn't have to travel far to play for the Bucks. His folks owned a farm fifteen miles west of downtown Breckenridge, and Jerry spent Saturday afternoons down at Bowen's Drugstore, eavesdropping on the conversations of his football heroes, dreaming someday he would be like them.

In Tubbs's three high school seasons, Breckenridge won two state titles while suffering only three defeats. Now, his mind was on the *Man* in Oklahoma. Tubbs would have crawled on hands and knees through cactus needles all the way to Norman to play for Bud Wilkinson. Before Tubbs hit the highway, a sophomore running back named Jake Sandefer III grabbed his hand and shook it hard. Jakie, as they called the boy, was about 120 pounds soaking wet. "Tell those folks up in Oklahoma that I'd sure like to play for 'em someday," Jakie said. "Give 'em a good word on me."

· · ·

On the second Saturday of October 1955, Jerry Tubbs wiped out the Texas Longhorns with three interceptions and twenty-seven tackles; Oklahoma 20, Texas 0, before 75,504 at the Cotton Bowl.

"That is the single greatest game ever played by an Oklahoma defender," Wilkinson told the sporting press. "I have never seen anything like it, nor will I ever see anything like it again."

Tubbs leaped to spear passes thrown by Joe Clements and manhandled halfback Walter Fondren, one of the best players in the Southwest Conference. Almost single-handedly, Tubbs shut down the Texas offense.

Several odd things happened before and during the Texas game that would have folks in Oklahoma talking for some time. Wilkinson unveiled a pregame motivational speech—it would be used three or four times later—that didn't make much sense. The speech included a story called "The Boy Who Took the Bird to the Wise Old Man":

Holding the sparrow in one hand, with only its head showing, the brash young man said to the wise old man, "Is it dead or alive?" The old man knew the youth's intent. If he said, "Dead," the boy would let the bird fly away. If he said, "Alive," the boy would squeeze the bird to death. So the old man skirted the issue by saying, "As you will, my son. As you will."

The players usually loved Wilkinson's motivational speeches, which were packed with conviction and purpose and served up with enough maple syrup to coat a Waffle House. The locker room was always silent when Bud spoke. This story, though, left the boys scratching their heads. But as the Great White Father said, "As you will . . . ," the Sooners tore through the door anyway, scattering the coaches and trainers and whooping like Comanches as they sprinted down the long Cotton Bowl tunnel onto the emerald grass field.

Their sudden arrival shocked a lot of folks, including the OU band members, who were still getting settled in the stands and didn't have instruments in hand. "Boomer Sooner" would have to wait.

Tubbs leaped and snatched Clements's first pass from the air at the Texas thirty-three, and the Sooners were on the board six plays later, Harris faking to Pricer and adroitly pitching to McDonald. The little halfback practically singed the grass as he whizzed past the Longhorns. Blackie Sherrod wrote in the *Fort Worth Press*: "Then this 157-pound fireball literally exploded at right end and was in the end zone before the Texas defense could get him bore-sighted."

McDonald hustled back to the huddle at the end of a play, and the act was becoming contagious. Instead of loitering and killing grass, the Sooners congregated quickly, and when Harris revealed the play and snap count Tubbs turned and ran to the line of scrimmage, his fellow linemen cantering right behind him. Between plays, the boys wearing orange jerseys and helmets stood with hands on hips, sucking wind like spent racehorses. Just as they were catching their breath, Wilkinson would send the alternate team onto the field— quarterback Jay O'Neal never missed a beat as the Sooners rolled down the field, over and through the expended Longhorns.

The alternates were in the game in the third quarter, and moving the ball with ease, when O'Neal pitched to fullback Dennit Morris, who slid out-of-bounds at the Texas nine in a tangle of arms and legs. The side judge marked the spot by dropping his cap on the yard marker. Then he dived into the pile of bodies to retrieve the football. Along came a female Sooner cheerleader, strutting along the boundary line. She spotted the cap, stopped, looked both ways, and kicked it all the way down to the four-yard line. Returning to the field, the official marked the ball precisely where his hat now lay. The Sooners, however, were held on downs and didn't score, a sign, perhaps, that God had disapproved of the ruse.

Even Wilkinson would laugh on Monday when, during the team

meeting, he ran the film projector back and forth, replaying the cheerleader's devilish deed.

In the fourth quarter against Texas, McDonald recorded the Sooners' fifth interception, returning the ball to the Longhorn seven. Harris then coyly read the defense. As the Texas end moved up the line to engage him, Harris pitched to McDonald, who skittered into the end zone. An entire nation was now talking about the Oklahoma Sooners.

• • •

Bar none, Kansas was the worst team in the Big Seven, going 2-17-1 the last two seasons. The Sooners had creamed the Jayhawks by the combined score of 110–0 in their previous two encounters. But the OU players knew what was coming Sunday afternoon, one day after they had walloped the dog out of Texas. Looking like a man facing the gallows, Wilkinson stepped to the lectern to open the team meeting at precisely four o'clock.

"Men. I have just completed a film session of the upcoming opponent. I have watched these films for eight hours. And I can tell you, men, Kansas is one of the best teams I have seen in a long, long time."

Sophomores always sat in the front, seniors in the back. The younger, more impressionable players, hung onto his every word while the older ones practically dozed. Bob Burris, Bo Bolinger, Joe Mobra, Cecil Morris, and Calvin Woodworth struggled to appear interested. But the sophomores couldn't take their eyes off the famous coach.

Wilkinson labored each day to scare the living daylights out of his players. It usually worked with the sophomores and juniors. But most players found the "off" button by their senior year. Oklahoma might be leading an opponent thirty-five–zip at half, and Wilkinson, with a long face, would stand before them and say, "Men, if you play hard in the second half, I think you can win. But it will take your best effort." Then the players would run back onto the field, checking the scoreboard over their shoulders to make sure they were still ahead.

The players half-assed their way through practice all week leading to the Kansas game. So Wilkinson was relieved when they finally checked into the Skirvin Hotel Friday afternoon in downtown Oklahoma City. Now he would have their attention.

Much of Wilkinson's frosty persona was adopted from Bernie Bierman, his coach at the University of Minnesota. The Golden Gophers won the national championship in all three of Wilkinson's years on the varsity—1934–36. So respected was "Wilky" that he called the plays as a sophomore playing *guard.* Later, he was moved to quarterback, which was really a blocking position in the single-wing offense. He not only called the plays but also became a key component in game planning.

So cold and aloof was Bierman that he would avoid his own players if he encountered them outside of the football complex. During practice, he sat on a chair on the sideline, far from the action, but the Golden Gophers felt those laser eyes stinging the backs of their necks. Bierman didn't need words to express his disappointment. Players were demoted or cut with no warning.

Bierman was dubbed the Gray Eagle by the sporting press, but the UM players, behind his back, called him the Gray Ghost.

During Bierman's reign from 1933 through the '50 season, most college coaches didn't dress up for the sideline, the rare exceptions being Paul Brown at Ohio State and Frank Leahy at Notre Dame. Bierman wore a suit and tie and, if the weather called for it, a fedora and an overcoat. He stood erect on the sideline, the spitting image of the man who would roam the sidelines in Oklahoma years later.

The similarities ran deep. Bierman compiled a twenty-eight-game winning streak and two more streaks of twenty-one. His Gophers won five national championships. Not a day passed when

Wilkinson didn't think of his former coach, and he often saw the old man in the mirror when he shaved.

In the fall of 1955, as the Sooners' winning streak rolled on, the Oklahoma freshman team was packing for a trip to Colorado to play the frosh of the Air Force Academy. Walking past the bus, Wilkinson heard the boys talking, laughing, and carrying on.

Bear Bryant would have yanked them off the bus and conducted a full-scale scrimmage on the spot. Instead, Wilkinson strolled onto the bus and waited until every eyeball was focused on his fatherly face. The bus fell silent.

"Men," he began, "there is one thing you need to know about Oklahoma football. Some people say it's *how* you play the game that counts. Well, at the University of Oklahoma, things are different. Here, *winning* is the only thing that matters." Then he casually exited the bus.

The trip from Norman to Denver required fifteen hours. Not another word was spoken until the bus pulled into the Air Force Academy. The Sooners were all business for the next two days and pulled off an impressive victory over the Falcons.

Now, if Wilkinson could only get the message across to the winningest football team in America. He worried that the Sooners were focused on nothing beyond Kappas and keg parties. After the Friday evening team meal at the Skirvin Hotel, Wilkinson gathered the team. "One of these days, you will face defeat," he said. "You don't know when it might happen. But it will happen. There is a team sitting out there right now waiting for you. Every team you play wants to beat you so badly they can already taste it."

The Kansas Jayhawks were truly the team that Wilkinson had imagined from the film projector. They stormed seventy-one yards down the field in eight plays, all on the ground, for the opening score. The crowd of 49,789 fans sat in stunned silence.

But it wasn't long before Harris had the offense cranking. McDonald side-armed a thirty-three-yard pass to John Bell on the eight-yard line. He scored on the next play, taking Harris's option pitch around right end. The alternates had their turn, and Jay O'Neal pitched to Carl Dodd, who scored around left end behind a thunderous block by Dennit Morris. Clearing the entire bench in the final quarter, the Sooners rolled to a 44–6 victory, and you could hear the yawn all the way to the wheat fields of Kansas.

Colorado, their next opponent, had been trouble for Oklahoma for three straight seasons—tying the Sooners in 1952 and losing by a touchdown in '53 and '54. But the Sooners, now the third-ranked team in the country, seemed to care less, even though the Buffs had won their first four games by the combined score of 73–19 and Dal Ward was known for coaching a rugged brand of the single wing.

Wilkinson proved to be psychic when the Buffs raced to a 14–0 lead. Two early fumbles had the Sooners behind the eight ball.

McDonald was so discombobulated on his first punt return that he dashed from the Sooner two-yard line to the eighteen, made a U-turn, and retreated to the one, where he was smothered by the Buffs. Harris fumbled on the next play. Now it was on the mind of every Sooner fan—*This might be the day.* The crowd of 57,663 at Owen Field could barely speak.

Wilkinson paced the sideline nervously, his eyes glued to the field and his mind working at ninety miles an hour. The Buffs were chewing up yards in huge chunks around end, and if the Sooners didn't turn this game around quickly, they would soon be faced with a mountain too tall to climb.

The Great White Father turned quickly and faced his players. "Where is Harris?" he yelled. "Where is Billy Carr Harris? I *need* him." Billy Carr ran toward his coach. "Get in there and stop them," Wilkinson demanded.

Billy Carr never expected to enter games until the Sooners led by plenty. He certainly didn't expect to hear Wilkinson calling his name with OU now trailing by fourteen points. But Wilkinson was convinced that Billy Carr, who weighed 165 pounds, was the answer.

No doubt, pound for pound, he was the toughest boy on the squad, but the Colorado linemen would outweigh him by more than thirty pounds. Fortunately, the stitches were out of his amputated fingers and most of the pain was gone.

Remarkably, the Colorado offense bogged down when the skinny end dug in his cleats. The Sooners forced a quick punt. Bob Burris scored four plays later, going sixteen yards around right end. McDonald then returned a punt in the right direction, all the way to the Colorado twenty-seven, and Burris scored again, making it fourteen-all.

Now the pace was quickening as the Sooners wasted no time between plays. They had caught McDonald fever. Instead of lying on the ground, the boys hopped up and hustled to the huddle. Harris called the plays faster, and the Sooners almost sprinted to the line of scrimmage. Colorado was overwhelmed. It didn't seem possible that Oklahoma could score again before halftime, but McDonald completed passes of eight yards to Bell and sixteen to Mobra, and alternate halfback Robert Derrick, a sprinter on the track team, bolted thirty-four yards to the two. Seconds later, McDonald vaulted over the goal, and the Sooners led 21–14 at halftime. An odd sight was sixty players literally sprinting to the locker room at halftime.

Wilkinson could sense the excitement emanating from the new hurry-up offense and didn't discourage it. The players were wide awake when he came to address them at halftime. Words of warning were no longer needed. "You're not out of the woods," he said. "Just keep working."

They didn't slow down a lick. Early in the third quarter, the Buffs' offense was forced to quick-kick on third down. The ball was rolling to a dead stop when Burris eighteen-wheeled one of the coverage men. McDonald picked it up and swivel-hipped his way to the Colorado thirteen. Four players later, Burris scored *again*. Fans knew this boy had the All-American genes.

The scrubs mopped up in the final quarter. But this time, Billy

Carr got to sit around with the first stringers on the sideline, smoking the make-believe cigar. After the Sooners won 56–21, Ward told the sporting press that Oklahoma was the fastest team he had ever witnessed. In his press conference, Wilkinson had a lot of ground to cover.

"Without a doubt, the greatest game ever played by Bobby Burris," he said. "Without a doubt." Asked to explain the new go-go offense, he said, "Tommy McDonald is a funny kid. He thinks he should score every play. When he doesn't, he gets mad and wants another crack at it. It's something God gave him. We didn't do it. The other boys picked up on it, and now the coaches are encouraging it. Of course, it has to be used in the right situation."

Wilkinson would spend the remainder of the season trying to hold down the scores. The final five opponents—Kansas State, Missouri, Iowa State, Nebraska, and Oklahoma A&M—were trounced by the collective score of 206–7. No team scored against the Sooners in the final four weeks.

On the Friday night before the Nebraska game, Jimmy Harris met up with an old friend. Kathy Ann Pollard had never forgotten their time together at Camp Lincoln and was anxious to see the star quarterback.

"But we're only going to do it one time," she said.

"Why?"

"Because you got a big game tomorrow. You're gonna need your energy." They sneaked into Kathy Ann's dorm room that night and, as promised, did it once.

Minutes before kickoff the next day, the Nebraska band unfurled a huge banner that read: "BEWARE, OU—THE END IS NEAR."

On the third play, Jimmy broke loose up the middle for seventeen yards. Before stumbling and falling, he blindly pitched to fullback Billy Pricer, who lumbered fifty-nine more yards to the Nebraska six. Jimmy felt a twinge in his right shoulder.

On the sideline, the team doctor told Jimmy, "Your shoulder's just slightly sprained. You'll be OK. But you shouldn't try to play any more today."

"Dammit!" Harris hollered.

"It's not that bad," the doctor said.

"Oh yeah, it is, Doc. I could have done it more than *once* last night. That's what pisses me off." The doctor looked puzzled as he walked away.

The Sooners tore through Nebraska 41–0 that day. The next week, in the season finale, Harris led them past Oklahoma A&M fifty-three–zip.

Now, danger lingered on the horizon. The heavyweight rematch was set.

Bud Wilkinson during his playing days as a quarterback for Minnesota in 1936. *University of Oklahoma*

Bud Wilkinson as a student at Shattuck Military School in 1932. *University of Oklahoma*

The 1952 backfield: (*left to right*): Buddy Leake, Heisman Trophy winner Billy Vessels, quarterback Eddie Crowder, and fullback Buck McPhail. *University of Oklahoma*

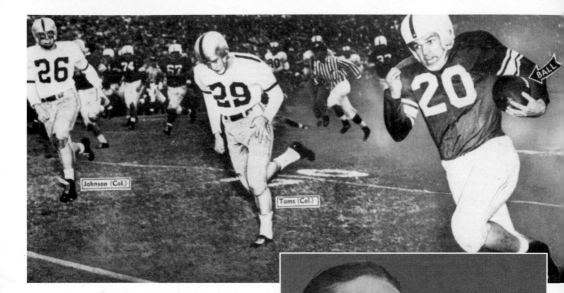

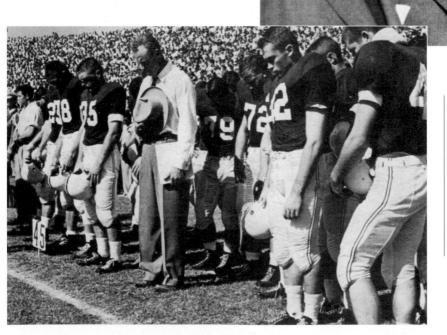

TOP: Merrill Green scores the winning touchdown, running fifty-one yards with thirty-six seconds left against Colorado for the 27–20 victory in 1953. It was the third win of the forty-seven-game winning streak. *University of Oklahoma*

RIGHT: Notre Dame coach Frank Leahy and Oklahoma coach Bud Wilkinson before the Oklahoma–Notre Dame game of 1953. *University of Oklahoma*

The Oklahoma football team on the side-line during prayer before the 1953 Texas game. *University of Oklahoma*

The 1953 starting lineup: **Front Row** (*left to right*): Max Boydston, Roger Nelson, J. D. Roberts, Kurt Burris, Melvin Brown, Don K. Brown, Carl Allison. **Back Row** (*left to right*): Larry Grigg, Gene Calame, Bob Burris, Jack Ging. *Bob Burris Collection*

Celebrating after the 7–0 win over Maryland in the 1954 Orange Bowl. In front row (*left to right*): Paul Burris, Gomer Jones, Bud Wilkinson, guard J. D. Roberts. *University of Oklahoma*

Jimmy Harris
stiff-arms a
Texas defender
in a 1954 game
at the Cotton
Bowl in Dallas.
*University of
Oklahoma*

Oklahoma halfback Larry
Grigg follows the block of
quarterback Gene Calame
(31) to score the winning
touchdown against
Maryland in the 1954
Orange Bowl. *University of
Oklahoma*

Left to right:
Coach Gomer
Jones, Jimmy
Harris, and Bud
Wilkinson confer
during the 1954
Texas–Oklahoma
game. *Jimmy
Harris Collection*

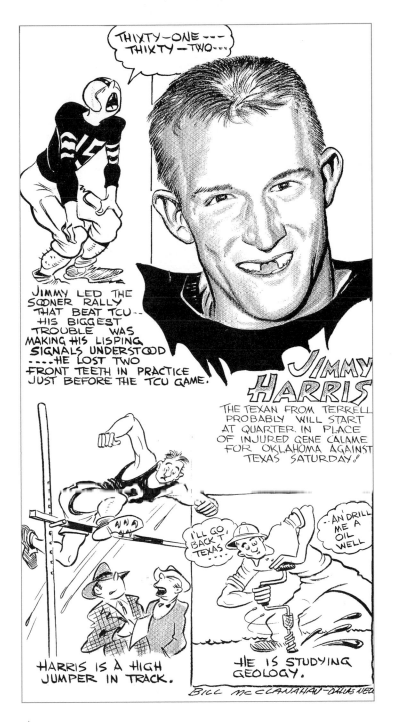

Cartoon of Jimmy Harris in the 1954 *Dallas Morning News.*
Dallas Morning News

Bud Wilkinson is carried off the field after a 7–0 victory over Maryland in the 1954 Orange Bowl.
University of Oklahoma

Left to right: Bob Loughridge (captain of '55 team), coach Gomer Jones, and Don K. Brown.
Bob Loughridge Collection

Sooner defenders Bob Loughridge (78), Carl Dodd (*center*), and Clendon Thomas (*right*) pursue Texas halfback Walter Fondren in the 1955 Oklahoma–Texas game. *Bob Loughridge Collection*

Quarterback Jimmy Harris runs the option against Texas in 1955. *University of Oklahoma*

Halfback Bob Burris scores against Colorado in 1955. *University of Oklahoma*

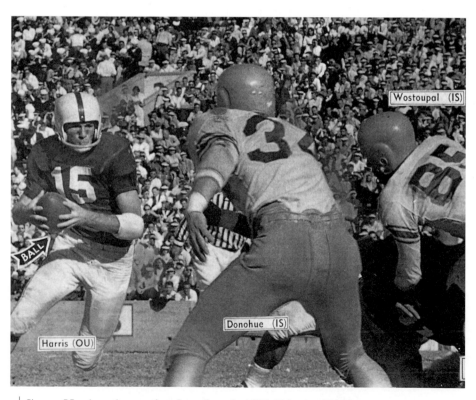

Jimmy Harris options against Iowa State in 1955. *University of Oklahoma*

Jimmy Harris (*left*)
and Ed Gray (*right*).
University of Oklahoma

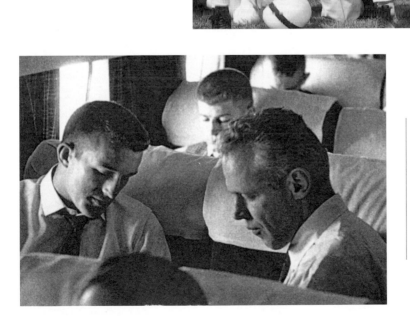

Left to right: Ed Gray,
Bud Wilkinson, and
Jerry Tubbs. Tubbs
and Gray were the
1956 co-captains.
University of Oklahoma

Jimmy Harris
(*left*) and Bud
Wilkinson
(*right*) study the
game plan on
the flight to a
1956 game.
*University of
Oklahoma*

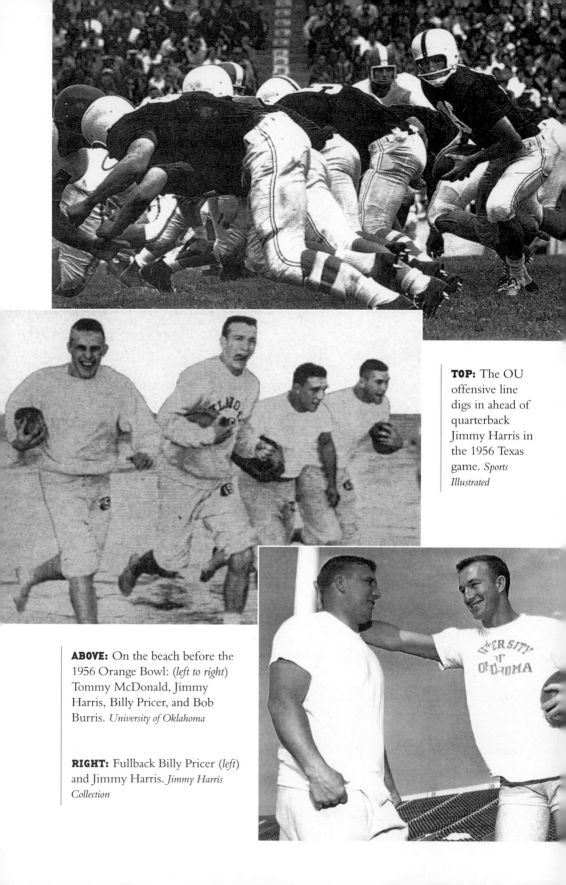

TOP: The OU offensive line digs in ahead of quarterback Jimmy Harris in the 1956 Texas game. *Sports Illustrated*

ABOVE: On the beach before the 1956 Orange Bowl: (*left to right*) Tommy McDonald, Jimmy Harris, Billy Pricer, and Bob Burris. *University of Oklahoma*

RIGHT: Fullback Billy Pricer (*left*) and Jimmy Harris. *Jimmy Harris Collection*

Program cover of the Oklahoma–Notre Dame game in 1956. *University of Oklahoma*

ABOVE: The Sooners in drag at a 1956 charity function: (*left to right*) Jimmy Harris, Tom Emerson, Clendon Thomas, Don Stiller, Billy Krisher, Buddy Oujesky, Bob Timberlake, Ed Gray, Carl Dodd, Dale Sherrod, and Jerry Tubbs. *University of Oklahoma*

RIGHT: Oklahoma center/linebacker Jerry Tubbs. *Jerry Tubbs Collection*

Jimmy Harris and Ed Gray remove their garters at the 1956 charity function.
University of Oklahoma

Left to right: John Herman Bell, W. W. Wilhite, Bob Loughridge, Norman Lamb, Carl Dodd, Henry Bonney, and Blackie Morrison in Las Vegas. *Bob Loughridge Collection.*

Hunting trip in 1956. **Front** (*left to right*): Dale Sherrod, John Bell, Ed Gray, Ken Northcutt, Lt. Governor Leo Winters, Kurt Burris, and Ray Goff. **Backfield:** Bob Burris, Billy Pricer, (quarterback) Jimmy Harris, and Tommy McDonald. *Jimmy Harris Collection*

Carl Dodd (*left*) and Jakie Sandefer celebrate after an Oklahoma victory. *University of Oklahoma*

Quarterback Jimmy Harris scores on a sneak against Notre Dame in 1956. *University of Oklahoma*

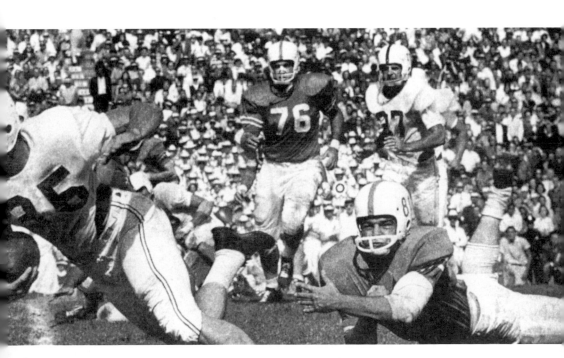

Halfback Clendon Thomas gains ground against Texas in 1957. *University of Oklahoma*

RIGHT: Halfback Jakie Sandefer in 1957. *Jakie Sandefer Collection*

BOTTOM: Game action against Oklahoma State in 1957. *University of Oklahoma*

Stiller (OU)

Dodd (OU)

E. Wood (OSU)

Morris (OU)

Thomas (OU)

BALL

D. Wood

Rector (OU)

Soergel (OSU)

Sandefer (OU)

Sewell (OSU)

10

HERMAN

The streak had swollen to twenty-nine games, and both the Associated Press and United Press now recognized the Sooners as national champs once more. Wilkinson had climbed the mountain again, but there was more climbing to do. Back in 1950, the great run had ended when Bear Bryant and the Kentucky Wildcats knocked Oklahoma from the summit with a heartbreaking defeat in the Sugar Bowl. Now it was Maryland and Jim Tatum's turn to vindicate their loss to OU in the '54 Orange Bowl.

So much had occurred the last two seasons that Bud Wilkinson needed to sit down and reflect. The Jimmy Harris experiment had exceeded expectations. The freshman class of '53 had actually performed beyond all forecasts. Wilkinson found himself almost precisely where he had been in December of '50, two games shy of his own record. But trouble lay ahead. The Orange Bowl was known to be a fickle lady.

Reasons existed to doubt the Sooners. For one, national champs hadn't fared well the last few years in bowl games, losing three of the last four. Maryland's national title was tainted two years earlier at the Orange Bowl. Now that the streak had risen to the tenth-longest in history, every team was shooting at the Sooners. The glare intensified each day as the national sporting press portrayed them as the new golden boys of college football.

Much of what was written was being thumbtacked to Maryland's bulletin board. "Knock those arrogant sonsabitches off their pedestal," Tatum told his Terps at least once a day.

No question, Maryland was loaded with talent, along with a few gallstones. Of all the college games played in '55, the Terps' 7–0 win over UCLA from start to finish was the most impressive. The UCLA Bruins, under Coach Red Sanders, had been a Top Ten team the previous four seasons. But they were held to minus twenty-one yards rushing against the Terps, prompting Sanders to rhapsodize, "Maryland is a majestic team, the greatest team of the era." Asked if he would renew the scheduling contract with this powerhouse, Sanders didn't hesitate. "I hope we never see them sumbucks again," he said.

But the Sooners seemed unfazed. Most had never even heard of Tatum, who had scooted out of Norman nine years earlier. None had been around on January 1, 1951, when the streak flamed out. They didn't know the meaning of losing the *big one,* though Wilkinson had often burned a mental image into their heads of how they would feel the day the winning died.

These Sooners were far different from the teams that had compiled the thirty-one-game streak from 1948 through '50. That was the end of the military era in college football. It was a time Wilkinson could depend on leadership from grizzled men like Harry Moore, who, at age twenty-nine, was the co-captain of the '50 team.

Wilkinson was only five years junior to Moore and, in truth, looked younger than the hardened center who had grown up working in the zinc smelters of northern Oklahoma while supporting an entire family following the death of his father. Harry worked from four in the morning till seven-thirty at night, often laboring three feet from an open flame. Moore joined the marines, and his military experience included battles at Guadalcanal and the Aleutian Islands.

Wilkinson often sought Moore's advice on team matters during the '50 season, and Harry always had an opinion.

"Harry, I'm having some discipline problems."

"F——, Coach," Moore would say. "If it were up to me, I'd kick their f—— asses off the team."

That logic wouldn't apply now. The Sooners of '55 were radically different. They were household names with futures in pro football. Some were media darlings. But they did have one thing in common with the boys from the class of '50—that unmistakable air of invincibility.

The player who scared the dickens out of everyone, and even inspired a few nightmares, was the studious and well-dressed son of a Pentecostal minister from the small town of Enid on the edge of wheat country in northern Oklahoma. John Bell, the seventh of twelve children, was as humble as his name. But his teammates learned not to be fooled.

At first blush, the six-foot, 190-pound end seemed as intimidating as a frat boy. He didn't talk loud or pound his own chest. His hair was combed, his faced shaved, and he would have looked quite at home hanging around with the premeds at the Bizzell Library. He wore tasseled loafers. But when Bell delivered his powerful right forearm shiver, the earth shook, ribs were broken, and chest plates were damaged. *Ugggggghhh* was the sound of air escaping from another Bell victim.

Bell was straight out of a Mickey Spillane novel—Mike Hammer, the two-fisted street guy on the lookout for crooks and the last guy you wanted to mess with. Three years earlier, in what would have been the spring of his senior year in high school, Bell dropped what he was doing in Enid and took off for Norman, where he participated in spring practice with the OU varsity.

Gomer Jones was quite curious to learn if the toughest high schooler in the state was really that hard-wired and ready to tackle the hairy-chested boys. Spring drills would be held for twenty-one days on the three practice fields just south of the stadium, and the smart money said the high school kid was overmatched.

"You sure you wanna do this?" Gomer asked.

"Why, yessir. When do we start?"

Truth is, Bell should have been focusing on recreational sports like backseat fondling and street rod racing. But he had graduated from high school a semester early, and instead of sitting around the local pool hall, he had packed for Norman, where he enrolled as a first-semester freshman with a full load of fifteen hours.

As a general rule, football players learned to hate football practice—the yelling, the cussing, the pounding, the vomiting, the gassers, and the donning of a cold, wet jock at six in the morning. But John Bell awoke that first morning of spring drills with nostrils flared. Here was a freak of nature, a boy who *loved* to practice football. He couldn't wait to inhale the pungent smell of sweat, blood, rubbing liniment, and soured practice uniforms, all mixed together.

Less than an hour into the first practice that March morning of '53, even before the sun had popped over the rim of Memorial Stadium, Bell had walloped practically every varsity player in sight. Upperclassmen walked around in a quandary asking, "Who the hell is that?" And this was a team that counted three future All-Americans— Kurt Burris, Max Boydston, and J. D. Roberts.

Roberts, the street-fighter of the OU team, was on a mission to put the punk in the hospital. He was now a snorting, snarling package of TNT when he lined up in front of the high schooler. "Kiss your ass good-bye!" J. D. hollered. The next thing he knew, J. D. was front side up, eyes spinning like lemons on a slot machine.

Most OU football players took their lumps no matter how hard the drill. Still, there were times when you tried to avoid some of the real bad-asses. Stepping into line for a hitting drill, a player would silently count the heads of the combatants in the other line. He was trying to determine whom he would face next. Players about to tangle with John Bell began developing a sudden case of leg cramps.

Gomer Jones crouched down in his catcher's stance to get a closer view of Bell at work. The Oklahoma line coach almost salivated at the sight of this teenager, knowing he would be around for three full years on the varsity, from 1954 through '56—that is, if the freshman coaches didn't screw him up, and Gomer wasn't about to allow that to happen.

Gomer sidled up to Wilkinson and said, "That boy right there, that Bell boy, he could play for us right now, this season."

The wheels were now spinning in Wilkinson's head. He was not above exploiting the rules, but this would be too risky. They would have to wait for this full-grown seventeen-year-old to get some age on him.

In the meantime, Bell was enjoying himself immensely around the OU campus. He had been assigned a sugar daddy, meaning he now had folding cash in his pocket and a closet full of new clothes. The second week of spring drills, he was set up with with a blind date, one of the prettiest girls from the Kappa Kappa Gamma house.

Around midnight, he walked his date back to her residence and kissed her good night. He couldn't take his eyes off the massive red brick house building where she resided. In fact, he stood for several minutes outside the house, marveling at the beautiful structure.

Weeks later, when he returned to Enid, Bell regaled his buddies with tall tales from life on campus.

"Golly," he said. "I took out this beautiful girl and you wouldn't believe where she lived, right there smack dab in the middle of campus in the biggest mansion you ever saw."

● ● ●

A nickname meant your teammates at least tolerated you. The '55 team, now packing for the Orange Bowl down in Miami, was filled with colorful monikers.

Quarterback Jimmy Harris, with his long nose and skinny face, was *the Joker*. Defensive end Don Stiller inherited a movie star's name because he looked like one—*Tab Hunter*. Guard Tom Emerson wore number 69 and was known as *Homo*. OU players thought Jay O'Neal was a pretty boy, so he became *Kissy*. Bob Timberlake was *Buns Timberlake* because he had a large butt. Billy Pricer ate a ton of food and was *Groceries*. Edmon Gray had a big nose and became known as *Beaky*. Fullback Dennit Morris, who produced quick touchdowns, became *Dennit in a Minute*. Clendon Thomas was simply *C. T.*

In the case of John Bell, players simply added his middle name—Herman. "John *Herman* Bell" soon came to evoke images of King Kong rumbling across campus. Everyone got out of his way.

Not a single sportswriter alive doubted that Oklahoma was the best team in America as the Sooners boarded the Braniff charter for Miami on the day after Christmas. Opponents in the '55 regular season had been outscored 365–54, the Sooners winning by the average score of 36–5.

Averaging 411 yards per game, the offense was number one in the land, and the defense ranked sixth. Not since the legendary Notre Dame and Army teams of the forties had a squad been so dominant for an entire season.

All that mattered, though, at this particular moment was the poker game taking shape at the back of the airplane. Players gathered in the final two rows, some already blocking the aisles and agitating the stewardesses. Most were carrying wads of large bills that had been accrued through the sale of tickets. Thanks to the national championship season, sugar daddies had dug deeper into their pockets to support the boys and their card games.

Most of the players wanted a shot at John Herman Bell, who fashioned himself as a gambler extraordinaire. You were almost certain to find Bell on the fourth floor of the Jeff House each afternoon with cards in hand. The fourth floor was more like an attic, shorter, more compact, and with a lower ceiling than the others. Everything but studying was tolerated in this hideaway. And John Herman was known to challenge a straight flush with two pair. It seemed that his enthusiasm for poker didn't quite match his grasp of the game or his run of empty hands. But John Herman still had plenty of money. The market for tickets to the OU–Texas game had been especially good.

Now, at thirty thousand feet, players were investing their money in a high-stakes game of Texas Hold 'Em.

"You know, John Herman, you can't be lucky in love and the cards at the same time," Jimmy Harris said. "And you've been by-God lucky in love lately."

"Look who's talking," Bell said. "If I were a god-dang quarterback, I'd be gettin' more."

"But you're not," Harris said with a sly grin. "And you'll never be." That drew a long "oooooh" from the players.

"Put your money where your mouth is," Bell snapped.

Jerry Tubbs, who was reading an economics textbook, overheard the remark.

"Ain't enough money in Oklahoma to fill up Jimmy's mouth," he said.

"Deal 'em," Harris said. The game was heating up.

Wilkinson heard the commotion from the first-class section. The coaches' wives were on the trip, so Bud and Gomer weren't flirting with the Braniff stewardesses. Wilkinson was worried about the collective swagger of his football team. Egos had been inflated to capacity. The national press was buzzing around the Sooners, and the OU sports information staff was quick to provide writers and broadcasters with anything they needed—quotes, stats, player interviews, or booze. At the time, Harold Keith was publishing the only media guide in America, and it was chock-full of enough information to fill up every sports page in America. For god's sake, Oklahoma had lost only five games since the second week of the *1948* season.

To most folks in America, Oklahoma was still a distant outpost on the southern plains, where the land was red and the people were dirty and dead broke. The sporting press, however, had a different take. Months earlier, the twenty-three-year-old centerfielder from Commerce, Oklahoma, had captured the imagination of every hardball fan in America. Mickey Mantle's thirty-two home runs not only led the American League but also had set the baseball world to talking.

Yes, the Sooners were now being touted as the New York Yankees of college football, having not lost a conference game in Wilkinson's eight-year tenure. And they were certain to improve in 1956 with the likes of Harris, McDonald, Tubbs, Bell, Pricer, Gray, and O'Neal returning for their senior season. Word spreading through college football was that the sportswriters planned to rank Oklahoma number one in '56 and the alternates number two.

The hype was giving Wilkinson a headache. He was worried about Jimmy Harris. Though he had played spectacularly, not losing a game as a starter, the quarterback was growing cockier by the day.

"Why can't you just be like Jay O'Neal?" Wilkinson would ask.

"Because I'm *not* Jay O'Neal."

Truer words had never been spoken. Harris was the consummate athlete: fast, rangy, and tough-minded. Outside of Pricer, Tubbs, and Bell, no Sooner hit harder. Opposing coaches were amazed at how a quarterback could be transformed into a headhunter on defense. No safety in America delivered a lick like Harris, and he likely would have gone both ways even in the era of two-platoon.

O'Neal was slightly built and slower than Harris. But his level of intelligence was almost beyond measurement. Jay had made a perfect 36 on the Academic Competency Test (ACT) as a senior in high school—a score that raised eyebrows in the dean's office. The day before O'Neal enrolled, Port Robertson received a phone call from Dean Glen C. Couch. He did everything but accuse the boy of cheating on the ACT and set down stringent requirements for his freshman year. Robertson called the young quarterback into his office and broke the news.

"Jay, the dean has some questions about your ACT score. You'll have to take calculus your first semester, and, son, that's a five-hour course. If you make it, fine. If you don't, well . . ."

"No problem."

O'Neal not only breezed through calculus; he also recorded a 4.0 grade point average his first semester. As the Sooners traveled to Miami for the Orange Bowl, O'Neal had yet to record anything below an A in any course for five straight semesters. And his team-mates found his photographic memory quite useful.

O'Neal was often surrounded by his teammates during the lunch hour at the Jeff House. Off the top of his head, he remembered every question from every test and, of course, every answer.

"There were twenty-five questions and here are the answers." Then he would reel them off without notes. "Number thirteen is a trick question. You'll think that the answer is D. But it's really C." O'Neal could even recall test questions and answers from semesters past.

O'Neal might have carried a higher IQ than Harris, but every quarterback under Wilkinson was on a level playing field when it came to knowing the game. Classwork was extensive. The coach demanded that his pupils study every situation, along with every down and distance, and know which play the coach wanted called. Wilkinson wanted the quarterbacks to think exactly as he thought. When an OU lineman was injured against Kansas, Wilkinson inserted Buddy Oujesky into the game. He whispered the play to Buddy before he ran onto the field. Oujesky trotted into the Sooner huddle, peered at Harris, and said, "Coach wants you to call the quick kick."

"Already got it called," Harris said proudly.

With Maryland and Jim Tatum coming up, Wilkinson was anxious to show off his shiny new toy—the go-go offense.

He told the quarterbacks, "There will be times in the game

when you might not even huddle. Just call the play at the line."
Three decades would pass before any team in the National Football
League attempted to execute such a sophisticated fast-breaking of-
fense.

For the first time in several weeks, John Herman Bell counted a
small profit from his efforts at poker. After team buses pulled to
the front of the Fontainebleau Hotel in Miami, Wilkinson gathered
the players in the lobby and said, "Put on shorts, T-shirts, and tennis shoes and meet in front of the hotel in ten minutes." Players
thought they were going to the beach. For the next hour, they
would run gassers on the grassy median, about ten yards wide,
dodging hedges and palm trees in front of the Fontainebleau.
Tourists stopped and stared—until they saw the Sooners bent over
and vomiting. The message was loud and clear. This was not a vacation, and the winning streak wasn't about to be surrendered to
Tatum.

Buses pulled out the next morning at seven for the ninety-minute
ride to the University of Miami, where the Sooners would practice
for five straight days leading to the Orange Bowl. They dressed in
full uniforms and practiced for two hours. After a quick lunch, they
rested briefly in the Miami athletic dorms and were back on the
practice field by two o'clock. It was dark when they returned to the
Fontainebleau, and meetings would consume the rest of the evening
until curfew.

Even the coaches' wives were getting in on the act. They were
constantly reminding the players' wives, "Don't have too much sex
this week. Cut him completely off the night before the game. Sex'll
sap him." Most disregarded the dictum.

Wilkinson dispatched graduate assistant Gene Calame to the Maryland hotel to hunt for misplaced playbooks. As Wilkinson might have
predicted, a man wearing a baseball cap pulled snugly down over his
forehead approached an OU coach in the Fontainebleau lobby.

"I believe that one of your players has lost his playbook," he said. As it turned out, it was a Maryland playbook—a fake one. It was a trick that Wilkinson had pulled on Tatum two years earlier.

After four days of grueling practices and long treks back and forth from the Miami campus, co-captains Bo Bolinger and Bob Loughridge, at the behest of his teammates, grudgingly approached Wilkinson about having Thursday night off. The coach agreed to give the Sooners two full hours of free time before an eleven o'clock curfew. Most were too tired to enjoy it.

Like most of the eastern teams, Maryland was big, strong, and loaded with players whose last names ended in vowels. Oklahoma focused its attention on two of the best players in the country—center/linebacker tackle Bob Pellegrini and tackle Mike Sandusky. Like the Sooners, the Maryland defense had shut out four opponents, and in ten games Maryland had allowed only fifty-seven points—three more than OU. They would outweigh the Sooners in the line by more than twenty pounds per man. So the Sooners spent the entire week in Miami practicing the go-go.

In spite of the marathon practices, the meetings, and the warnings about too much sex, the Sooners couldn't have played much worse in the first quarter.

Maryland halfback Ed Vereb swept right end, reversed field, and took off against the alternate defense. He was sixty-six yards down the field when he was caught from behind by a diving O'Neal, whose body was parallel with the ground when he knocked Vereb down at the Sooner twenty-four. O'Neal was slower than Vereb but made the play on grit alone. His effort paid off as Maryland quarterback Bob Tamburello was hit by Wayne Greenlee on the next play and fumbled into the arms of Don Stiller.

The Maryland offense was on a roll again late in the second quarter. The Terps had possession at the Sooner ten-yard line when Vereb faked the pass, made a U-turn, and sprinted into the end zone just seconds before the halftime gun. Tubbs blocked the extra point attempt, and the Sooners were down 6–0.

Wilkinson was livid in the OU dressing room. "If you don't get your shit together, you're going to get the hell beat out of you," he snapped. "You're screwing it all up." His eyes were now on fire.

Wilkinson had never used profanity on the players. He often cussed a blue streak at the game officials, but not around the team. His outburst, though, shocked them back to reality.

Before returning to the field for the third quarter, Wilkinson made it clear that the huddle was now a thing of the past. Plays were to be called at the line of scrimmage.

Early in the third quarter, the Sooners tore down the field in quick bursts behind the hurry-up offense. McDonald completed a nineteen-yard pass to Burris, moving the ball to the Maryland seven. McDonald then followed blocks by Mobra, Woodworth, and Bolinger to the four. He took Harris's blind option pitch around right end, scoring on the next play.

Late in the third quarter, Maryland's defensive line was on the brink of exhaustion. Pelligrini and Sandusky were having trouble getting off the ground before the next snap. They often tried to hold the ball carrier on the ground until they could catch their breath.

At one point, Sandusky was down on one knee, his shirttail flopping out and the laces on both shoes untied, when the Sooners sprinted to the line. Pellegrini tried to help Sandusky to his feet, but the big lineman yelled, "Get outta my way. Here come those bastards again!"

The alternates ran over Maryland, and O'Neal scored the second OU touchdown on a sneak from the one. Midway through the fourth quarter, Sooner cornerback Carl Dodd intercepted Larry Beightol's pass, returning it eighty-two yards for a touchdown.

Near exhaustion, both teams stumbled and staggered off the field at the final gun. Oklahoma had won 20–6.

"Oklahoma is the best team in the country," Tatum said. After thirty straight wins, it was a sentiment shared by a nation of college football fans.

. . .

Sen. Robert S. Kerr was the most powerful and influential man in the history of Oklahoma and by the midfifties had the U.S. Senate by the *cojones*. In Washington, they dubbed him the "uncrowned king of Congress."

Before his fabulous success in politics, Kerr had plunged headfirst into Big Oil, founding one of the largest energy companies in the history of the country—Kerr-McGee Industries.

With millions in the bank, he ran for governor and won in 1943 and served through '47 before being elected to the U.S. Senate in '48. He despised the state's image born out of John Steinbeck's *The Grapes of Wrath*. He spit out the word "Okie" like brackish water.

One of Kerr's greatest deeds was making certain that Wilkinson would finish his coaching career in Oklahoma. Impressed by the positive national publicity generated by Wilkinson, Kerr set out to raise a quarter-million dollars for the coach. His personal Beechcraft was flown all over the state, where the rich and the powerful were asked to contribute $3,000 each. The limit of each gift was set to avoid federal and state gift taxes.

Kerr, of course, had yet another motive to placate Wilkinson. Rumors already abounded that the coach would someday enter politics, and Kerr wasn't about to lose his Senate seat to this miracle worker.

Money, of course, had become a major incentive to Wilkinson's long-term commitment to OU. He was now the highest-paid coach in America at $102,000 per year—an unheard-of coaching salary at the time—and *The Bud Wilkinson Show*, thanks to generous advertising dollars, had become a money machine. His $40,000 mortgage had been paid off by a group called the Touchdown Club, and the cars driven by Bud and Mary Wilkinson were provided cost-free by wealthy boosters. When Kerr presented him with the $250,000 gift, Wilkinson gave $50,000 to Gomer Jones. The two men celebrated that night with enough old-fashioneds to float the navy.

Compared to the desolate thirties, the midfifties in Oklahoma were a time of celebration, and Kerr was one of the most fun-loving people around. He cheerfully played the tuba and knocked down bowling pins to launch charity drives.

Two weeks after the Sooners had whipped Maryland in the Orange Bowl, the senator was having Sunday lunch at his Oklahoma City residence when his son, Bill, mentioned a fraternity activity about to take place at OU. Students had finished semester finals and were now on winter break. Bill was the president of the Phi Delta Theta pledge class, and it was time for the freshmen to take their "walk"—normally just a slobbering drunk weekend down in Dallas.

But the '56 pledges were far more creative than the ones before them. Bill was already planning a trip to Las Vegas, some twelve hundred miles away. A caravan of cars would tackle the two-laners through Amarillo and Albuquerque and Flagstaff, Arizona, where the mountain highways were famous for their death toll. The trip would take more than two full days, if the boys were lucky enough to arrive alive.

The senator peered across the table at his son and said, "Can you get forty boys to go?"

"Why, sure. Yessir."

"Well, TWA owes me a favor. I'll get the airlines to fly you boys out there and back."

Bill Kerr couldn't believe his ears. This would be the trip of a lifetime for some of the Phi Delts. Many had never traveled by air, much less on a private charter. Furthermore, the pledges could invite some of the upperclass Phi Delts. Football stars like Bob Loughridge, Carl Dodd, and even John Herman Bell, an avid cardplayer, would make the trip.

The boys were full of piss and vinegar when they boarded the four-engine Convair 121, identical to the aircraft that ferried Pres. Dwight Eisenhower about the country. They were greeted by four attractive stewardesses, who were quick to inform the boys that they, too, would be "laying over" the two nights in Las Vegas.

"Pinch me! Pinch me!" John Herman bellowed as he climbed the stairway to the aircraft.

"Calm down, John Herman," Phi Delt junior Dick Champlin said. "And don't lose *all* your money on the flight to Vegas." While he loved the party life, Champlin seemed more mature than the others and had aspirations to become senior class president in the fall of '56.

Many of the frat boys did lose every red cent on the four-hour flight. Meanwhile, Champlin was focusing all of his energy on TWA stewardess Mary Lou Darling, age twenty-one, five-two, brown hair, D cup.

Miss Darling followed Champlin off the plane, down the long corridor of McCarran Airport, and straight to the rental car counter. While most of the boys hailed cabs to the Flamingo Hotel, Champlin was going in style—a red convertible.

At the hotel, while the other boys tackled the dice and blackjack tables, Champlin arranged for show tickets. Bing Crosby was performing that night at the Flamingo. Dick made sure that he and Mary Lou had a table close to the front.

The Flamingo had been built a decade earlier by legendary mafioso Benjamin "Bugsy" Siegel. When Siegel first visited Las Vegas in 1940, he had written it off as nothing more than another bowl of blowing dust in the middle of the Mojave Desert. A little research, though, revealed just how much money could be made off legal gambling. Bugsy did an about-face, convincing Meyer Lansky, Lucky Luciano, Frank Costello, and other mobsters to back him in the construction of the Flamingo, budgeted at $2 million. By the time it was completed in 1946, the hotel and casino's construction costs had soared to $6 million, and the grand opening attracted a smattering of gamblers and virtually no action. Bugsy was suddenly in deep trouble with the eastern Mafia. Some of the mob bosses suspected Bugsy of skimming off the construction funds and having his girlfriend, Virginia Hill, park the money in Swiss bank accounts. On June 20, 1947, Bugsy was sitting in Hill's mansion in Beverly Hills when two steel-jacketed slugs from an army carbine tore through his face. Authorities found one of his eyes on the dining room floor, fifteen feet from the body.

If only Bugsy could have seen the place in January of 1956. Four casinos dotted the dusty landscape, and dozens were either under construction or in the planning stages. The Flamingo was a beehive of activity, attracting the rich and the famous from the Los Angeles basin, the geriatric set from Arizona, and some college boys from Oklahoma.

While Dick Champlin doted over Mary Lou, the cash-poor boys were cooking up money schemes. One of the brave Phi Delts approached the casino money cage and said, "We're here in Senator Kerr's party. Will y'all cash our checks?"

"Why, of course."

The boys were suddenly back in the chips, and it was time to gamble. The casino manager opened a bar tab for all of the Phi Delts, and Champlin learned that his show tickets had been comped. The boys didn't know it, but they were walking around rich.

The first night of this adventure, John Herman Bell's luck made a U-turn. Every hand was coming up twenty-one. He had never seen so many aces and jacks wedded to each other. Chips were piling up on the table, and the Phi Delts gathered in a large circle to cheer their football hero. Never before had John Herman counted as much money as when he cashed out three hours later.

When the Sooners' defensive end wasn't busy with football or cards, it seemed that women were falling at his feet. So it wasn't surprising that the fraternity brothers found Champlin in a state of depression at the casino bar a few hours later.

"Where's Mary Lou?"

"Up in John Herman's room."

"Figures."

The next night, John Herman charged the blackjack tables again with all of his might. "I will take this place to its knees," he said. An hour later, he was charging through the front door of the Flamingo, roaring off in a rented convertible. He was tapped. So angry was John Herman that he decided to take a drive through the desert at high speed. Luckily for Mary Lou, she wasn't along for this ride.

The next morning, the Phi Delts gathered in the lobby of the Flamingo when they heard the news. Everything—the hotel bill, the bar bill, the shows, and the meals—had already been paid off by Senator Kerr and all of their checks torn up. They owed nothing. Now they had about an hour to get to the airport. Then they found John Herman Bell, sitting in one of the lobby chairs with a hollow stare.

"What's wrong?"

"I lost the car."

"Oh."

For moral support, frat brothers Lanny Ross, Norman Lamb, and Sooner tackle Bob Loughridge accompanied John Herman to the rental car counter. Bell was lucky that he could still count Ross as a friend; he had pounded him into bloody oblivion three years earlier during a high school game. Lamb felt obligated to tag along since he had been the Enid quarterback and was one of John Herman's life-long friends. Loughridge had about $150 in his pocket, thanks to his luck at craps, and knew his buddy might need some cash.

"I've lost something," Bell told the counter attendant.

"Oh, that's OK, sir. People lose their keys all of the time."

"Ma'am, I didn't lose the keys."

"Then what'd you lose?"

"The car."

For more than an hour, Bell, Ross, Lamb, and Loughridge rode around the desert in a black pickup truck with a toothless driver whose breath smelled like kerosene. They finally spotted the convertible five miles from the casino, axle-deep in sand. It took a good half hour of huffing, puffing, and pushing to get it free.

The chartered flight was more than an hour late leaving Las Vegas. John Herman took a seat near the back and thought about something Jimmy Harris had said weeks earlier on the flight to Miami: "You can't be lucky in love and the cards."

But what if it's just a one-night stand? John Herman thought to himself.

11

FAT CATS

More than two decades after the repeal of Prohibition in America, bootlegging was still a cottage industry in Oklahoma. In 1956, only two other states—Mississippi and North Carolina—held the line against Satan's firewater. The only alcohol you could legally purchase in Oklahoma was three-two beer (3.2 percent alcohol). Most folks called it *headache beer* and swore it was nothing more than a workout for the kidneys.

Just as the swingers in New York, Philadelphia, Baltimore, Chicago, and Detroit refused *not* to booze in the twenties, Oklahomans rebelled in the fifties. You could acquire the hard stuff by either driving into the bordering states, operating a still in the basement, or hiring yourself a bootlegger.

Back in the Roaring Twenties, when the Mafia grabbed America by the throat and crime boss Meyer Lansky said, "We are now bigger than U.S. Steel," bootleggers ascended into the income brackets of doctors and lawyers and the elite. The profession became as essential to organized crime as the chicken to the egg.

Now, Bud Wilkinson had a bootlegger. Gomer Jones had a bootlegger. George Cross had a bootlegger. Doc Rountree had a bootlegger. Practically every upstanding doctor and lawyer in Oklahoma City and Norman with a taste for drink took delivery at the back door. If the man of the house was away, the bootlegger had *carte blanche* to inspect the liquor cabinet and fill the order accordingly.

Oklahoma students got their booze from a bootlegger who parked his car on the bridge above the Canadian River, the line of demarcation between Cleveland and McLain Counties. If the county sheriff pursued him from the west, he drove into Cleveland County. If he sensed trouble coming from the east, he drove into McLain County.

When the University of Oklahoma wanted to throw a party, officials often turned to E. G. "Big Boy" Johnson, a tall, rawboned man who, in his midfifties, was quick with a joke and a drink. Big Boy's laugh seemed to rumble up from his socks. He was the life of any social gathering, especially the shindigs held at his spacious two-story wood-frame house on Main Street in Norman.

No one was more tightly tethered to Oklahoma football than Big Boy. When the Sooners were struggling in the depressing thirties, Big Boy bought 125 season tickets and handed them out to contractors and friends to stir interest in the program. In the thirties, when OU tackle Dub Wheeler's concentration was drifting, Big Boy paid off Dub's debts and came to the financial aid of his wife and children. Dub turned his season around, winning All-American honors in 1935. Three years later, at the height of the recruiting battle for "Indian" Jack Jacobs, Big Boy stashed the quarterback/punter at his lake house in Arkansas. Players of the late forties like Myrle Greathouse, Darrell Royal, Bill Jennings, and Dee Andros often ate breakfast, lunch, and dinner at Big Boy's. Some OU players were regularly treated to "loans" from Big Boy, who also picked up the tab for expensive suits at McCall's Men Store.

One more reason Big Boy was so worshiped was the lavish parties at his house, where the booze flowed and deals were cut. The backyard was often filled with rich and powerful people, along with the aroma of Big Boy's barbeque chicken. OU president George L. Cross once wrote Big Boy a letter of thanks: "I want to express my sincere appreciation for the fine service you have been performing for the University of Oklahoma in arranging for the entertainment of important groups of persons coming to the University for meetings." Cross also added this postscript: "In my opinion, you are the best public relations agency the University has."

Big Boy soothed a throbbing headache. Thanks to "Prohibition" in Oklahoma and rules against drinking at OU, cocktail parties were out of the question at the president's mansion, situated squarely at the center of campus. When Cross needed to woo legislators or football boosters, it was done at Big Boy's.

Though Cross was not a serious drinker, he and his wife, Cleo, enjoyed martinis. Discretion became a top priority. Even more worrisome were the empty bottles—*they might be discovered in the trash cans*. Cross racked his brain for a solution. He revealed his plan one Sunday morning at two o'clock when he arose from bed, swung open the front door, and flung the vodka bottles into his own front yard. He slept well that night, knowing passersby would think that college revelers had desecrated the president's lawn. Garbage collectors would soon be along to clean up the mess.

Along with being one of the most ambitious men of his time, Cross possessed a dry sense of humor that could be disarming. Members of the board of regents were often stung by the president's little jokes and didn't speak to him for long stretches.

Five years earlier, Cross had become concerned with issues of a downward-spiraling university. In 1950, the same year the Sooners had won their first national championship, attendance dropped by more than twenty-five hundred students in one semester, leaving the university with fewer than eight thousand students for the first time since the war. Cross needed a bigger budget and went before the Oklahoma House-Senate Appropriations Committee asking for $10.6 million, an amount that exceeded Gov. Johnston Murray's request by $3.6 million. Following his passionate thirty-minute plea, which Cross judged to be a success, the floor was opened for questions.

A sleepy-eyed senator said, "I would like to ask the good doctor why he thinks he needs so much money to run this university?" Cross was floored. Then he pulled himself up and delivered one of the most famous lines in the history of the University of Oklahoma:

"Sir, I would like to build a university the football team can be proud of."

The room fell silent. Seconds later, it was filled with laughter. But Cross didn't get the funds.

In spite of the gentle irony, the quote appeared in newspapers across America, including *Time* and *Life* magazines. Friends traveling abroad mailed Cross clippings of the quote from three foreign newspapers.

A month after being turned down on his budget request, Cross attended a banquet honoring Muskogee football players and learned the true meaning of academics at OU. After a round of speeches, the Muskogee Quarterback Club presented Wilkinson with a brand-new Cadillac. As a testimonial to "higher education," the OU president received a cigarette lighter.

• • •

In Big Boy Johnson's game room, on a cold January morning in 1947, Bud Wilkinson pledged himself to Oklahoma. In fact, it was straight-up three o'clock when Wilkinson finally relented. For hours, he had tried to convince both Cross and Big Boy that he was too young at thirty-one to be a head coach. Big Boy mixed up a round of old-fashioneds, Bud's favorite, when the hay was in the barn.

About eighteen months later, Bud and Mary Wilkinson arrived at Big Boy's house to have dinner and drinks on a Thursday night before the Texas game in 1948—an evening that Bud would never forget. He left Big Boy's feeling lighthearted, and two days later a Wilkinson-coached team beat the Texas Longhorns for the first time.

It was no secret that Wilkinson was obsessive about his superstitions. He wore the same suit on the sideline of every Sooner game. He arrived at the stadium at precisely the same time every game day. During every practice, he wore a new pair of white socks. Not just a clean pair—a brand-new pair.

So it was not surprising after the 1948 defeat of Texas that Wilkinson would trek to Big Boy's house, only a few blocks from his own, every Thursday night during the football season. Sometimes he took Mary and the two boys, Jay and Pat. Sometimes, Gomer and the rest of the coaching staff would come for drinks. Bud, who had a key to the house, didn't mind going alone if the Johnsons were out of town. He would mix an old-fashioned, take a long drink, and lie on the game room floor in the dark, his body soaking up the lucky vibes.

One more factor caused Bud to gravitate to Big Boy like a bug to a light. On the night he signed on, Johnson had promised to launch a fund-raising club to assist the football program in its quest for more national championships. He promised money galore from the big guns. The Sooners would have cash to spend on the best players, while remaining competitive with all of the big-time money machines churning out Top Ten teams across America.

Years later, on the day the letter arrived from the NCAA in the fall of '53, Wilkinson promised Cross that everything inside the OU football program was on the up and up. "There is nothing to fear," he said. Rumors had persisted for years that Oklahoma players were on the dole for cars, clothes and, yes, the gold standard for all dirty programs, cold, hard cash. The Texas schools were forever firing off letters to the NCAA offices to snitch on Wilkinson and "Big Boy" Johnson, along with oilmen Eddie Chiles and Roy Guffey and Quintin Little, a member of the Oklahoma board of regents and a man who had opened his heart and his wallet to Sooner football.

Guffey was Jimmy Harris's sugar daddy and, along with paying a huge premium for game tickets, had bankrolled a trip to James K. Wilson, an expensive men's store in Dallas, after Jimmy signed with the Sooners in the spring of '53.

Cross was unaware at the moment that Coach Gomer Jones had a vast amount of cashed locked away in his desk drawer for the purpose of paying for players' tickets. Jones paid ten times face value. He also paid "advances" on ticket money if a certain star player was strapped for cash.

As Cross dug deeper, he learned that funny money was everywhere. There was no system of checks and balances inside the athletic department. When university administrators tried to track expenditures, they were often led down blind alleys or treated as if they had no business sticking their noses into football matters. The Athletic Council, established in 1928 for the purpose of raising stadium money, was still a separate corporate body that collected and disbursed money that was rarely accounted for. In reality, the Athletic Council was a closed society that no one had tried to crack. Until Cross came knocking.

The issue of illegal aid became more complex when Big Boy Johnson, as promised, invited some of the wealthiest supporters of OU football to his home for dinner and drinks and arm-twisting in 1947. This was about six months after Wilkinson had signed his first head coaching contract at OU. In total, seventy-six men gathered at the house on Main Street that night. The nucleus of the Touchdown Club was formed, the only resistance coming from Harrison Smith, an influential Oklahoma City businessman.

In the spring of 1948, the Touchdown Club gathered again in Big Boy's backyard, where lights were strung and the booze flowed. To commence the fund, supporters were encouraged to stuff large bills into a cowboy hat.

Big Boy worked out a plan to sway Harrison Smith. He decided to play to the *big man's* ego—naming him the first president of the Touchdown Club. It was Big Boy's plan to stay in the background while becoming the driving force behind the war chest. He had promised Wilkinson money, and, by god, there would be plenty of it.

The first task of the Touchdown Club was to "ransom" running back Lindell Pearson back from the University of Arkansas. After verbally committing to the Sooners, Pearson didn't show up for the first day of freshman practice. A group of Oklahoma City businessmen hired a private detective, who discovered that Pearson was holed up in Fayetteville, having been lured to the Ozarks by gifts and cash. "The Lindell Pearson Ransom Fund" attracted thousands, and the boy was quickly back in his home state, where he lettered two seasons for the Sooners.

By the mid-1950s, the NCAA enforcement division had quite a large file on this illegal activity at OU. Cross made two trips to Kansas City, hoping to dissuade executive director Walter Byers. But Byers was having nothing to do with it, citing boxes of letters accusing Oklahoma of operating a slush fund. Most were postmarked from Texas, where members of the Southwest Conference had turned green with envy.

The SWC football powerhouses had struggled in the fifties while the Oklahoma Sooners soared to the top. Only Arkansas was cracking the Top Twenty on a regular basis. The Texas schools blamed the imbalance on the burgeoning slush fund at OU. They failed to mention that the Oklahoma recruiters were whipping them at every turn in their own backyard—especially in West Texas, where the majority of the leading blue-chippers were playing high school ball.

Word got around that every OU recruiter was toting a wad. Wilkinson practically had an air force at his disposal, beginning with the fleet of twenty-two planes owned by Halliburton Oil and made available by Clyde Davis, Bud's friend and golfing buddy. If recruits needed to be transported from West Texas to Norman, Bud could depend on Eddie Chiles and his fourteen-seat Dove aircraft. The university's Beechcraft Bonanza was almost always available.

As the rumors swirled about dirty laundry, Cross called Wilkinson into his office and asked if money was changing hands. Wilkinson admitted that some players had been paid, that the ticket business was healthy. But he pointed out that Oklahoma was an equal opportunity employer—linemen as well as backs and ends were reaping the benefits.

Then Cross picked up the trail of Arthur Wood, an Oklahoma City accountant who was overseeing a stash of money earmarked for the football program. Wood freely admitted to Cross that he had disbursed funds for years to Bill Jennings, OU's chief recruiter. The demand for money became so great, Wood said, that more had to be raised by the Touchdown Club. NCAA enforcers interviewed Wood, but he refused to open his books. When Byers persisted, Wood moved himself to Reno, Nevada, in the mid-1950s, taking the financial records with him.

The NCAA slapped the university with two years' probation for offering numerous inducements. Then the media got involved. Some wild stories flew. A newspaper columnist in Denver publicly questioned why Sen. Joe McCarthy had sat in the Oklahoma rooting section during the 1954 Orange Bowl. The sweet irony was that "Tailgunner Joe," the famous Communist baiter, had pulled for "Big Red."

True Magazine printed an investigative piece with this headline: **"Oklahoma and the Touchdown Club—How Does a Third-rate College Football Team Suddenly Become One of the Best in the Country?"**

Paul Gardner, author of the story, wrote: "It isn't so hard when there are seven hundred millionaires helping it along." It was doubtful during that period that seven hundred millionaires could find their way to Oklahoma.

For three decades, Grantland Rice, along with most sportswriters, had elevated college players to Greek gods and coaches to Einsteins. But now he was taking a hammer and chisel to the great game, accusing coaches and university presidents of proselytizing athletes.

Rice wrote in *Sport* magazine: "Certainly no game could look to be strictly amateur to a college player when he began to count up the immense sums taken in largely through the ability to crash a line, throw a pass, run around end, or make a tackle. Being normal human beings, many of these young men naturally wanted their share of the swag. And more than a few got paid—up to $10,000 a year. I have been reading lately statements by many college presidents that, 'as far as they know,' their alumni have given their players no financial aid. In too many cases, 'as far as they know' is about as far as a midget can throw an elephant."

Indeed, these were scandalous times in college football. To maintain a Top Twenty status, many universities were forced to meet a payroll. The Oklahoma program was like so many others of the time: it was soiled.

While it was true that the Texas schools were envious of Wilkinson, the Sooners were willing to pay the price for success. It wouldn't be the last time that NCAA came snooping around. They had yet to find the end of this money trail.

12

CROSSROADS

Prentice Gautt rarely ventured beyond the boundaries of the neighborhood, and most of his life had been lived within blocks of the house where he was born on Northeast Fourth Street on the edge of the Deep Deuce in Oklahoma City. Weeks and months often passed when he didn't see a white person. Prentice had one dream locked up inside him, and today he was unleashing it on the world— scaling those invisible walls.

When Prentice dreamed beyond his own backyard, he could see a man with wavy white hair dressed in a gray flannel suit. Prentice listened to every game coached by the man, and on Sundays, precisely at four o'clock, he was seated on the floor in front of the small television in the family room, worshiping. He never missed *The Bud Wilkinson Show.*

For years, football was the lifeboat that rescued Prentice from his sadness. The Gautt family had been upside down since his mother had died during childbirth when Prentice was four. The baby could not be saved, and in the blink of an eye Prentice had lost his mother and a baby brother. Both passed away in the very house where the family would continue to live. A brother and two older sisters were sent away to live with a relative in Muskogee.

Though Prentice still had his father, Jack Gautt, he often felt empty and alone. Jack was an automobile mechanic badly in need of a job; he didn't have enough money to buy a car. He entered a partnership with a friend in an auto parts business, but the business quickly foundered simply because a black man was unable to network inside the white community to find the parts that he needed to sell. As the business collapsed, Jack drank. His brother, Bob, owned a beer joint next door, and Prentice was starting to see his father less and less. Bob's Tavern now occupied Jack's days and nights.

This emptiness eased a bit when Jack Gautt remarried, bringing Sarah into his life. She was personable and quite attentive. At least, he had someone to talk to. One Sunday afternoon after watching *The Bud Wilkinson Show*, Prentice turned to Sarah and said, "Mom, I think the only way I'll ever meet Bud Wilkinson is if I join the Air National Guard."

"What do you mean, Prentice?"

The boy pointed to the TV screen where Wilkinson's face appeared. The coach was in the midst of a commercial for the Air National Guard. Then Prentice smiled.

"Mom, I really want to play for the Sooners."

"Prentice, this is something that you need to think about. In my opinion, you need to go someplace where roads have already been crossed. The first black man to cross the road is usually the one who gets killed."

From the Deep Deuce you could gaze west upon the tall buildings of downtown Oklahoma City, where the bustle of the streets and sidewalks was captivating. But if your skin was black in the early 1950s, you could look but not touch, see but not feel. To the Negroes living on the east side in that six-block area, the white man was a bully and a racist. Many white folks knew these practices were morally wrong, but the separation of the races went unchecked. Time marched on with little change.

In these tense times, Negroes were wary about crossing into

white man's territory or venturing into downtown, where they were allowed to shop at department stores but not to dine in the cafeterias or restaurants or stay in the hotels. They were shooed away like chickens from the dining counter at Katz Drug Store at the corner of Main and Robinson. They were free to spend their money at John A. Brown's department store, but not to dine inside the luncheonette. Orders for Negroes were placed in paper sacks, and the food was to be eaten on the streets or sidewalks. Only two public rest rooms were accessible to Negroes—one at the Union Bus Station and the other in the basement of the county courthouse. Black men often carried tin cups in their coat pockets for the purpose of urination.

Oklahoma City in this period was not unlike most places south of an imaginary line that extended across the northern borders of Oklahoma, Arkansas, Tennessee, and North Carolina. Jim Crow laws were rigorously obeyed, and America's tug-of-war over civil rights was still years away.

This day, a Friday in June of 1952, Prentice was crossing the road and shooting for the moon. He summoned his two best friends, Willie Hodges and Theodore Green, also fourteen years old, and explained his secret plan.

"Hope you guys got some guts," Prentice said. "Because we're gonna have some *fun* today."

They would board the city bus on Durland and ride into the center of downtown, where they would hop off and sprint about six blocks and catch the Interurban, the bus that connected Oklahoma City to outlying towns, and they would sit in the back row and watch the farms and ranches and silos slide past. They would gaze at the white picket fences and freshly painted red barns along the two-lane highway. They would see horses and cows and inhale both the pungent and pleasant odors of life on the other side of the wall.

June in Oklahoma was the rainy season, and the rolling pastures held an emerald glow. After they'd boarded the Interurban, it seemed surreal to be out of the Deep Deuce, away from all the concrete, steel, and brick—away from the blues and jazz and the nightlife and the smoke of Second Street. The Deep Deuce was the all-black sector just east of downtown that was filled with drugstores, bars, pool halls, dry cleaners, churches, hotels, schools, and a brothel or two. Saturday nights, entertainers like Count Basie and Lionel Hampton came to Second Street.

As he listened to the tires singing on the pavement, Theodore said, "You sure you wanna do this?"

"I'm not sure," Prentice said. "But it might be my last chance."

"What do you mean?"

"I figure I'll wind up in Minnesota or Michigan after I graduate. That's where they let colored boys play ball."

"So you'll never see Oklahoma again."

"That could be so."

There was much to think about on the twenty-minute ride into this strange land, and Prentice kept asking himself if they could pull it off. Everything would have to fall just right.

The University of Oklahoma was the glistening centerpiece of Norman—ten thousand students and twenty-seven thousand residents peacefully co-existing in this pastoral tree-lined town in the midst of the American dream, a town of white picket fences and manicured lawns and shiny new Chevys. Of course, it was lily white. The only black man working in Norman was old Uncle Amos, now in his sixties and still called the shoeshine boy. Uncle Amos had to drive forty miles each way every day to pop that rag at the Campus Corner, just around the corner from OU. And *this* was the world that Prentice Gautt dreamed of someday invading.

For years he had often wondered what Norman really looked like as he listened to the games on the radio. In the fall, he could envision the windblown leaves and the bright colors, the roar of the crowd emanating from Owen Field that echoed down Lindsey Street, the smell of hamburgers grilling, the lurid colors of the 140-piece OU band, the snap and crackle of the snare drums.

Now, as the bus hissed to a stop, the boys knew they were somewhere in Norman. For several minutes they stood on the corner of Lindsey and Oak, their eyes combing the streets and the green lawns, their heads swiveling this way and that. Many white people passed, but none seemed willing to converse with three black youths or to even acknowledge their presence. In his soft voice, Prentice asked a passerby, "Sir, where do the Sooners play?"

The man never looked at Prentice, nor did he speak, but finally pointed in an eastern direction, down Lindsey Street, and walked away. In the blink of an eye, the three boys were off and running, and six blocks later they saw the magnificent edifice known as Memorial Stadium rising in the distance like Oz. Year after year, as he listened to the Sooner broadcasts, he tried to imagine the fifty-five thousand seats rising to the sky and the thick grass of Owen Field, named several decades ago for Benjamin Gilbert Owen, the first coach of the Sooners in 1905 and the man who compiled four unbeaten seasons in twenty-one years that brought immense pride to the young state.

Playing in Prentice's head was "Boomer Sooner," the school fight song, and he could hear play-by-play man Bill Bryan painting the pictures of heroes as they tore-ass across the spinach green field. Prentice had imagined tall fences with razor wire strung along the top and armed guards ringing the complex. Instead, only a five-foot concrete barrier stood between the boys and their dream. They listened for threatening voices but heard none. Their eyes scanned the parking lots around the stadium and they saw no one. Squirrels were busy with a nest in an elm tree, and a cottonwood snowed white flecks. Birds sang. And before you could say, "Bud Wilkinson," the boys were over the wall, scurrying down the fifty-odd steps through the end zone stands and sprinting onto the field. Amazingly, on this sunny summer day, no one was watching. The coaches and most of the athletic department officials were on vacation, and the sleepy campus had virtually cleared out with the end of the semester.

Prentice heard his voice echoing across the field and into the vacuous concrete grandstand, and it startled him.

"Hey, look at me! I'm Billy Vessels!"

He dodged an imaginary tackler and stiff-armed another. Theodore and Willie knew that Prentice was one of the fastest athletes in the state. But they were still mesmerized by his speed and fluidity this day. His feet never seemed to touch down. Thanks to the combination of adrenaline, raw energy, and the realization of his dream, Prentice was defying gravity, and for several seconds he appeared to be in flight.

"Hey, Prentice!" Theodore yelled. "No man alive could tackle you today."

"Maybe Jim Thorpe," Willie said. "But I think he's dead."

In their rush to reach Norman, they had forgotten to bring a football. But it didn't stop them from faking hand-offs and deep passes and long touchdown runs. They raced wide-eyed from end zone to end zone without breathing hard. Prentice could feel the imaginary eyes of Bud Wilkinson tracking his every move, and he knew *Coach* would approve. After scoring his sixth touchdown of the day, Prentice yelled, "Let's get out of here before they catch us!"

They dashed up the end zone steps, and any college coach would have been amazed at their speed.

Out on the sidewalk, an old man with a crew cut glared at the boys.

"You niggers need to get outta town before sundown. We don't allow no niggers around here after dark."

He was referring to the law of Cleveland County, which didn't allow Negroes to sleep within the city limits. At the time, only a handful of black students were enrolled at the university, and they were treated like aliens. They were seated in stalls in the back of the classroom or out in the halls.

"Yessir, we're going," Prentice said, his eyes scanning the block for police. "We're headed for the bus right now."

But as he jogged away, Prentice couldn't help himself. Emotions had been boiling in his gut too long.

He stopped and turned toward the man.

"Sir, with all due respect, I plan to be back."

13

FAST TRACK

On the morning of September 1, 1956, the winningest college football team in America was awakened in three shifts at the Jefferson House. The Oklahoma Sooners had adorned the cover of every college preseason football magazine in America, and why not? They were the defending national champs and working on a thirty-game winning streak.

The first to enter the locker room on this opening day of preseason drills was the man who loved practice more than anyone else— John Herman Bell. He burst through the door at 5:00 A.M. sharp and now stood over a vat of something reddish purple.

Trainer Ken Rawlinson walked into the locker room and stood next to Bell. He also stared down at the concoction.

"You will be able to keep this down," Rawlinson said. "I know it looks awful. But there's some real good stuff in there."

For decades, preseason football practices across America were known to produce orange and purple splotches all over the dusty fields—purple from grape juice and orange from orange juice. When the boys became overheated, they invariably threw up, leaving stains.

So it became Rawlinson's mission to mix a drink that would replenish fluids and minerals and remain in the stomach. The vat was slowly drawing a curious crowd of players who had made their way across campus to the stadium. They dreaded the thought of drinking from it.

Bell stuck his nose into the pot, sniffed, and said, "Kenny, I gotta ask you something. You sure you didn't just cut a steer's throat and drain out the blood?"

John Herman had a way with words—a way that sent shivers down everyone's spine.

"Kenny," Bell continued, "I think we'll just call this stuff monkey blood. Whadaya say?"

Each OU player would have trusted Rawlinson with his life. For years, he had fixed their injuries and sent them back into action much faster than anyone could have expected. If he wanted them to drink monkey blood, they would drink monkey blood. His concoction was said to contain fifteen different juices mixed together. All the players knew was that it looked bad, smelled horrible, and tasted worse.

Preseason practice at the University of Oklahoma was far different from practice at most big-time football programs in America. The simple reason was that Bud Wilkinson was a man ahead of his time. He smiled upon things that were progressive. He appreciated a trainer like Rawlinson, one of the few in the business who could do more than tape ankles.

In this blood-and-thunder era of college football, most coaches subjected their players to vicious hitting drills, along with torturous scrimmages. They wanted to hear bodies colliding, see snot flying. They wanted to see the boys running countless gassers after practice, until their legs wobbled and they fell face-first into the dust. This was how Knute Rockne had done it and how Bear Bryant still did it. The theory was passed along to every college coach.

But the message never registered with Wilkinson.

The Great White Father believed in working the boys hard, all right, but didn't revel in the sight of blood and exposed bone. If a player seemed reluctant to hit, he was taken aside and told to "let your fears go." But he was not driven into the ground like a fence post for the purpose of making him a man.

This is not to suggest that Wilkinson didn't have calluses. When a player was injured, and unable to leave the field on his own, the Sooners never missed a beat. The practice was moved over a few feet while the trainers attended to the fallen boy.

It was getting dark late one afternoon when Wilkinson moved the practice over a few feet while one of the Sooners writhed on the ground. Halfback Jack Santee, known for his dry wit, raised his hand and said, "Coach, may I make a suggestion? If we are to continue to practice, shouldn't you at least hang a lantern over our injured comrade?"

Wilkinson didn't even smile.

Most coaches visualized football as a war game, and that was understandable considering that America had been fighting wars for the majority of the last fifteen years. Wilkinson, however, thought of football as a cross between a chess match and ballet.

On the practice field, he was light on his feet, moving from station to station, from player to player, teaching fundamentals, speaking in a soft, steady voice and employing an economy of words. Wilkinson never regressed to rage. His eyes were sharp and clear like a predator's. He saw everything. The Sooners were spread over three different practice fields, and if a player made the tiniest mistake at the farthest distance, Wilkinson saw it. If a player committed a series of mistakes, he was called to the side. Many times, the player was surprised at what the *Man* had to say.

"Clendon. Are you having trouble with your girlfriend?"

"No, sir," Clendon Thomas would say.

"Are you having trouble with schoolwork?"

"No, sir."

"Clendon, you *are* having trouble with football. You need to concentrate." Then the Great White Father would walk away, a cold vapor trailing him.

Wilkinson's practices were shorter than most. The staff actually worked longer at planning practices than executing them. But the OU coaches could squeeze more work into an hour and twenty minutes than most coaches could accomplish in three hours. Everything was planned to the minute, to the second.

Each morning, the players were awakened in three shifts to avoid long lines in the dining room and the training room, where ankles were taped. During practice, each drill was timed with a stopwatch, and when time was up the boys sprinted across the field to the next one.

As the Sooners were prepping for the Texas game in the '55 season, Wilkinson was unhapppy with both the energy level and the focus of an afternoon workout. He repetitively advised his players that they needed to work harder. Then he called them together for a meeting.

They couldn't believe their ears. Wilkinson told them to take leave from the practice field, to get dressed, and to find something else to do. They had expected to run stadium steps until sundown. Instead, they walked to the locker room in a state of shock. Never had a coach told them to just take off, to haul ass. But the psychology worked. The next day, the Sooners had their best practice of the entire season.

Wilkinson's first priority when two-a-days kicked off each September was to melt five to ten pounds off every player and then spend a few days with light hitting and short scrimmages. The early days were reserved for finding the hitters. Wilkinson firmly believed that if a college freshman hadn't already developed a taste for knocking heads and kicking butt, he was better suited for baseball or golf. Most of his players had plowed, worked cattle, buried drilling pipe, or strung barbed wire. Their hides had been toughened by hard labor beneath a searing sun. Many had been scrapping and streetfighting the better part of their lives.

Wilkinson loved to polish. The same plays were run over and

over. The same fundamentals were taught time and again. Timing was of the essence. Before long, the Oklahoma Sooners were a ballet in cleats.

Though he was Machiavellian, the Great White Father understood that he couldn't handle every task, find every flaw. Though his list of confidants was short, the men he came to trust were granted far-ranging power.

Wilkinson couldn't have found a more effective chief assistant if he had hopped a plane to New York and stolen either Tom Landry or Vince Lombardi off the Giants' staff. Gomer Jones was fire to Wilkinson's ice. No two men could have possibly looked more different, and acted more different while managing to walk shoulder to shoulder through both crisis and calm. Wearing an overcoat and fedora on the sideline, Wilkinson looked as though he had walked straight out of Central Casting. In the same getup, Gomer resembled a pudgy hit man.

Wilkinson needed Jones the same way that Astaire needed Rogers, that Ricky needed Lucy. And together, they did 99.9 percent of all the meaningful coaching at the University of Oklahoma. Bud built the perfect model, and Gomer made it run like a Chevy off the showroom floor. On practice days, Gomer roamed the fields, teaching fundamentals like a drill instructor. One of his obsessions was the "wave drill" that taught the Sooners how to discipline their feet. They were instructed never to take a crossover step and to keep their shoulders square to the line of scrimmage, a key component in the proper technique of carrying the ball, blocking, and tackling.

In spite of this great attention to detail, Gomer never let practice sessions become too serious. He loved to outwit the new recruits.

"Scatter out in bunches and pair off in threes!" he would holler. The players took off running in several directions, as if they understood.

Another Gomerism was "that Jimmy Harris is richer than three feet up a bull's ass." Translation: The boy has talent.

Gomer resembled Lou Costello. He was short and overweight and full of warmth and goodwill. It seemed that he was always on the players' side, even when he was chewing them out, and that was generally the case.

He had been an All-American guard for Francis Schmidt at Ohio State in the thirties, spent one season with the Cleveland Rams of the NFL, and returned to his alma mater to coach before entering the military. Wilkinson called him to Oklahoma as his chief assistant in 1947.

Though Wilkinson treated the rest of the staff like so much fodder, he did encourage discussion and debate. Coaches' meetings were often transformed into political caucuses, where the floor was opened to votes. After the secret ballots were tallied, Wilkinson would say, "Gentlemen, as you know, this is a democracy we are running here. Therefore, I should inform you of the unfortunate outcome. You have lost by the count of one to nine."

During the heat of a game the previous fall, Wilkinson even shot down graduate assistant coach Gene Dan Calame, a former quarterback he admired. As they stood on the sideline, the third-year law student said, "Coach, I thought we were going to run the swinging gate in this situation."

"That is why I am the chief and you are but an Indian," Wilkinson said, his eyes never leaving the field.

The other man in Wilkinson's inner circle was Port Robertson, who, in effect, was the *czar* of everything. Wilkinson wanted to distance himself from the chore of discipline, and he knew the ex-soldier would labor twenty hours a day and that he would kick some tailbone. By nature, Wilkinson didn't like to get his hands dirty, and Port loved dirt.

During Christmas break a year earlier, little Tommy McDonald had slipped off campus without running the stadium sets that Port had ordered for breaking team rules. After attending his final class that fall semester, McDonald grabbed the first bus back to Albuquerque, some six hundred miles away. This was a touchy matter, since Wilkinson had come to appreciate McDonald's speed and capacity to break the big play. Port found the coach sitting upright behind his desk, wearing a starched white shirt and red tie. Again, he was signing letters. After explaining the McDonald matter, Port waited for an answer, but Wilkinson never looked up: "Port, do what you feel is right."

Robertson telephoned McDonald's mother in New Mexico, and Tommy was on the next bus back. After running up and down seventy-two stadium steps until he puked, McDonald was en route back to Albuquerque for the holidays.

The players were scared stiff of Robertson, who possessed uncanny strength and was the master of hand-to-hand combat. As the OU wrestling coach, he also happened to tutor the greatest college wrestler in the history of the sport—Danny "Homicide" Hodge, a man with hands strong enough to bend the handles on pliers. One afternoon, Hodge grabbed Robertson from behind in a bear hug and starting squeezing. His face now turning purple, Port calmly said, "Danny, you are hurting me." Port managed to slowly twist his body to the point where he was now face-to-face with Hodge. "Stop it or I will hurt you." Danny didn't stop. Port hit the wrestler with an open hand to the forehead, dropping him unconscious to the mat.

Buddy Burris, the All-American guard who blocked punts with his face, became quite intoxicated while playing Cardinal Puff, the classic drinking game, one night in the late forties. He stumbled into the Jeff House and, one by one, wrestled four or five teammates to the floor. Finally, one of the Sooners spoke up: "Hey, Port is right over there. Why don't you take him on?"

Burris leveled his eyes on the balding middle-aged man.

"I am not *that* drunk," he slurred.

Robertson liked to drive the bony middle joint of his thumb into a boy's sternum and listen to him beg for mercy. At age forty-six, there wasn't a college boy he couldn't whip or a frat house he couldn't clean out. It didn't take long for the boys to learn they should not curse around him.

This became powerfully evident one summer during two-a-days when freshman guard Doc Hearon became dizzy and nauseated while practicing beneath a blazing sun. Doc was on his backside when he saw an odd-looking figure standing next to Wilkinson. "Who the hell is that Al Capone–looking sonofabitch?" he hollered.

With his dark features, square jaw, and receding hairline, Port did look like Scarface without the scar. He walked to the middle of the field and said in a firm but quiet voice, "You will come with me." They walked to the west stands, where Doc Hearon was introduced to a hell he had never imagined.

"How long will I be running?" Doc said.

"Until I finish reading the morning paper."

"How far along are you?"

"Page one."

Port had barely turned to the metro section when Doc collapsed on row thirty-three. "There will be no puking or sleeping on my time, peahead," Port said.

This abhorrence of cussing was the result of a World War II experience. On June 6, 1944, he had stormed the beachhead at Omaha and marched across France as a captain in charge of an artillery unit. He was six feet deep in a foxhole in the Normandy forest known as *Cerisy la Foret*, having led the artillery division of the Second Infantry to Hill 29, where they were stymied. This was between *Bayeux* and *Saint-Lo*. The hand grenade landed a few feet from Port, who only had time to talk his way out of this one: *God, if you won't let that thing go off, I will never cuss again, I will never drink again, and I will go to church every Sunday.* God was listening.

Two days later, Port was holed up again when the German eighty-eights successfully pinpointed their target. He flew twenty feet into the air, and all he could remember was the ground spinning beneath him. He prayed that Mother Earth would be transformed into a soft wrestling mat. Instead, he landed on gravel and rock, but he somehow lived to fight another day. With German bullets flying out of a hedgerow, the rugged soldier urinated on himself.

Port later explained, "A man who said he wasn't scared over there in Europe was one big *liar.*"

At five each morning, Port rumbled down the hallways of Jeff House yelling, "Get up, peahead. You're running today. Get up!" All Sooners were known as "peahead." If Port happened to call you by your full name—James Bedford Harris, for example—your number was really up. The west stands had seventy-two steps, and the minimum punishment was twenty round-trips. The boys normally started puking by the tenth trip.

• • •

On the seventh day of preseason drills, Wilkinson stopped everybody in their tracks. He ordered left end Don Stiller to split out by about fifteen yards and moved Tommy from left halfback to right flanker. Pricer and Thomas shifted into a split backfield, also known as the pro set, and Jimmy Harris was transformed into a passing quarterback. Just as Y. A. Tittle and Charlie Connerly dropped seven steps to pass, so was Jimmy setting up in the pocket. The Sooners were soon chucking the ball all over the lot and moving at will. Then, as rapidly as he had shifted the Sooners to the passing offense, the Sooners were back in the Split-T two days later.

During preseason camp, Harris had a telephone installed in his dorm room at the Jeff House, and it was the first one that anyone could remember. It rang morning, noon, and night, and most of the time Johnny "the Gnat" Pellow came sprinting down the hall to answer it. Now some people might have mistaken the Gnat's intention as an attempt at cutting into Jimmy's action. Not true. He was taking messages from all of the OU coeds, hoping to impress the quarterback with his team-first attitude. Jimmy responded in kind, and the Gnat started getting more carries and catching more passes in practice.

Clendon Thomas was also getting more action, and it was pissing Tommy McDonald off. Thomas was now Harris's roommate and was getting the lion's share of carries during practice.

"Jimmy, I need the ball more," Tommy said between every play.

McDonald moved to a different beat, and some folks thought he was a showoff—Elvis in cleats. Wilkinson didn't cotton to vanity and was wary about discussing anything with the sporting press that might smack of individual acclaim. Tommy didn't care. He kept track of his own statistics.

The '56 Oklahoma media guide was chock-full of pertinent information about the Sooners, and the cover was decorated with a photograph of Carl Dodd dashing eighty-two yards for a touchdown in the Orange Bowl. But nowhere in the fifty-eight-page booklet was there an individual statistic. That didn't deter McDonald, who kept track of every yard he gained—passing, receiving, rushing, and returning kicks—and wasn't bashful about tooting his own horn. As he watched McDonald doodle in his stat book one afternoon, Jimmy Harris groused, "Tommy, you'll *never* be a team man—in football or in life."

The biggest sports names of the time were Bob Cousy in the NBA, Otto Graham in the NFL, and Mickey Mantle—all bereft of pretension. The great Bill Russell, who led the University of San Francisco to consecutive NCAA hoops titles, was known as the silent warrior. The most colorful star of the time was Detroit Lion quarterback Bobby Layne. But even the hard-drinking, loquacious Texan had a way of buttoning it up when he stepped between the lines.

The fifties were captured in black-and-white, most often by still photographers. Elvis Presley had arrived on the scene, as had James

Dean, but Oklahomans were not swept away—not at the moment, anyway. The traditional system of authority held, especially in sports, and you heard a lot more about the Yankees, Browns, Lions, Celtics, and Sooners than you did about Mantle, Graham, Layne, Cousy, and McDonald.

This is not to say that Tommy was some kind of rebel without a cause. He was just *different.* Some folks thought he could strut sitting down.

After his first practice with the varsity back in 1954, he sat down and cried. It bothered Wilkinson to no end that a player would openly display tears, but when the little halfback explained he merely was distraught over what he considered a lousy practice, Wilkinson smiled.

Though Wilkinson was light-years ahead of the competition in matters of strategy, infrastructure, conditioning, and recruiting, he rarely shared with the sporting press his views on singular achievement. In that regard, he was still from the old school. His signature innovation was the alternates—a group of second stringers who were never treated like second class. They normally entered the game on either the third or fourth possession of the game, and Wilkinson never panicked and dispatched the first teamers if the opponent was about to score. The alternates were not scrubs, and the Sooners were normally no worse on the scoreboard when the second stringers had completed their tour of duty. In this era of the archaic one-platoon system, most teams were casting their lot with the starting eleven and perhaps two or three other key substitutes. The top studs across the country were playing sixty minutes. Wilkinson, however, was able to circumvent the system by keeping twenty-two players in the loop and often went much deeper into the bench. Individual stats didn't mean a lot to the Great White Father. Team play did.

Of course, most of the data in Tommy's little book was quite impressive. In 1955, he became the first OU player ever to score a touchdown in every single game, including the Orange Bowl, and completed seventeen of twenty-four passes without an interception for a percentage of 70.6.

The galling part was that Tommy was always begging for the football, and it irritated quarterback Jimmy Harris to no end. It really hit the fan at the end of the 1955 season when the announcement came that the OU public relations machine had cranked out two more All-Americans—guard Bo Bolinger and McDonald. Bolinger, a scrapper from Muskogee, clearly deserved the honor. McDonald? Well, his teammates weren't sure.

Just the idea of somebody flaunting All-American status sent Jimmy Harris into orbit.

One of the first lessons taught in the southern and western sectors of America was humility. Boys who resisted came to learn about the razor strap and the hickory stick. Most fathers had fought their way through either the Great Depression or World War II or both, and they passed along hard lessons about life. They demanded that a boy avoid pretension the same way he avoided the Communist Party. Boys needing a father figure, like Harris, could depend on their high school coach to drive home these values, normally through the use of a three-foot paddle with holes on the end.

One afternoon, Gomer Jones tried to explain the concept to Tommy: "Oklahoma's been humbled by droughts, tornadoes, Indian raids, floods, and the Dust Bowl. Boys grow up strong and with a lot of ambition in Oklahoma, but they don't brag."

It wasn't the only lecture that Tommy would hear. On the values of hard work in the classroom and the need to improve his grades, Port Robertson once said, "Tommy, I could enroll you in Sandbox One, and all you'd do is cover yourself up."

For the most part, the Sooners were sons of farmers and ranchers and men who had labored long hours beneath a broiling sun just to feed a family. Wilkinson looked for boys with calluses on their fingers and tenacity in their bones, because they readily accepted the lessons of teamwork and were less likely to keep their own stat book.

McDonald was hard to catch and harder to understand. Not that anyone questioned his courage. With the game on the line, you wanted the football in Tommy's hands. He was fast and agile—could stop on a dime and start again on a half-dime. To borrow a term from baseball, McDonald was a five-tool player. He could run, pass, catch, block, and tackle. About half of the Sooners wore the single-bar face masks, but not Tommy. He never ducked a hit and loved to bury his face into the sternum of a pile-driving running back. He was always the first one off the ground and back to the huddle, and no one could explain it.

Sports had yet to reach the age of the stopwatch and the scouting combine, but it was evident that McDonald was the fastest halfback lugging a football in America. During the '55 season, he finished third nationally in scoring with 96 points, fourteenth in total offense with 967 yards, and eleventh in rushing with 707 yards. All of this was accomplished without the use of the upper third of his left thumb, which had been severed in a motorcycle accident. A daredevil also lurked within. During the spring months, OU jocks often got their kicks from diving off the Highway 77 suspension bridge into the South Canadian River, about three miles from campus. Most of the players would dive from the highway, about ten feet above the water, but wouldn't go much higher. McDonald, however, climbed all the way to the top, dropping fifty feet into about eight feet of water. It scared the dickens out of everybody but Tommy.

Watching the little stuntman, Bob Burris hollered, "Coach Wilkinson'd kill me if he could see this!"

"Why'd he kill you?"

"Because I let you kill *yourself*."

His air of confidence turned teammates against McDonald.

Tackle Ed Gray was the team's comic and an easygoing sort, but he was often agitated that McDonald badgered Harris for the football. It was a rule that only one player, the quarterback, was allowed to talk in the huddle. During practice one day, Gray dropped into his three-point stance and whispered across the line to defensive tackle Doyle Jennings, "Here comes the little shit on two. Knock his ass off." Gray moved out of the way and let Jennings hit Tommy like a Mack truck, knocking him three yards into the backfield. Standing over the little running back, who was trying to clear his head, Gray said, "You see, Tommy boy, you ain't going nowhere without us."

Fullback Billy Pricer might pal around with McDonald one minute and ventilate on his cockiness the next. In the team's hotel lobby one Saturday morning, a group of OU fans approached Pricer and asked if he was "the great Tommy McDonald."

"Oh, yeah, I'm Tommy," said Pricer. He preened for the crowd while trying not to laugh. He was about forty pounds heavier and looked older than Tommy, thanks to dark features.

"Oh, Tommy, are the Sooners going to win today?"

"I don't care *anything* about winning," said the fake McDonald. "All I care about is making All-American." Then Pricer pivoted and walked away, leaving the admirers flattened by the arrogance.

14

ON THE BRINK

The Oklahoma Sooners were now *expected* to win the national championship in the fall of '56, and some of the greatest headliners of the era felt obliged to make sure that it didn't happen. Among the powers ranked in the preseason Top Ten were Tennessee coached by Bowden Wyatt, Georgia Tech under Bobby Dodd, Texas A&M led by Bear Bryant, and Iowa tutored by Forest Evashevski. Wilkinson's Sooners were 80–7–3 over the past nine seasons, and every team in America wanted a piece of them.

The year's list of leading Heisman Trophy candidates read like a *Who's Who:* Earl Morrall, Len Dawson, Jimmy Brown, Paul Hornung, John Brodie, Sonny Jurgensen, Johnny Majors, John David Crow, Jimmy Taylor, Sam Huff, Jack Pardee, Alex Karras, and Lou Michaels. Two more from Oklahoma would be added to that list, McDonald and Tubbs.

Not everyone was sure that the Sooners would survive another season without a defeat. Herman Hickman wrote in *Sports Illustrated:* "The Sooners are sure to be surprised somewhere along the line. Armageddon will be at South Bend on October 27."

Perhaps, but Wilkinson had the best senior class in the history of OU football, along with a thirty-game winning streak. Just three years earlier, when they were freshmen, Wilkinson had told the boys that with the right amount of dedication and commitment they would someday be national champions. He didn't mention they might win two.

Of course, when great players come together, egos will clash and headaches will arise. Wilkinson was worried about the rift between Harris and McDonald but wasn't sure how to fix it. He had briefly benched Harris during spring drills in an effort to get his attention.

"You're not working hard enough," the coach said.

"I know."

"Why don't you do something?"

"I will."

"Jimmy, practice is still important."

"Yes, sir."

"Jimmy, your attitude must change."

Harris's mind always drifted in the spring, when a young man's fancy turns to beer parties and sorority row. There was so much action in Norman and Oklahoma City: thirty-cent highballs at the Officers Club on the naval base, and the jazz and the hot women at the Uptown Pit in Oklahoma City.

Jimmy knew he could run the Split-T offense in his sleep. Everyone knew that he was the best all-round athlete playing quarterback in America, even though his passes over thirty yards looked like wounded birds flopping to reach the tree. And outside of Jerry Tubbs and John Herman Bell, Harris was the toughest hitter on defense.

What irritated Wilkinson was that Jimmy could turn his concentration on and off like a faucet. Days and counting till the start of the '56 season, Jimmy's eyes were riveted to the task once more.

One player whose focus never faded was Billy Pricer, the greatest team player Wilkinson had ever coached. Billy didn't care if he was blocking, running, scoring touchdowns, or carrying the water bucket. Pricer wouldn't have complained if the coaches tied his shoelaces together and told him to run gassers into the next week. He also happened to be tougher than boot leather. The last of fourteen children born to John and Cora Pricer, Billy was reared in a small wood-frame house on the wrong side of the tracks in Perry, Oklahoma, a dusty crossroads town about fifty miles north of Oklahoma City. Perry might have been the center of the oil-pumping universe, but the Pricers were not oilys and had no relatives in the drilling elite. The house with three bedrooms and one bathroom was terribly overcrowded. A carpenter, John Pricer struggled mightily just to make ends meet, laboring fourteen hours a day, six days a week, and never had the time to see his son play ball or wrestle in high school, even though Billy was the best all-round high school athlete in Oklahoma. Billy was an all-state fullback and catcher and made the all-state wrestling team three straight years.

Perry was known as the the high school wrestling capital of Oklahoma, and all of the studs graduated straight to Norman, where Port Robertson sowed those seeds into national championships. Port salivated for Pricer, but Wilkinson ticketed him exclusively for football. Eventually the day would come when Robertson couldn't resist temptation, and Pricer couldn't resist temptation, and they would be united in the dark little cell known as the wrestling room inside Memorial Stadium, where the OU wrestlers grunted and sweated for several hours each day.

When Billy Pricer had accepted the challenge to wrestle in the spring of 1955, he also shook hands with a harsh reality. In thirty days, he would have to lose *forty-three pounds.* It didn't seem fair, but Port pegged him for the 167-pound class, even though 177 would have been far more comfortable. But Danny Hodge, also from Perry, now ruled the sport of college wrestling in the same manner that Bill Russell and Wilt Chamberlain had come to dominate college basketball. Hodge *owned* the 177-pound class. So Pricer's challenge was to become a magician and make one-fifth of his body disappear. Quite a task for a man who loved food so much that he was called Groceries.

Pricer knew firsthand there was no need to even think about

stepping onto Hodge's turf. They had grown up together in Perry. In fact, everyone on the OU campus, especially the football players, learned to give Hodge a wide berth. He possessed supernatural strength in his hands, which were known to break ulna, radial, and metacarpus bones like dry twigs. Around campus, he was humble, polite, and studious. But lurking inside the six-foot, 180-pound frame was the strength of three men, along with a predator's instinct.

Still, Hodge was so down-to-earth that he rode his bicycle to class on the tree-lined campus and, during the lunch hour, parked it outside of the Jeff House cafeteria, where both the wrestlers and football players took their meals. One afternoon, he was taken aback when he discovered one of the freshman football players joy-riding his bike.

Hodge, who spoke with a slight lisp, said, "Give me back my bi-thickle."

The freshman laughed. He wouldn't have known Hodge from Hank Williams. "I ain't givin' you back your bi-thickle." Anger now boiling inside him, Hodge managed to wait patiently, hoping the boy would come to his senses. Luckily, Billy Pricer emerged through the back door of the Jeff House and sized up the situation. He marched to the middle of the street, seized the handlebars, and stared at the boy.

"You see that man standing over there?" He pointed to Hodge.

"Yes, sir."

"Well, that man has been beating me up every day since the first grade. And this is *his* bicycle." The freshman leaped from the seat and tore-ass faster down Lindsey Street than anyone had ever seen him run.

Naturally, the sudden loss of weight took its toll on Pricer's body. He ate nothing but salads and drank nothing but water for one full month. Each day, he joined his fellow wrestlers on the ten-mile run through the Canadian River bottoms with weights strapped to his body—wrestling championships were forged in pain. The pounds melted away, and so did much of the muscle. His eyes sank back into his head and he looked like a walking ghost. Though he finally made his weight, Pricer didn't have the strength to climb into his own bunk at night, needing a boost up from his roommate, Bob Burris. It had been obvious for weeks that Pricer was a walking dead man and had no prayer of winning that first match. He lost, of course. Wilkinson then wasted no time marching onto Port's turf and demanding that he leave the big fullback alone. Pricer was to spend the rest of his days at OU lifting, running, eating, gaining weight, going to class, and prepping himself to become an All-American fullback.

In spite of the tough exterior, a warm heart beat inside Pricer. One of his best buddies was Owen "Bully" Hewett, a boy with cerebral palsy who worked on the training and equipment staff. A familiar sight was Billy riding Bully's bicycle across campus with Bully in hot pursuit. Or the two of them playfully wrestling on the campus lawn.

At the same time, you didn't want to cross Pricer. Weeks after his strength returned, he was studying in his room at the Jeff House when in strutted Edward "Wahoo" McDaniel, a freshman from West Texas and a boy who had quite a reputation as both a fullback and wrestler. Some predicted he would be the next Billy Pricer. Wahoo loved to drink, womanize, play cards, and talk loud. He also managed to piss off the wrong man. In a flash, Billy flew down from the top bunk, flipped Wahoo over, pinned him, and now had his hand on the boy's throat. Burris almost needed a crowbar to pry Billy off.

When the fight ended, Burris fell into a chair and laughed. "Billy Pricer, I sure feel safe rooming with you."

· · ·

Burris was among the handful of players who had graduated the previous spring. Clendon Thomas would assume his starting spot at right halfback. Guard Bo Bolinger would be replaced by a muscled-up boy from Midwest City, Bill Krisher, the first real weight lifter at OU and statuesque at six-two and 220 pounds. Krisher was an active member of a new organization called the Fellowship of Christian Athletes and the kind of boy who was made for the public relations machine.

Truth is, some of Krisher's teammates thought he was a goody two-shoes and slightly overrated. He was powerful but heavy-legged and tended to get blocked out of the hole by smaller guards. On offense, though, he would be playing alongside the best center in America, Jerry Tubbs, while being tutored by Gomer Jones, the game's foremost fundamentalist.

Thomas was the player that had everyone talking. Though Burris had been roundly respected, Thomas was a little taller, a little faster, and more capable of breaking the big play. Now the Sooners had four potential All-Americans in the backfield, and the sight of Harris, McDonald, Pricer, and Thomas together was almost chilling. Two years earlier, though, few folks would have given this backfield much of a chance when Thomas arrived on campus as a gangly and somewhat laconic halfback from Southeast High School and a team that had won but two games in three years. So impressive was Thomas in his first two days of practice that he was dropped from third string to the AOs, which stood for "All Others." Thomas looked around and realized he had already hit rock bottom.

What a waste. In high school, he had been clocked at 21.3 seconds for 220 yards, and that was wearing baseball shoes on a football field chalked with squiggly lines. Tucked into the southeastern corner of Oklahoma City, Clendon's high school had no track, no track team, no track shoes, and but one stopwatch. Though it was evident Thomas had speed, his smooth strides suggested a lack of desire—coaches thought he was loafing. Hope for the boy was fading when Clendon finally did it: he knocked the living daylights out of somebody.

That somebody was fullback Bill Brown, a boy with a square, powerful chin. He went down like a sack of potatoes, snot flying everywhere. As the dust settled, assistant coach Leon Manley ran toward Thomas and shouted, "Are you Carl Dodd?"

"Are you kidding?" Clendon said. "Hell no, I'm not Carl Dodd." Each player's name was taped to the front of his helmet, and Clendon's had faded beyond clarity. "My name's Clendon Thomas, and you are *not* running *my* ass *off*." Manley passed that story along to Wilkinson, and it wasn't long before Thomas climbed all the way to first team, never to look back.

Arriving on the Norman campus that September was a boy who didn't blend in—at least at first. Jakie Sandefer, a speedy sophomore halfback, wheeled into Norman in the middle of the afternoon in a brand-new red Thunderbird convertible—top rolled down. He was the son of the rich oil tycoon from Breckenridge—Jake Sandefer himself. In his own right, Jakie was a fine runner and receiver and one of the fastest boys coming out of Texas the last five years. More important, he had received a solid recommendation from Jerry Tubbs during his recruitment at OU. After two years of watching Tubbs dominate every player he faced, recruiters were burning up the highway from Norman to West Texas to see if there were any more players like him in the tiny boomtown.

As the red Thunderbird pulled into the parking lot at the Jeff House, sophomore center Bob Harrison yelled, "Hey, Jakie, why don't you get your daddy to buy the whole doggone university? Then we could all make straight A's."

Harrison was under the microscope himself, but for different reasons. Like the Burris boys, he had grown up plowing the fields; his family owned a thousand-acre farm in the little West Texas town of Stamford, where they tended to row crops, chiefly cotton and maize. Harrison drove a tractor, chopped cotton, and pulled bolls. He got the nickname Hog from Jakie due to the speed with which he devoured mass quantities of food at the Jeff House. No one called him Bob anymore. It was either Hog Harrison or Hoggy Harrison, and both were OK with him. But the OU players learned not to be fooled by that easygoing spirit. Stepping onto the field, Hoggy was transformed into a wild man. Coaches were already comparing him to Tubbs.

Like Tubbs, Hog Harrison had to practically fight his way out of Texas. The grown-ups were always saying, "Now, son, you'd better think twice about signing with that Wilkinson feller. We might just lock the gates to Texas and not let you back in." He also had to ward off the temptation of a large cash offer from the Aggies.

Now, two years later, Harrison was right where he wanted to be, the center/linebacker for the OU alternates and the heir apparent to Tubbs's starting job for the 1957 season.

The alternate team was taking shape, and the backfield was almost set—Jay O'Neal at quarterback, Carl Dodd at right halfback, Dennit Morris at fullback, and Jakie Sandefer playing left halfback.

Not in his nine years of coaching could Wilkinson remember the Sooners being more fit and ready for the start of a season when the starting lineup was posted two days before the season opener against North Carolina:

End—Don Stiller
Tackle—Wayne Greenlee
Guard—Ken Northcutt
Center—Jerry Tubbs
Guard—Bill Krisher
Tackle—Tom Emerson
End—John Bell
Halfback—Tommy McDonald
Halfback—Clendon Thomas
Fullback—Billy Pricer
Quarterback—Jimmy Harris

Jim Tatum's single greatest mistake of his coaching career was bolting Oklahoma after the 1946 season, just as the Sooners were turning the corner toward national prominence. Lately, he had been roaming the countryside like a little lost sheep, having left Maryland and returned to North Carolina, where his career had begun back in 1942. He was still nursing scars from losses to the Sooners in the Orange Bowls of 1954 and '56 and his Tar Heels were eighteen-point underdogs in the season opener at Owen Field.

In the first quarter, the Tar Heels didn't seem to know if they were in Oklahoma or Oz. The OU alternates scored first when David Baker, playing at left halfback for the injured Sandefer, was tackled at the ten-yard line, then twisted his body and lateraled to quarterback Jay O'Neal, who scored standing up, the touchdown netting seventeen yards.

Not to be outdone by the second stringers, Oklahoma's starters tore through North Carolina. Running between the tackles, Clendon Thomas burst through a hole in the center of the line at the eleven and found a wide-open running lane to the end zone. Once again, a lateral had set up the score—Thomas picking off a North Carolina pass and then pitching to McDonald, who sprinted forty yards to the North Carolina twenty.

Driving for the third touchdown, Harris gained thirteen yards around right end to the Tar Heels' six-yard line and, on the next play, rolled left and fired a bullet to McDonald, curling back toward the post. Tommy now had a touchdown in twelve consecutive games, and the Sooners led at halftime 21–0.

The third team produced two touchdowns in the second half, and defensive end Steve Jennings, a burgeoning force with the alternates, tackled Bill Marquette for a safety to complete the scoring. It was another runaway, with fifty-nine players participating and Oklahoma winning 36–0.

Some teams play for winning records, others for conference

championships. Elite teams set their sights on national titles, but there is yet a higher calling—the journey to greatness. This day, in spite of tying their own thirty-one-game winning streak, no celebration was staged. Why? The Sooners dreamed of something much larger.

Against North Carolina, guard Ken Northcutt and tackle Wayne Greenlee had suffered strikingly similar injuries, breaking the fibula about three inches above the ankle. Both would be in casts for several weeks. Into their places walked Buddy Oujesky and Ed Gray from the alternates.

Kansas State had lost the four previous games to Oklahoma by the combined score of 144–13, and *the Streak* seemed safe with the Wildcats coming to town. Ninety seconds into the game, McDonald carried twenty-eight yards to the KSU sixteen, and Clendon Thomas scored on the next play, slanting behind blocks by Tubbs and Oujesky.

On the Sooners' second drive, McDonald carried from the fourteen to the seven, and Thomas again took advantage of the opportunity, scoring on the very next play. Late in the first quarter, McDonald carried six yards to the sixteen, and, once more, Thomas got the call from Harris, scoring his third touchdown on the very next snap. David Baker's fifty-seven-yard punt return for a touchdown made it 27–0 at halftime.

Wilkinson decided to give the starters one more series in the second half. With all four backs sharing the ball, they hammered it down the field and, from the KSU eight-yard line, Pricer broke three tackles on a seven-yard run. Then he scored on the next play. Wilkinson informed the starters that their day was over. They had played all of eighteen minutes, slightly more than one quarter.

The rest of the game was a laugher. Late in the game, the crowd chanted, "We want Pellow! We want Pellow!" The little halfback they called the Gnat slipped through a hole at left tackle and scored from the six-yard line. Wilkinson instructed his quarterbacks not to throw another pass, but the Sooners couldn't help themselves from the end zone, scoring twice more in the 66–0 romp.

What happened on the OU sideline was even uglier. McDonald's eyes were like daggers when he approached Harris.

"You sonofabitch!" he bellowed. "I knew you'd do this to me."

"Do what?"

"I didn't get my touchdown today."

Harris roared with laughter. "Shit, Tommy, it's not my fault."

As he stomped off, McDonald said, "You're going to hear about this."

Harris shrugged. "What the hell am I supposed to do? Every touchdown was from twenty yards out."

In truth, the only "gimme" touchdown for the starters was Pricer's one-yard run, and he had set that one up by himself, running over three Wildcats. The other touchdowns by the first team, all scored by Thomas, were from the sixteen, the seven, and the sixteen. Naturally, Harris had the last word.

"It's like I said, Tommy. You'll never be a team man."

Yes, and the Sooners were unbeaten, unscored upon, and the unanimous choice as America's number-one team—with the Texas game next on national television. Success, however, didn't always equate to happiness for a team still walking a tightwire.

15

DYNASTY

The players were getting antsy with fifteen minutes and counting until kickoff against Texas. Wilkinson had yet to return to the locker room following pregame warm-ups, and the Sooners were itchy for their pep talk. Lying on the floor in the middle of the room, Edmon Gray rolled over and said, "I sure wish the old man would show up and tell us that dumb bird story again."

Gray, a tall bird himself with long arms, was the free spirit of the Sooners, and Wilkinson displayed an uncommon fondness for the boy. He was dubbed Beaky because of his expansive nose. In the world according to the Great White Father, players were to be seen and not heard. You were *not* to speak to Bud Wilkinson unless spoken to first, but this edict had somehow eluded Beaky Gray.

One afternoon, during preseason practice in '56, Beaky approached Wilkinson, who at the moment was the picture of concentration standing alone on the practice field, his eyes riveted to the action. Beaky removed his helmet, bowed his head, and seemed poised for prayer. The other players couldn't believe their eyes; no one had ever encroached upon Wilkinson's force field at such a time.

"You know, Coach," Beaky began, his eyes now set on Wilkinson, "I think you've been using me wrong. I'm *really* a quarterback."

If Beaky was a quarterback, then Tommy McDonald was a shot-putter. Wilkinson smiled that go-away smile, and Gray trotted back to his position in the line, a place he would occupy for the rest of his days at the University of Oklahoma.

While his teammates called him Beaky, the boy referred to himself in the third person as "Gray Boy." He would say, "Gray Boy's gotta go to class now" or "Gray Boy is havin' *some* fun."

Though he was slated for the alternates, Beaky was selected as a co-captain, along with Jerry Tubbs. An injury had opened the door for Beaky's move into the starting lineup. The captains were elected by popular vote of the team, although the players knew that Wilkinson didn't preside over a democracy. They figured he counted the ballots while setting fire to them. He wanted regular, hard working guys to be captains, not the big stars like Jimmy Harris and McDonald. And the coach, in spite of the cold river that ran through him, was warmed by the presence of Edmon "Beaky" Gray.

At the team banquet the previous spring, Beaky had approached Mary Wilkinson and asked her to dance. Everyone in the room held their breath, almost expecting Port Robertson to appear from somewhere and drag Beaky by his left ear into the stadium, where he would run steps for days. But the coach graciously smiled and seemed to enjoy the moment. Mrs. Wilkinson happened to be an attractive woman who possessed a great sense of humor. Again, Beaky had accurately sized up the situation and loved the attention as they moved gracefully across the dance floor together.

Now, with only ten minutes remaining before kickoff at the Cotton Bowl, Wilkinson slowly entered the locker room with the expression of someone about to deliver the news of a death. The room fell silent.

"Gentlemen, I think that you know that you didn't practice well this week," he said. "But it is no disgrace to lose to a team such as Texas. Even so, when they beat you, just remember that you are still Oklahoma, and keep your heads held high."

He turned and sauntered out the door, leaving them with many thoughts, many questions. The Sooners were riding a thirty-two-game winning streak and Texas stank. They'd be lucky to win three games in '56, and their coach was about to get fired. Now, as they sat in stunned silence, the OU players wondered if the 'Horns had some kind of secret weapon. What did Wilkinson know that he wasn't sharing?

The referee had no more stuck his head through the door to fetch the Sooners for kickoff when he was almost stampeded. What ensued was a mad calf scramble down the long concrete tunnel of the Cotton Bowl, steel-tipped cleats throwing sparks and players knocking into each other, the Sooners almost running up the backs of the Longhorns, who had paused at the edge of the field, waiting for their band to strike up the school fight song. They arrived at the bench five minutes before Bud, Gomer, and the rest of the coaches.

On the opening kickoff, Tommy McDonald rocketed fifty-four yards straight up the middle, and the big show was on. It was a crisp and sunny day in Dallas, and the crowd of 76,017 was split straight down the middle, half wearing burnt orange and the other half dressed in crimson. Several thousand fanatics had reveled in the downtown streets the previous night, swilling booze and picking fights and then posting bail a few hours before kickoff. An impromptu football game had broken out on Commerce Street at midnight, an empty bottle of whiskey serving as the ball. Those who didn't want to drink, fight, and see women raise their blouses for dollar bills made a short trip to the Cotton Bowl Friday night to experience Elvis Presley. According to the *Dallas Morning News,* the fans saw Elvis "do a staggering, shuffle-footed dance with the microphone. Sometimes he went into a really classic Indian war dance. Other times it was the sheer voodoo acrobatics as he threw his famous pelvis from the fifty-yard-line to the thirty-five."

Saturday, the Longhorns were the underdogs by three touchdowns, and the Texans in their Stetsons and boots were gobbling up those points and throwing down stacks of hundreds. Between belts of Old Charter, the Texans cursed the likes of Jimmy Harris and Jerry Tubbs, traitors who had bolted the state. Of the twenty-two players on OU's first and second teams, nine were from Texas. Longhorn fans were really furious when the Sooners mowed down their defense in a seven-play drive after Tommy's kick return, with Clendon Thomas shooting two yards between Bill Krisher and Tom Emerson for the opening touchdown.

In his heart, Wilkinson knew the Sooners would win. But he'd concocted a dandy little game plan anyway with plenty of tricks. Stuck at their thirty-six-yard line, facing third-and-long, Harris stepped behind center and stuck his hands beneath Jerry Tubbs's backside. When fullback Billy Pricer took two steps backward, the Longhorns knew what was coming—the quick kick. Tubbs snapped the ball between the legs of Harris and straight to Pricer. As the safeties turned and beat cheeks toward the end zone, Pricer swung his leg, but the ball did not spring from his foot. Instead, Pricer handed the ball backward to Thomas, now swinging around left end on the old Statue of Liberty. As the better part of the Texas defense retreated, the long-legged halfback actually ran past a couple of embarrassed Longhorns going his way. The Texas players finally responded to the yelling and cursing of the coaches and woke up in time to stop Thomas at the twenty-yard line following a gain of forty-four yards.

Three plays later, with two Longhorns clinging to his knees at the five-yard line, Harris pivoted and pitched perfectly to McDonald, who trotted around right end into the end zone. After the second botched PAT kick, Oklahoma led 12–0.

On rare occasions did the Sooners shoot for the moon. But in the final seconds before halftime, Harris retreated into the pocket and uncorked a pass that would have folks talking for decades. It was Unitas to Berry, Van Brocklin to Crazylegs Hirsch. For the first time in his career, Harris threw a pass of more than thirty yards that didn't flap like a duck, and McDonald caught it on full stride at the Texas eighteen. It was a remarkable catch considering that McDonald was fully extended and actually snagged the back half of the ball, stabbing it with the stub of a left thumb. The touchdown covered fifty-three yards and ignited a celebration that had everyone scratching their heads. After crossing the goal, McDonald sprinted back up the field and jumped into the waiting arms of Harris, wrapping his legs around the quarterback's waist and his arms around his neck.

Standing on the sideline, Gomer Jones said with proper sarcasm, "Would you just look at that little lovefest?"

The Sooners led 19–0 at halftime, and while the Longhorns trudged to the dressing room Texas fans checked their pockets to make sure they had enough cash to pay off all wagers. Things would only get worse. Oklahoma eighteen-wheeled Texas with an eighty-yard drive to open the second half, the most impressive moment a twenty-seven-yard completion from McDonald to John Herman Bell, who slid out-of-bounds, kicking up chalk inches from the goal line. Thomas was a cinch in that situation. Harris slipped him the ball at right tackle and he barreled into the end zone. McDonald fumed, believing Harris was playing favorites again.

"You're a selfish sonofabitch!" Tommy hollered as they trotted toward the sideline.

"It's good to see you're still a team man," Harris shot back.

Gomer grinned as the two boys ran past. "Now *that's* the spirit."

The alternates scored twice, giving credence to opinions that they were the number-two team in America, right behind the OU starters, of course. This group could have beaten most college teams, including some in the Top Ten. From left to right, they were end Ross Coyle, tackle Byron Searcy, guard Steve Jennings, center Hog Harrison, guard Doyle Jennings, tackle Benton Ladd, and end Bob Timberlake. In the backfield were halfbacks David Baker and Carl Dodd, fullback Dennit Morris, and quarterback Jay O'Neal.

In the final seconds against Texas, cornerback Ernie Day returned an interception twenty-eight yards for a touchdown, and the Sooners walked away with a 45–0 victory, the second-most lopsided score in the forty-nine game history of the rivalry, the Sooners having defeated Texas 50–0 in 1908.

No one could measure just how badly Wilkinson wanted to beat Texas. This was his eighth victory in the last nine years over the hated 'Horns. The Sooners had used a fake quick kick, the swinging gate formation, and a rare bomb from Harris to McDonald. In spite of his hissy fit, McDonald enjoyed the most productive day of his career, with 140 rushing yards, 61 receiving yards, and 27 passing yards. He outgained the entire Texas team.

The Sooners had played three games and outscored the opposition 147–0. It was time to party.

Rarely did Wilkinson turn the boys loose, but it was tradition after the Texas game that they could stay in Dallas overnight provided they had transporation back to Norman and would arrive in time for the four o'clock Sunday meeting. As he strolled onto the bus outside of the Cotton Bowl, Bud turned to Gomer and said, "You know, our boys are going to be celebrating all night." Indeed, the Braniff chartered flight back to Norman was virtually empty.

The Sooners headed straight for Lou Ann's, a few miles from the Cotton Bowl and located on Greenville Avenue, northeast of downtown Dallas. By the time they arrived, the place was packed with OU students, who had partied till dawn, cheered for the Sooners, and collected their bets and now wanted more.

Lou Ann's was a cavernous saloon with enough space and dance floors to accommodate up to three bands and hundreds of revelers. More important, it offered something that folks couldn't find in Oklahoma—mixed drinks. In the crowd were Charlie Rountree, the biggest party animal on campus, and Lanny Ross, the Phi Delt who had helped John Herman Bell rescue his car from the Las Vegas desert a year earlier. The first man on the dance floor was Bell, who loved to dance and didn't fret over who he was dancing with.

The unluckiest boy in the world was the one going steady with the girl now dancing with John Herman. Bell had casually approached the twenty-year-old, who wore an ultratight red sweater, taking her by the hand and leading her onto the crowded dance floor. She smiled prettily and did nothing to resist. Now the boyfriend had smoke pouring from his ears. John Herman pulled her closer, pressing her ample breasts against his chest. She smiled brightly. The jealous boyfriend suffered another serious misfortune. He didn't know that this was *the* John Herman Bell.

Minutes later, Lanny Ross saw John Herman stroll through a back gate with three boys on his heels. Ross hustled across the saloon just in time to witness the final blows. Back inside, Lanny told Rountree, "I hurried out there to see if John Herman needed help. By the time I got there, he'd whipped all three of 'em."

Bell was back on the dance floor within minutes, his only concern being the rip around the right armpit of his brand-new sports coat. As always, he was dressed impeccably. He would send the jacket back to the manufacturer with the explanation that the jacket had been "accidentally" damaged. After the garment was inspected, it was returned to Bell with this reply: "We have detected human blood on the jacket. You were FIGHTING."

Billy Carr Harris was running late for the party at Lou Ann's. He had checked into the Adolphus Hotel in downtown Dallas after the game and now was waiting for an elevator to carry him to the lobby. The Adolphus was one of the most elegant hotels in the city, known for its first-class entertainment in the Venetian Room.

After Harris rode the elevator down several floors, the doors opened and a man wearing a tuxedo popped in. Harris studied the dapper gentleman and said, "Don't I know you? You really look familiar. I know that I've seen you before." There was no response.

Finally, the Sooner football player stuck out his hand and said with a broad, friendly smile, "Hi, I'm Billy Carr Harris from Ardmore, Oklahoma."

The other man's smile was even broader as he extended his hand. "Hi, I'm Tony Bennett from New York, New York."

• • •

The Kansas fans in Lawrence streamed onto the field and climbed the goalposts. Tears had been shed on the Sooner sideline, and now the players were cussing and slamming their helmets against locker-room walls.

In his newsletter the following week, Wilkinson wrote: "Unfortunately our players and our fans were disappointed that we didn't win by a larger score."

All the Sooners had done was whip the Kansas Jayhawks by the final of 36–12. Strangely, Sooner fans making the drive north across the border booed their team in victory. They were outraged that Kansas had registered two touchdowns, the first time an opponent had scored on Oklahoma during the regular season in *eight* straight games. Blanked during that skein were Missouri, Iowa State, Nebraska, Oklahoma A&M, North Carolina, Kansas State, and Texas.

Sooner guard Buddy Oujesky was knocked unconscious during the first quarter. He was somewhere over the rainbow until his head cleared. He returned to Kansas late in the game. Sitting on the bench, looking up at the scoreboard, he saw a "12" hanging underneath "Jayhawks." Buddy grabbed his helmet and charged onto the field. The Jayhawks were in the midst of running a play. Coaches had to sprint onto the field and drag Buddy to the sideline. All the while, he was madly yelling, "They got twelve points! I *gotta* do something! How the hell'd they get twelve points!"

Buddy wasn't the only Sooner goofy with anger. The Sooners had stomped around and cried after both touchdowns—the first on a two-yard sneak by quarterback Bob Marshall, the second a twelve-yard reception by Lynn McCarthy. That's when boos rained down from the OU section. Wilkinson couldn't believe his ears and lectured the fans in his newsletter: "When a team is fortunate enough to win several games consecutively, some of its followers lose their sense of perspective and are not satisfied unless every opponent on the schedule is defeated by a truly large score. Such an attitude is bad for the game."

While the Sooners refused to celebrate, another Oklahoman was taking a champagne shower. It had been the greatest season for Mickey Mantle, now the hottest commodity in baseball, having won the Triple Crown, along with being selected the Most Valuable Player in the American League. He hit 52 home runs, had 130 RBIs, and held off Ted Williams down the stretch to win the batting title with a .352 average. The Yankees won the World Series in seven games over Brooklyn.

Life was good in Oklahoma, even when the Sooners were winning by something less than five touchdowns. The winning streak now stood at thirty-four games.

• • •

Prentice Gautt's reasons for choosing Oklahoma had little to do with civil rights or racial equality or the ministry of Martin Luther King. Prentice simply wanted to play for Bud Wilkinson, to tear-ass across the grass of Owen Field, to fullfill a childhood dream.

Now, less than two months after enrolling at the University of Oklahoma, he simply wanted to get across the Oklahoma campus without hearing one more fellow student say, "Hey, boy, how 'bout a shine?" He wanted to close his ears and his eyes and to numb himself against the pain. If he could have lived in a bubble, Prentice Gautt would have gladly moved in yesterday.

At times, Prentice believed he could make his hearing stop. *Sticks and stones will break my bones, but words will never hurt me.* In the weeks after enrolling at OU, he tried to blend in but always stood out. Then, out of self-defense, he attempted to shut all of his senses down. He hummed and sang to himself as he walked across campus, as he strapped on shoulder pads for practice. *I have to be more intelligent than everyone else. I have to use my mind.* Every minute of his free time was spent studying in his dorm room. *No wonder I am making such good grades.* Prentice didn't have a roommate at the Jeff House, but at least he had a room. The other Negro students were commuters, preferring to get out of town before dark.

Ahead, situated on Lindsey Street, Prentice made out the Four-story Jefferson House that was home. Surely a structure named after Pres. Thomas Jefferson, the great thinker, would be a safe haven for a man with black skin.

After spending almost a month with his new teammates, Prentice was starting to feel a bit more at ease. Guys like Brewster Hobby had made life easier. Brewster often walked the campus with Prentice and kept watch over him.

Smiling as he entered the Jeff House, Prentice turned the corner and walked straight toward a room where a gaggle of freshman teammates were playing cards and talking loudly. Prentice heard the voices before he saw their faces. He knew they were talking about him.

"I see that nigger's leg sticking out of a pile, and I kick that nigger's leg." That was the voice of Wahoo McDaniel.

"I see that nigger laying on the ground, and I kick that nigger." That was the voice of Bobby Boyd.

"I see that nigger's hand, I step on that nigger's hand." That was the voice of Larry Munnerlyn.

Prentice stopped in his tracks and tried to turn around before the others saw him. But it was too late. He had been moving too fast, feeling too good, forgetting where he was. He trundled down the hallway, numbing himself to the pain.

It was a conversation Prentice would never forget.

Hobby had been standing just around the corner and absorbed the entire scene. He marched into the room that belonged to Wahoo McDaniel, a big fullback and linebacker.

"I don't know who you sonsabitches think you are," Hobby said. "But you just hurt a good man's feelings. You jackasses from Texas are rude." Brewster's face was so red that it looked ready to explode. "Hell, boys, Prentice is a *great* man."

It might have been a coincidence that all three agitators were from Texas. Edward "Wahoo" McDaniel, a Choctaw-Chickasaw Indian, had played football at Midland Lee, where the mascot was a Confederate Rebel and the school song "Dixie." Boyd was a running back from Garland, a small town on the outskirts of Dallas and one of the state's strongholds of the Ku Klux Klan. Munnerlyn hailed from Breckenridge, the hometown of Jerry Tubbs and Jakie Sandefer, though neither of those boys was racist.

Munnerlyn's elevator didn't go all the way to the top. On a five-dollar bet, he would drink—actually chug—an entire quart of motor oil. Such a novelty was Munnerlyn that he found himself chug-a-lugging several times a week, normally in front of large cheering crowds. Another bizarre habit was sleeping on a piece of plywood with his dorm window propped open, come rain or winter freeze.

The boys listened to Hobby's lecture and felt a little embarrassed. They knew that Gautt had been a good soldier, had kept his mouth shut, and had taken care of business.

"I'll apologize to him; I promise I will," Wahoo said. "In fact, I'll take him to a movie." Though nobody believed him, Wahoo did appear contrite.

"You know," Hobby said, "being an Indian, you oughta know what Prentice is going through." Wahoo heard the abuse himself. It was a bit shocking, but one of his professors had taken umbrage at his presence. "Is there a Wahoo in this class?" he said one morning. "Well, you know, Wahoo, the only good Indian is a *dead* Indian."

More hurtful than the racial slurs he heard across campus was the treatment that Gautt received from Port Robertson. Port called every player peahead. But Prentice was called Prentice out of a nervous kind of respect. And it made him feel uneasy.

"More than anything, I just want to be one of the guys," Prentice told Wilkinson during their weekly meeting. "Just treat me like you would everyone else."

While watching high school film of Prentice, Wilkinson had made note of his aggressive streak. He was a vicious hitter and drilled the other boys into the ground. But at OU, he had turned passive.

"Prentice," Wilkinson said after the first couple of weeks of practice, "I am not seeing the old competitive fire. I'm wondering if you are holding back." Wilkinson stopped there, hoping Prentice would glean the message without hearing the words. As Prentice walked across campus an hour later, it hit him like a haymaker: *I am afraid of success. If I succeed, I stick out even more.* That day, he became one of the boys—that day he started knocking the crap out of everybody he crossed.

A few weeks later, as the team bus pulled away from Tulsa University, Prentice felt good about his performance that night against the Golden Hurricane freshman team. Many of the players had shaken his hand when he scored a touchdown in the second half; Brewster Hobby had practically mauled him. More important, his teammates were no longer walking around him as if he were a swamp. He was also appreciative of the support from graduate assistant Bob Burris and assistant coach Eddie Crowder, both ex–Sooner stars.

Prentice actually smiled and cut up a little on the bus ride until he realized they would be stopping for dinner. Jim Crow laws practically forbade blacks from eating at white diners in any part of Oklahoma, and Prentice had experienced firsthand the whites' callousness to black people on his rare trips into downtown Oklahoma City as a youth. He didn't know, though, that Robertson had called ahead to Beverly's Chicken Corner to make certain they would serve the Negro.

With a victory under their belt and a big dinner on the stove, the Sooners were in heaven when they strolled into Beverly's and smelled the frying chicken and saw the mashed potatoes, creamed gravy, biscuits, corn on the cob, coleslaw, and baked beans. They were sitting at several tables, laughing and joking, when the waiter, a thick man with greasy hair, walked around the corner and spotted Prentice.

"Oh no," he said. "Ain't no nigger gettin' served in here."

Port Robertson had yet to enter the restaurant, so Brewster Hobby handled the situation. He turned over his plate. "Sir, we're football players. We play together and we eat together. If Prentice here doesn't get to eat, we all leave."

Every player turned over his plate and stood up. "We all stick together," center Jim Davis said. "We don't eat without Prentice."

Wahoo glowered at the waiter. "If you weren't so old, we'd take you out in the parkin' lot and whip your dog ass."

Port was beside himself when he saw the boys filing toward the bus. He tried to reason with the restaurant manager, who was satisfied to allow fifty hungry boys and a wad of cash to leave the premises. They found a pancake house about five miles down the road, and the manager was more than happy to accept Port's money—cash in advance, of course.

But Prentice wasn't about to budge from the bus. He was sobbing. In the last few weeks, he had been called a baboon, spook, coon, nig, and shoeshine boy. But being embarrassed in front of his teammates, the boys who were finally starting to accept him, was devastating.

Port sat down next to Prentice. "Son," he said. "Those boys in that restaurant stood up for you tonight. The least that you can do is act like a man. Walk in there and join them."

Prentice raised his head slowly.

"I'll go in there if you'll promise me one favor."

"What is that?"

"That you'll start calling me peahead."

16

NOTRE DAME

Bud Wilkinson seemed different, almost breezy, as he strolled into the quarterbacks' meeting on the morning of the biggest game of the year, a glorious and sunny October 27, 1956, in South Bend, Indiana.

He gazed about the room and leveled his eyes on Jimmy Harris. "We are going to beat the hell out of these guys today." Wilkinson studied the quarterback's expression before turning to leave the room.

Not once had Jimmy ever heard the man say *"hell"* or uncork a prediction. He wanted to believe it didn't happen. That was not the style of the man in the gray flannel suit.

Of course, Jimmy understood the magnitude of this day for Wilkinson. Everyone did. The Fighting Irish represented the flaw in the Oklahoma tapestry, the *glitch* on the canvas. Losses to Notre Dame in the 1952 and '53 seasons were the difference between Wilkinson being a football god and a great coach. Eight losses littered his ten seasons that included five bowl games, and only Texas and Notre Dame had whipped him twice; the singular losses were delivered by TCU, Santa Clara, Kentucky, and Texas A&M.

Not once had Wilkinson beaten the Irish, and, appropriately, Notre Dame had been the last team to beat Oklahoma before the winning streak was launched. Now *the Streak* stood at thirty-four games.

The Notre Dame defeat back in '53 tore at Wilkinson's gut and stoked his ulcers. He pledged to himself that he would never again lose to *those people;* at times, the Irish came to consume his being.

Preparation for Notre Dame had begun on the seventh day of preseason practice, two months earlier. That's when Wilkinson introduced wide receivers to the Sooners' offense. End Don Stiller was split to the left side and Clendon Thomas shifted to right flanker. The pro formation had been the Sooners' own little secret— until today.

Though Oklahoma was the country's top-ranked team, the Irish were America's darlings. Paul Hornung, with his wavy blond hair and blue eyes, was the cover boy of *Sports Illustrated*. Most of the sporting press considered Hornung the best player in college football, and the eastern writers were in his corner.

Few people knew at the time knew that Hornung also had an appetite for gambling. But a big bettor from Oklahoma by the name of Billy Ray Cisco knew all about the boy's habit. Hornung received a call the week of the game from the Ada oilman, a man who loved to wager on his beloved Sooners.

"I'll lay y'all twenty-five points," he told Hornung. "Get up the money and we'll have us a bet."

Twenty-five points was too juicy, and besides, the Irish had their pride. No way they could lose to Oklahoma by that margin. So Hornung and teammate Sherrill Sipes started collecting money from their teammates. Freshmen were backed into corners, all of their money fleeced. A pot of money was collected that would be matched against the oilman's bankroll. The bet was on.

Though Notre Dame had the greatest winning history of college football, these were not the Irish of Leahy and Rockne. Now, Notre Dame was experiencing growing pains under twenty-eight-year-old coach Terry Brennan, by far the youngest head coach of his time. Brennan was quoted as saying in *Sports Illustrated,* "Oklahoma might not be the greatest team in the history of college football, but then again it may. They'll be out to prove that against us. Oklahoma is in a funny position. If they lose, or just barely squeak by, you'll hear that old story. Oklahoma builds its records against mediocre teams. So, naturally, they'll be out to beat us by ten touchdowns."

From top to bottom, Wilkinson had built these Sooners to beat Notre Dame. The Irish were known for recruiting large, muscle-bound boys from the Midwest and East Coast. They came from steel mills and factories. The Sooners were a bunch of lean, fast, hard-boned country boys.

Brennan's prayer was that the Irish could outmuscle and possibly intimidate the smaller Sooners. That's why the entire Notre Dame team crashed through the Oklahoma calisthenic circle an hour before kickoff, raising hell and barking like dogs—a blatant effort to bully and rattle the Sooners. Another team might have responded by fighting back—Bell and Pricer, among others, wanted to kick ass. The Irish players were now in their faces, shouting obscenities, calling them rednecks. But Wilkinson rushed to the scene and road-blocked the melee. He sent the Sooners back to the locker room earlier than usual, and the crowd cheered, as if the Irish had run the visitors off the field.

It was a sparkling day—sixty-four degrees, with virtually no wind. The crowd of 60,128 was the largest in the history of Notre Dame Stadium. High in the stands were a thousand or so rowdy OU students who had traveled by train to Chicago, leaving the Norman station at four o'clock Friday morning, and then been bussed from Chicago to South Bend a few hours before kickoff. The clever OU revelers had smuggled their bootleg whiskey bottles onto the train in hatboxes brought on board by coeds, who had been encouraged to leave their hats in Oklahoma.

NBC was broadcasting the game to millions while tinkering with a new concept—"living color." America's color TV sets still numbered in the thousands, but the network was hustling to beat ABC and CBS.

Wilkinson was still steaming when he prepared to speak to the team minutes before kickoff; his anger had never been more evident. "What you witnessed out there was unethical," he almost spat. "I want you to go out there and beat them thirty-five to nothing."

The Sooners charged onto the field like Confederate soldiers. They didn't stop until they reached the end zone three minutes into the game. The first three plays of the game were pitches to McDonald, with Harris laying the clearing blocks. From the Notre Dame fourteen, Harris rolled right behind Pricer and Thomas and zinged a strike to John Herman Bell at the right sideline, five yards deep in the end zone. The big tight end got one foot down inside the boundary, and the official was quick to signal touchdown.

After the commercial break, NBC surprised its audience with a replay of the catch. In fact, the network used "stop action," showing Bell's right foot tapping down inches from the sideline. Almost a decade would pass before Roone Arledge of ABC perfected this concept and dubbed it instant replay.

Michigan State had throttled Notre Dame the previous week, inspiring rumors that Hornung's thumb was too sore to take center snaps. Now, the Irish shifted into the single wing on the first play with Hornung trying to sweep right end. Buddy Oujesky slid off his back, and then it was Jerry Tubbs's turn. It was the titanic tackle that football fans would talk about for decades. With a long running start, Tubbs plowed into the quarterback at the twenty-two, driving his helmet into Hornung's ribs. The two were airborne for three full yards, all the way back to the nineteen, as Tubbs rode the quarterback like a mule. Hornung managed to stand up and stagger back to the huddle as the Notre Dame fans held their breath.

But the "Golden Boy" would come back spitting like a wet snake. He drove the Irish deep into OU territory in a matter of minutes. As a testament to Wilkinson's faith in the alternates, he didn't hesitate to send them into action when the Irish reached the Sooners' twenty-six. Stirred by the fierce tackling of linebackers Hog Harrison and Dennit Morris, OU stopped the Irish on downs at the eighteen.

Oddly enough, OU halfback Carl Dodd quick-kicked on first down and the strategy was successful, the ball sailing and then rolling a distance of sixty yards. Then the second-string defense took out the whipping stick once more.

With the ball at the Notre Dame thirty-two, Steve Jennings surged through two blockers and nailed quarterback Bob Williams two yards deep in the backfield before he could hand off, and the ball rolled free to the twenty-one, where the Irish recovered. On fourth down, Jennings flew through the line, blocking Dean Studor's punt. End Bob Timberlake plucked the ball from the air and rumbled to the three-yard-line.

Jay O'Neal sneaked the ball into the end zone on the next play, and the Sooners led 13–0.

When the starters returned for the first play of the second quarter, the Sooners unveiled the big surprise—the pro set. McDonald rolled right, passing twenty yards to Thomas, then gained fifteen yards on the halfback counter. Back in the Split-T, Thomas took the quick hand-off from Harris at right guard, blasting it into the end zone from the eleven. OU was up nineteen–zip.

Minutes later, the Irish marched inside the OU five-yard line. With Tubbs out of the game, Hornung liked his chances against the alternates. He didn't know that Hog Harrison was the spitting image of Tubbs and just as ill-tempered on the field. On fourth down from the two, Harrison stopped Hornung in his tracks, and once more, the Irish first stringers had lost the ball on downs to the alternates.

According to the consensus of college football experts, Tubbs and Pricer was the best linebacker tandem in the country. But Morris and Harrison could have easily won the vote as number two. One more reason for the effectiveness of the alternates was the play of end Steve Jennings and tackle Byron Searcy, who, in some eyes, were better than the first stringers. The Sooners were so deep in talent that, in many cases, it was impossible to separate the first and second team on talent alone.

All hopes for a comeback were crushed a minute before halftime when halfback Jim Morse fluttered a halfback pass into a covey of Sooners and McDonald stole it and sprinted fifty-seven yards to the end zone. This time, NBC's replay focused on Pricer, who harried the passer and laid the clearing block for McDonald. Again, the network utilized stop action, this time to highlight both of Pricer's deeds.

Thanks to the pro set, McDonald passed forty yards to Thomas early in the third quarter, Harris dashed seventeen yards around left end to the four, and Thomas scored on the dive play. In the fourth quarter, Thomas returned an interception thirty-five yards for a touchdown, with NBC illuminating Bell's clearing block.

The Oklahoma students, filled with drink and adrenaline, poured onto the field at the final gun. Charlie Rountree carried a cup filled with scotch, and he handed it off to his pal Jimmy Harris. The celebration was on. Gomer Jones hugged Harris and caught a whiff of his breath as they ran off the field. "Dammit, Jimmy," he said, "why didn't you save me a shot of that hooch?"

Of the 40–0 victory Red Smith wrote in the *New York Times*: "If there is an abler, wiser unit anywhere than Wilkinson's first eleven, it must be kept under armed guard. If there has been a college team in recent years with greater overall speed, these eyes did not see it. Withering speed in the backfield and shattering speed in the line made it easy for Oklahoma to trample Terry Brennan's forces in the most frightful demonstration of man's inhumanity to man the farm belt has witnessed since the Dearborn Massacre."

Hornung was more succinct: "That is the best team I ever played against."

. . .

The Big Cigars were always buzzing in and out of Bud Wilkinson's life. He loved to spend time with the oil-rich because they were fun-loving guys who would laugh and drink and smoke cigars on the golf course or take him on their private planes to private places where they could flirt with women and dance with temptation.

Wilkinson changed personalities when he changed out of the gray flannel suit. The metamorphosis could be witnessed about an hour after games at Owen Field, after he had walked the twenty blocks from the stadium to his house, tucked away on a quiet Norman street lined by a canopy of trees. Minutes after strolling through the front door, he shed the coat and tie, along with the public image that had been so finely tuned. He mixed a stiff drink, took a seat on the kitchen counter, and started regaling the oilys with stories he would have never shared with the common press. A few writers came to the house after games, but they were inner circle friends who would never repeat the whiskey talk. Wilkinson picked and chose his reporters carefully, making certain they would never publicize his *other* life. The trusted writers were Volney Meece of the *Oklahoma Times,* Dick Snider of the *Topeka Capital-Journal,* and Maury White of the *Des Moines Register.* Wilkinson had become close friends with Snider and was already making plans for the young, bright, and personable writer. He would utilize Snider in some capacity when his football days were through.

You could always find Jack and Jimmy Vickers of the Vickers Oil Company at the Wilkinson home after games, along with Clyde Davis, the chairman of oil operations for Halliburton Energy. Also running with the Wilkinson pack was U.S. Congressman Mike Monroney, who was at the house after every home game. They were the mainstays of Bud's party circle.

Along with being a big wheel in Big Oil, Davis was in charge of the Halliburton Air Force, a fleet of twenty-two airplanes at his disposal day or night. Davis and Wilkinson might fly off for a weekend of golf in Southern California or make the short trek to Enid, where Bud often entertained a black-haired woman in her twenties. She was the secretary of Homer Paine, the manager of Johnston Grain Company in Enid. Paine happened to play tackle for Wilkinson from 1946 through '48 and was an all-conference selection twice. His secretary had an attractive figure and was one of the most coveted women in several counties. Bud made regular trips to Enid, even during the season. But she wasn't the only woman to catch his eye.

Back in 1954, in preparation for the Colorado game in Boulder, Wilkinson had insisted that the Sooners travel three days early to the Rocky Mountains to acclimate themselves to the altitude. As they arrived at the Brown Hotel, located in an exclusive suburb of Denver, coaches and players received their room keys in the hotel lobby from business manager Ken Farris. Edmon Gray grabbed his key and headed to the elevator. On the ninth floor, he inserted the key into the door and entered the room. His broad smile quickly melted. Sitting on his bed were Wilkinson and one of the Braniff stewardesses. Actually, it was Wilkinson's bed, and Gray had been given the wrong key.

Always the showman, he smiled broadly and said, "The Gray Boy made a boo-boo. Gray Boy must be goin' now." With his heart pounding, the big tackle sprinted all the way to the elevator.

When in the company of his trusted buddies and away from the prying public eye, Wilkinson let his hair down. If a woman with an attractive body happened to pass by, he would say, "Now, that is one fine athlete."

During after-parties in Norman, he was often asked why Tommy McDonald smiled so much.

"Have you seen his girlfriend?" he'd answer.

Indeed, Ann Campbell was a dark-haired beauty who turned

heads wherever she walked on the Oklahoma campus. She'd captured the Miss Oklahoma contest hands down, then finished as one
of the five finalists at the Miss America pageant. Rumors flew that
she was actually offered the crown but turned it down because then
she would have to spend a year away from Tommy. The couple had
dated for two years, and Ann had recently moved into an apartment
close to the Jeff House so she could be closer to the OU football
hero. Of Indian descent, she had grown up in Oklahoma City and
attended Northeast High School. The student body viewed Tommy
and Ann as the ideal couple.

Relaxing on the kitchen counter, Wilkinson would smile at his
all-male audience and say, "Boy, that Tommy McDonald is a *very*
lucky guy."

Wilkinson was a scratch golfer, but his game actually seemed to
improve the more he indulged. One reason he gravitated toward
Jimmy and Jack Vickers was because they would take a nip on the
course. A round of golf normally consumed four hours, and that was
a lot of time to drink. It was true that Wilkinson rarely cared what he
was drinking—gin, scotch, vodka or rum—he could mix the perfect
martini and old-fashioned.

Every spring, college football coaches across America gathered for
a three-day convention, normally at a large city in the South. Sooner
or later, three men would get together in one of the hotel rooms.
They were Paul "Bear" Bryant of Texas A&M, Frank Howard of
Clemson, and Wilkinson.

Bryant and Howard were legendary for their consumptive powers, but Bud, according to his polished image, was a conservative
church-going man who enjoyed nothing stronger than milk. Truth
is, Bud could drink the others under the table and walk away smiling
and in complete control. Along with a great mutual respect for each
other's talent, Bryant and Wilkinson were also the best of drinking
buddies. No one was more notorious for his indulgence than

Bryant. Bud and Bear were known for socking it away into the wee hours of the morning while playing make-believe football games with the little men.

Bud loved to knock it around with the guys while keeping one eye on the girls. He loved the bar at the Skirvin Hotel in Oklahoma City, where friends would gather to drink and sing. Wilkinson knew the words to almost every college fight song, and there was nothing he enjoyed more than breaking into song. He might belt out "On Wisconsin" and "Hail to the Victors" and even "Eyes of Texas" until the last dog went home. Or he might sing, "I want a girl just like the girl who married dear old Dad." Each verse was sung without a single slur. And the next morning, as he marched across the hotel lobby, his eyes did not see the previous evening's drinking crowd. He was known to walk straight past longtime friends without so much as looking their way. With the dawn of a new day, he had a public image to protect.

Wilkinson sang in bars, and he sang in church, and *never* the two shall meet. The Great White Father was a loving father of sons Pat and Jay and seemingly a dedicated husband. But he could shift gears into the fast lane in the blink of an eye. Women often threw themselves at him. It was not unusual on road trips for women to follow him into the hotel elevator with hopes of a warm introduction. Some had groping hands and others stuffed phone numbers into his coat pocket. They had seen the handsome face in the newspaper and on football telecasts. They tracked him as a groupie might track a rock 'n' roll star.

Of course, the next morning, Wilkinson might be found at St. John's Episcopal Church in Norman, where he had the strongest voice in the choir.

In spite of the six-figure income, his money bought virtually nothing. The Touchdown Club had paid off his mortgage, Sen. Robert Kerr helped stuff a quarter-million in his bank account, and a car dealer named Ralph Bolen provided him a new Oldsmobile 98 every six months. The V-8 engine with 300-plus horsepower could provide a fast ride, and Wilkinson loved speeding down the highway with the pedal to the metal. He would tell his passenger, "Don't worry; these troopers around here know me. They always let me go."

Bud loved cigars and an occasional cigarette, but like many men of the time, *never* in public. He bought boxes of fifty Antonio 'n' Cleopatra cigars at the local drugstore, and they went fast. He kept a box in the office and one at home. Friends often bought him cigarette lighters, ranging from the cheapest to the most expensive gold-plated models from Tiffany's. Bud never carried the lighters. "I would be admitting that I am smoking, and I am not there yet," he told friends. Though he smoked constantly in his office, he never allowed the players to witness the act. In his preseason letter to the players, he once wrote: "Smoking is definitely harmful to physical condition. If you sincerely desire to be as good as you can be, to be fair to yourself and fair to the team, you will give up smoking."

Gomer Jones smoked three packs of Lucky Strikes a day. Thanks to the clouds of smoke produced by Bud and Gomer, you could barely see across the room during staff meetings.

Though Wilkinson was at the office at six in the morning, friends noticed the inner flame was flickering. He was spending more time on the golf course, more time drinking, and more time traveling with the Halliburton Air Force. His friends wondered if winning had become mundane. He had climbed the tallest mountain to slay Notre Dame. Now, what challenge remained?

17

JAGGED EDGE

Now they stood trembling inside the Quonset hut constructed of corrugated steel on a frigid afternoon when the wind sliced down from the Arctic and snow was piled high along both sidelines.

Bud Wilkinson's eyes burned a hole in the players now standing before him. He had just witnessed the worst first half of football he could remember anyplace, anytime. The Sooners trailed Colorado 19–6, and reports were being transmitted from Boulder across America that the King was dead—the winning streak would die at thirty-five games.

The Great White Father had but one thing to say. He said it loudly.

"Gentlemen, the jerseys you are wearing are part of the great tradition of Oklahoma football. They are symbolic of our grand history. You do not deserve to wear those jerseys. Take *off* those jerseys." As the players undressed, Wilkinson walked through the door and into the gray Colorado afternoon.

It was the first time anyone could remember Bud yelling. Now, without their jerseys, the Oklahoma Sooners were frightened and freezing as they stood in the semidarkness, the wind howling and blasting through the windows that should have been covered by the canopy now locked down on the hut's roof.

The Colorado athletic department either lacked the funds or

didn't care about building a visitor's locker room. So the enemy was left out in the cold, in a stark room filled with naked lightbulbs at the rear of the compound. The Sooners were so far from the action that they could only dimly hear the raucous celebration already under way inside the stadium.

The first half had been hell, and there was blood in the water. Colorado's signature single-wing offense rumbled up and down Folsom Field, embarrassing the number-one team in the country, a team flatter than a tortilla at kickoff and pooped by the second quarter. Wilkinson had brought the Sooners to Denver on Wednesday night for the purpose of acclimating them to the altitude. They had practiced in the snow Thursday and Friday on a golf course next to the hotel; then the sky dried up. Saturday broke dark and cloudy, and the Sooners' play had been as depressing as the day itself.

The players were having trouble breathing only minutes into the game. Boulder provided a tremendous advantage for the Buffs, whose lungs were accustomed to the thin air.

The bumbling Sooners were backed up to their ten-yard line on third down when Billy Pricer retreated two steps and received the snap from Jerry Tubbs. Seems the Buffs had been watching Oklahoma film. Guard John Wooten sniffed out the quick kick, angled inside, and smothered it. The ball bounced twice in the end zone and straight into the arms of John "The Beast" Bayuk for the opening score.

Minutes later, from the Colorado thirty-five-yard line, Jimmy Harris faked to Pricer, sidestepped Wooten, and hit McDonald in stride down the middle of the field at the ten. Tommy rambled into the end zone untouched, and Harris, who had missed three kicks against Texas, shanked yet another one. The Buffs led 7–6.

McDonald, playing with a cold and a sore throat, fielded a punt over his shoulder at the Sooner thirty, retreated five steps, faked left, paused, and danced a cha-cha step. Now the coverage team descended. But Tommy had the Buffs right where he wanted them.

He skittered to the right, found the sideline, and was gone like a bullet. On reaching the end zone, he turned to see a red flag lying at the Colorado thirty. The Sooners had committed a personal foul even before the ball was kicked, and the Buffs' offense was now back in business.

They rolled down the field, tearing off huge chunks of turf, but braked inside the ten-yard line as the Oklahoma alternates fought back. On fourth-and-goal from the ten, Boyd Dowler stepped under center, turned, and handed to Howard Cook, who then handed to Eddie Dove going the other direction. Dove strolled around left end into the end zone on the double reverse and Colorado led 13–7.

A fifty-five-yard touchdown run by Bayuk was nullified by a penalty on the Buffs' next possession, but it didn't matter. They chipped away at the Sooners with short gains, and, on reaching the Sooner nine, Dowler again stepped under center, then pitched to Bob Stansky, and with thirty-six seconds left before halftime, Colorado was ahead 19–6.

Wilkinson made a brief appearance at the hut, told the boys to get undressed, and left. Twenty minutes later, the referee stepped inside the shadowy room and reminded the Sooners it was time to play ball.

"By the way, you boys'd better get dressed," he said. "We still got a second half of football left."

"Mr. Referee," captain Jerry Tubbs said, "we haven't seen our coach in quite some time. We'll be out there directly."

A moment later, Wilkinson slid silently through the back door, and now his face was about two inches behind one of the naked bulbs. He looked scary. He had little to say.

"Gentlemen, there is only one person in this stadium who believes you are going to win this game. That person is *me*."

Billy Pricer was so overcome with emotion that he turned and charged the twenty-foot steel door like a raging bull. Sliding it open was not an option. Ramming the door with his helmet and shoulder pads, he knocked it cleanly off the runners. He retreated five steps and charged again, this time shoving the massive roadblock ten feet to the right. Players poured through the hole and sprinted down the tunnel toward the field. Assistant coaches ran after the players, screaming, "Put your jerseys back on! Put your jerseys back on!"

The Sooners were so adrenaline-charged they could have flown over the Rockies. But they couldn't even make a first down. Just minutes into the second half, Harris peered at the chains on the sideline and realized it was fourth-and-two at the Oklahoma twenty-eight. He eased into the huddle and said, "Guys, this is the game and *my* ass. But we're goin' for it anyway. Twenty-two on two. Dig in, dammit. Break!" Twenty-two was old reliable—Clendon Thomas straight ahead off right tackle. This time, the hole was clogged, but Thomas angled left and found an opening worth three yards. *You can start breathing again,* Harris told himself.

Then the real Sooners stood up. On nothing but running plays, Pricer gained six yards, McDonald sixteen, Thomas six, Pricer three, McDonald twenty-seven, Thomas two, McDonald two, and McDonald two more. On fourth-and-four from the five-yard line, McDonald took the pitch from Harris, rolled right, and flipped the touchdown pass to Thomas. It was the most important score of the season and one of the biggest in OU history. Harris's kick cut the lead to 19–13.

The day turned darker, and the clouds now seemed to skim along the rim of the stadium. Harris lit a fire when he returned a punt seventeen yards, and fifteen more yards were tacked on for a late hit. The Sooners were in business at the Colorado forty-eight.

Oklahoma sliced up the Buffs, moving the ball on the ground all the way to the twelve-yard line, where McDonald pump-faked to Thomas and swept right end for the touchdown. Tommy, who usually bounced up like a rubber ball, lay on the ground for several seconds, feeling the hot poker burning a hole in his damaged right knee. He was near exhaustion when he held for the extra point, and Jimmy's kick sailed through the uprights: Oklahoma, 20–19. Snowballs and Coke bottles sailed out of the stands, and the Sooners were reminded by coaches to keep their helmets on at all times.

A few minutes later, the alternates moved the ball to the Buffs' sixteen, whereupon the starters returned. Harris rolled left and fired a touchdown pass to Thomas in the left corner. The kick made it 27–19 with five minutes to play. By now the Buffaloes were spent, and the Sooners were able to run out the final minutes for the streak-saving victory. Oklahoma had done the unthinkable, throwing three touchdown passes and still winning.

As they trudged from Folsom Field, it began to snow. Not once had it rained, hailed, sleeted, or snowed during a game coached by Wilkinson. But if the game had lasted two minutes longer, that streak would have been broken.

• • •

John Herman Bell was dealing cards on the fourth floor of the Jeff House when he felt a cold chill. His eyes studied the fireplace that had never been used, to his memory, in four years at the jock dorm.

"Why don't we have any danged firewood?" he asked the gambling crowd.

John Herman had an idea. His eyes surveyed the cluster of little desks, constructed of white oak, that had been purchased by Port Robertson for the purpose of studying. They were about as worn as the fireplace.

The big end grabbed one of the desks, turned it upside down, and slammed it to the floor, breaking it into about ten pieces.

"Now we have firewood." Somebody had a can of gasoline in his dorm room and, within minutes, six little desks were roasting.

Assistant coach Sam Lyle happened to saunter into the room the next morning and saw pieces of broken furniture and a heap of ashes in the fireplace. A radio had been left behind on the card table. At a time when TV sets were still scarce, a radio held value.

About an hour later, Port Robertson set his eyes upon the little music box and said, "I just bet we can find the owner of this."

Norman Lamb was a former all-state quarterback from Enid who had won fame by passing to John Bell. He was on his way to Norman to play quarterback for the Sooners when he cracked his fifth lumbar playing junior college football. Because Lamb was both intelligent and personable, Wilkinson wanted to utilize his talents as a Jeff House proctor and student assistant coach. Lamb was attending OU on a full athletic scholarship. It was his radio that Robertson now clutched.

Port had a way of making sure the boys were always thinking about him. He hung a clipboard at the head of the dining line at the Jeff House, where hundreds of eyeballs saw it each day. A hungry boy would lose his appetite if his name appeared on the list with these typewritten words next to it: SEE ME IMMEDIATELY—PGR. It meant that your ass was grass.

Monday morning, each of the Jeff House cardplayers dreaded the trip through the breakfast line. They really dreaded reading these words: WHOEVER OWNS A MISSING RADIO, SEE ME IMMEDIATELY—PGR.

Norman Lamb, John Herman Bell, and several others spent the next twenty minutes playing with their food. Then they slowly and silently marched as a unit over to the field house to see *the Man*.

"Peaheads," he said. "Those desks cost money. So I'm hitting you where it hurts. Fork over your ticket money."

Lamb stood at the back of the room, summoning his courage.

"Port, is there any chance I can have my radio back?"

"Just as soon as you boys run stadium steps and pay for those desks."

Due to soreness in their legs and backsides and a shortage of money, the card games ceased for about a week, until the gamblers could approach Gomer about an advance on next season's tickets.

"John Herman," Gomer said. "Seems to me that you are graduating. How are you going to come up with Texas tickets?"

He shrugged and said, "Ah, Gomer, I'll think of something. Right now I need a stake."

Thanks to the thirty-six-game winning streak, the Sooners were virtually swimming in their own newspaper ink. The press recorded every move they made. With the exception of Wilkinson, few people knew that the Sooners were emotionally out of gas and that practice sessions were going nowhere. Everyone was talking and writing about *the Streak*, not realizing it had become a ball-and-chain for the players.

Wilkinson prayed the Sooners could win their final four games, capture yet another national title, and break the all-time record for consecutive wins set from 1908 through '14 by the Washington Huskies. Anything after forty straight wins would be gravy. Besides, with so many seniors graduating, the '57 season held no guarantees.

Though the fans had reveled in *the Streak*, the players didn't walk around patting themselves on the back because of it. There were no signs inside the locker room or the stadium reminding everyone just how many the Sooners had won.

Perhaps as important to the seniors was leaving the University of Oklahoma without a loss in three varsity seasons. Actually, it would be four seasons. The '53 freshman team didn't lose.

Jerry Tubbs wasn't much for speeches but took it upon himself to address the team one afternoon as the boys were dressing for the afternoon workout.

"Guys, I think that a lot of y'all know that everybody is talkin' about the Streak," he said. "Seems that everybody is also talkin' about who's gonna make All-American, who's gonna win the Heisman Trophy, all of that stuff. Me, I'd just like walk off this campus having never lost. I think every senior in this room feels the same way."

The team's concentration level, thanks to Tubbs's speech, was much higher that day, and Wilkinson could feel a renewal of the collective spirit as the Sooners prepared for Iowa State.

The final four opponents—Iowa State, Missouri, Nebraska, and

Oklahoma A&M—were not exactly famine, pestilence, destruction, and death. Only a handful of players on those teams could make OU's third and fourth strings.

The week after that rugged trip to the Rocky Mountains, the OU defense registered its tenth shutout in the last twelve regular-season games as the Sooners whipped Iowa State 44–0. Tubbs bowled over about the half of the Cyclones on a forty-yard interception return in the first half.

But they were crestfallen two days later when the new Associated Press poll promoted Tennessee to number one. Though the Sooners received ninety-two first-place votes to Tennessee's fifty-eight, the Volunteers climbed into the top spot while the Sooners, for the first time in almost two seasons, slid to second.

Five days later, the Missouri Tigers had yet another reason to sweat bullets as their buses pulled into Norman.

Jack Ogle, the OU public-address announcer, became the Sooners' twelfth man that day. In the second quarter, he announced that Tennessee had whipped Missouri 27–7. Now the Sooners were ready to run through steel doors again.

The starters played so well in the first half that Wilkinson dismissed them at halftime. The fourth and fifth stringers were on the field the better part of the fourth quarter as Oklahoma rolled to a 67–14 victory. Wilkinson looked almost sick in the locker room, trying to explain it to the press.

"I couldn't do anything," he said. "I couldn't turn off the faucet. You can't ask your boys to turn if off."

With McDonald, Tubbs, Harris, Thomas, Pricer, Gray, and Bell exiting the field so early, Harold Keith was having trouble keeping the public-relations machine on track. Tubbs and McDonald were viable candidates for the Heisman Trophy, and several others were favorites for the All-American teams.

Other little games were starting to play out between the Sooner stars. Thomas and McDonald were dueling for the national scoring title, and Thomas was getting all the help his roommate, Jimmy Harris, could muster. McDonald threw fits whenever Harris called Thomas's number in the huddle.

Robertson approached Harris one day and said, "Jimmy, are you getting your rest? Coach Wilkinson is getting a little worried. What time did you go to bed last night?"

"Oh, about nine."

"OK then, what time did you get up and go home?"

When Harris was not making the scene with Donna Sue, he was at the Uptown Pit in Oklahoma City with Charlie Rountree, who had been selected the social chairman of the SAE fraternity but unofficially filled that position for the entire campus. Since Charlie didn't go home much anymore to Nichols Hills, he was having his grades sent to the Uptown Pit. When Charlie emerged through the front door at night, the band stopped in midsong and started playing his favorite song, "Take the A Train."

During a break one night, drummer Freddie Peck came over to Charlie's table. "Young man," he said pointedly. "I've been meaning to talk to you about that grade in English."

With a third consecutive unbeaten season on the line, Gomer Jones was now fretting over the nightlife of his star quarterback. Jimmy was spending too much time with Doc Rountree's boy. So he telephoned the doctor at his office in Oklahoma City.

"Doc, your son, Charlie, has been keeping our quarterback out *way* too late," he said.

"I haven't seen that little peckerhead in weeks," Doc Rountree said. "But when I do . . ."

"Don't worry about it, Doc. Why don't you just come on down to Norman so we can drink some more bourbon."

Thirty minutes after the final surgery that day, Doc Rountree was sitting in Gomer's living room, a large glass filled with amber liquid in his hand. For the next four hours, the names of Jimmy Harris and Charlie Rountree never came up. The two were happy for an excuse to fill their glasses.

Back in the dark ages of college football, the newspapermen predicted that the thirty-nine-game winning streak that belonged to the Washington Huskies would never be broken. The Sooners were now one victory away from tying it. Coming to Norman were the Nebraska Cornhuskers, a team that had not defeated OU since 1941 and was now a four-touchdown underdog.

Oklahoma's routine since Wilkinson became the head coach was to stay each night before home games at the Skirvin Hotel in Oklahoma City, some twenty miles from campus. After team meetings, the players always went to a movie on Friday night, walking a few blocks from the hotel. This night, when the lights went down, Jimmy Harris stood up and walked out. Gomer punched Port Robertson in the arm and said, "Where the hell's he going?"

"Aw, he hasn't seen one of these movies in three years," Port said.

Harris was off to see Kathy Ann Pollard, the girl he had met at Camp Lincoln two years earlier, the one who had consented to one roll in the hay when the Sooners traveled to Nebraska the previous season. Jimmy wasn't planning to make curfew this night and didn't care if he was all used up the next day. Kathy had just arrived on the train from Lincoln.

Harris was actually at his best the following day, scoring twice, including a thirty-one-yard burst up the middle, and the Sooners compiled 506 yards rushing and 150 passing. The Cornhuskers had dreaded this day, knowing that Oklahoma wanted to impress the pollsters. Though Wilkinson cleared the bench once more, the first team went back onto the field with two minutes to play, and Harris led them for one more touchdown. The national record for thirty-nine straight wins had been tied, as the Sooners won 54–6. There was no doubt which team the pollsters would vote number one.

Oklahoma A&M didn't have a prayer in the final game, and the

Aggies knew it. About the only matter left to settle was the national scoring title, and Thomas held a one-touchdown lead over McDonald.

All afternoon, Harris ignored McDonald's pleas to carry the football. Once, when Pricer broke a long run through the middle, McDonald ran behind the big fullback, yelling, "Pitch me the ball! Pitch me the ball!"

In the final minutes of the game, McDonald had one last shot to tie Thomas for the scoring crown. Thomas was out of the game with an injury, and the stage now belonged to Tommy. The ball was at the A&M seven. Harris handed off to McDonald and he tore into the line with all of his might. It took half of the Aggie defense to stop him at the two.

On the next play, Tommy begged once more, and Pricer bellowed, "Shut up!" Then tackle Beaky Gray had something to say.

"Jimmy, I have never scored a touchdown in my life. This might be my last chance ever. Whadaya say?"

Harris smiled that familiar gap-toothed smile. Then he shuffled the lineup. He switched Pricer to Gray's spot at left tackle and moved Robert Derrick to fullback. Gray would line up at right halfback.

"OK, boys," Harris said in the huddle. "Let's hope that Bud doesn't kick my ass over this one."

The OU contingent was in a stir when they spotted the number 77 in the backfield. Wilkinson merely smiled.

Harris called old reliable—the play responsible for the majority of Thomas's touchdowns. He handed the ball to Gray at right tackle. The big man bowed his neck and shoulders and barreled across the goal, bowling over three Aggies, knocking two on their backsides.

Gray ripped off his helmet and sprinted to the sideline. He handed the football to Wilkinson, who smiled like a proud father. Gray said, "Coach, you've been using me wrong all these years." As they hugged, tiny tears now wet the eyes of the Great White Father.

In the final seconds, the starters were inserted back into the game for one play and then asked to take a curtain call. They removed their helmets and walked slowly to the sideline, the Sooner fans cheering wildly. Tears streamed down Harris's cheeks as he approached Wilkinson, whose hand was extended. Harris hugged his coach and said, "Bud, I gotta tell you something. You are the father I never really had." Now they both were crying.

Wilkinson knew in his heart that he would never see another competitor the likes of Jimmy Harris.

It was the greatest season by the greatest college team ever to suit up. The Sooners outscored their opponents 466–51—a per-game average score of 47–5. Six teams were shut out. The Sooners finished first in virtually every statistical category, including 481 yards per game and 391 rushing, a national record. Thomas beat out McDonald by one touchdown, nineteen to eighteen.

And the Sooners now held the national record for forty straight wins.

Harold Keith stoked the OU public relations machine until it belched smoke. McDonald finished second in the Heisman balloting, and Tubbs was fourth. In effect, they canceled each other out, allowing Paul Hornung, who had thrown four interceptions against the Sooners, to walk away with the trophy despite Notre Dame's 2–8 record. Hornung's statistics were quite unimpressive. He finished the season with three touchdown passes and thirteen interceptions. It was the first and only time a Heisman winner would come from a losing team.

Tubbs won the Walter Camp Award as the nation's best player, and McDonald was equally honored with the Maxwell Award. McDonald and Tubbs were everybody's All-Americans, while Gray, Thomas, and Krisher were included on the second teams. Amazingly, Harris made no All-American teams, but he couldn't have cared less.

The most impressive aspect was that each senior—Jimmy Harris, Jerry Tubbs, Tommy McDonald, John Herman Bell, Edmon Gray,

Billy Pricer, Jay O'Neal, Billy Carr Harris, Hugh Ballard, Bill Brown, Delbert Long, and Tom Emerson—never played in a losing college game.

Thanks to backwater rules of the Big Seven, the Sooners would not be playing in a bowl game. Conference officials continued to vote down a resolution that would have allowed a team to participate in bowl games in back-to-back seasons. America would be cheated out of one last bow from the Sooners.

Harris, McDonald, Tubbs, and Pricer were headed to the National Football League. Scouts predicted that McDonald and Tubbs would enjoy long and successful careers and that Harris and Pricer would have their moments in the sun. Gray and Bell were off to the Canadian Football League. O'Neal announced his intention to work as an assistant coach under Wilkinson. Emerson and Billy Carr Harris planned to further their educations, Harris at the University of Oklahoma law school and Emerson studying for his master's in zoology.

Their successful lives were only beginning.

18

ONE FOR BILLY

Folks from Hollis to Idabel were madder than wet hens in the fall of 1957 regarding the comments of Dr. George Lynn Cross, the number-one Sooners fan now turned traitor.

"I honestly believe that a loss might be good for the football program," the OU president told a booster group. "I think we've lost all perspective. I think that some of our fans have become downright spoiled." Those remarks, delivered with great sincerity, were printed in virtually every Oklahoma newspaper.

The weight of the world was settling down on Norman. Bud Wilkinson often appeared preoccupied, and he struggled to maintain his focus even during the most casual conversations. He talked to people but didn't see them. He didn't sleep well. He often visited the training room in the middle of the night, seeking relaxation on a vibrating table that had been installed by Ken Rawlinson. The trainers often found him sound asleep when the room was opened for business in the morning.

The sporting press hung around the OU campus like ghouls, and every fan outside of Oklahoma was ready for the forty-game streak to crash like the stock market of '29. Now the Sooners were embarking on the '57 season without seven starters from the previous year, not to mention great leaders like Jerry Tubbs and Edmon Gray. After three seasons of subtle change, the Sooners had been fractured by graduation.

On the chartered flight from Norman to Pittsburgh for the opening game that season, Byron Searcy, a senior with a serious mind, was experiencing grave doubts. Solid men like Billy Pricer and John Herman Bell had been replaced by Wahoo McDaniel, Larry Munnerlyn, and Bobby Boyd, boys now cutting up and talking loudly in the back of the plane at a time when they should have been studying their playbooks.

Searcy turned to Buddy Oujesky. "We're gonna lose a game, maybe *games,* this year. I got a real bad feeling."

"I sure wish those guys'd shut up." Oujesky turned to study the three clowns in the back row and wondered what had happened to the good old days.

No one understood Wilkinson's infatuation with McDaniel, whom he called by the boy's first name—Edward. The big fullback and linebacker had been a prize when he arrived in Norman out of Midland, Texas, but *overrated* more aptly described him now; it was the word his teammates were using, anyway. Munnerlyn had turned nuttier than an outhouse rat, and there was enough motor oil oozing through his system to lubricate every engine on the stock car circuit.

Another sideshow was taking shape. Everyone was talking about the first Negro to ever suit up for the Oklahoma varsity.

After a strong showing on the freshman team in '56, Prentice Gautt struggled to adjust to the larger challenge and was floundering on the fourth string. A handful of players seemed supportive, but the majority still threw the *n*-word around like poker chips in the Jeff House card room. Again Prentice had lost his appetite for hitting, and the coaches were concerned. He had dropped several punts in practice.

Wilkinson approached Gautt the week before the season opener with some startling news: "You're not even going to make the traveling squad. Prentice, you must let go of your fears."

Gautt listened to his coach and managed to work his way up the depth chart and now was challenging Bobby Boyd for his spot on the alternates.

Gautt's isolation was magnified by the coaches' failure to assign him a roommate for road trips. He would be the only player without one. It seemed that when Prentice wasn't practicing football or going to class, he spent every minute alone. Wilkinson noted that many of his players walked around Gautt as if he were a poisonous snake. But Jakie Sandefer approached the coach when the Sooners arrived at the team's hotel in Pittsburgh and said, "I'll be Prentice's roommate. I got nothing against Negro people. Besides, Prentice is a good man."

This was ironic, since Sandefer's full name was Jefferson Davis Sandefer III, the last three Sandefer men having been named for the president of the Confederacy. Racial turmoil was starting to sweep the South, from Montgomery to Little Rock, and now Prentice had a roommate whose name conjured up images of Dixie.

As the season approached, Prentice's presence stirred more controversy. Wilkinson spent more time reading his mail than he did writing letters. The hate mail arrived in large bundles, and most of it deeply disturbed the coach. Undercover police officers attended practices, and they would be on the sideline at Owen Field when the season began. Most of the mail was so incendiary that Wilkinson determined it would destroy what self-confidence Gautt had left, so the letters would remain locked up in his office.

The mailbag had also become a cross to bear for one George L. Cross. Oklahomans had experienced drought, depression, and denigration the last forty-odd years. Cross's theory that *the Streak* had become an albatross was unacceptable to the fans. Dreamers believed that several years might pass before the Sooners lost again. Realists merely prayed for one more unbeaten season. Regardless, folks wanted to bask in the national spotlight for a bit longer, anyway.

In spite of these conflicts, Johnny "the Gnat" Pellow, the 160-pound halfback from Enid, was having the September of a lifetime. He had just been promoted to the starting lineup. Again, Wilkinson was picking on Clendon Thomas, who had appeared laconic during practice. Thomas, a second-team All-American in '56, had recently been voted a Sooner co-captain. Those honors meant nothing to Wilkinson. Thomas was demoted all the way to fourth string.

The Gnat, the beneficiary of that temporary promotion, was overjoyed for a reason that superseded football. Starters, even temporary ones, were issued brand-new white socks and T-shirts. That stuff would wear well around campus with his new blue jeans and polished Weejuns. The Gnat was now going around in style.

Over the years, Thomas had learned not to sweat preseason demotions. He knew that his name would show up on the *real* 1957 lineup when Wilkinson finally got around to posting it:

End—Don Stiller
Tackle—Byron Searcy
Guard—Ken Northcutt
Center—Hog Harrison
Guard—Billy Krisher
Tackle—Doyle Jennings
End—Joe Rector
Halfback—Jakie Sandefer
Halfback—Clendon Thomas
Fullback—Dennit Morris
Quarterback—Carl Dodd

The line was solid. The Sooners had actually lost little ground with Hoggy Harrison's promotion to starting center and linebacker, in spite of the fact that Jerry Tubbs was voted the best college player in '56. Harrison was *the* recruiting prize of Texas two years earlier, and a man named Bear Bryant almost corraled him for Texas A&M. Bryant viewed Harrison as the next Charlie Krueger, the most highly recruited player in the history of Aggieland after John David Crow himself. Bryant visited Stamford three times, and that was two more trips than he made for any other blue-chipper. Bob thought he had seen the last of Bear Bryant until he walked into the house one day after school.

It was bridge day, and the dining room table was packed with card-playing women from the neighborhood. Bob normally said hello to the ladies, then headed straight to his tractor. But the scene this day stopped him in his tracks. Smack-dab in the middle of the hen party was a tall man with dark features and swept-back hair. Dressed in a coat and tie, he was getting ready to bid.

"Well, hello, Bob," Bryant said. "Your mother here says that you might just be changing your mind about the ol' Aggies." Harrison was in the process of learning one of the great truths about this coaching legend: that Bryant could change personalities as rapidly as he changed clothes. No, this wasn't the same man who had supervised a ten-day preseason hell camp down in Texas, running off seventy-six players and almost killing two others. Here was a man who could warm the pulpit and play bridge with the ladies right after church.

Though the Sooners line was in great shape, a million questions centered on the quarterback position. Neither Carl Dodd nor David Baker had ever played the position, and Wilkinson's string of great luck looked to have run out. Since 1946, the lineage of signal callers at OU had been "General" Jack Mitchell, Darrell Royal, Claude Arnold, Eddie Crowder, Gene Calame, and Jimmy Harris; three All-Americans emerged from the group, and collectively they had produced a record of 103–11.

Dodd and Baker were really born to play halfback. Neither possessed a strong and accurate passing arm. They would never be able to fill the shoes of Harris, remembered as *the quarterback who never lost a game*. It was the opinion of many that Harris was OU's greatest quarterback. Neither Dodd nor Baker could come close to matching Jimmy's talents at handling the ball and running the option. Quite naturally, they also lacked his cocksureness.

The running game would have to carry the Sooners in '57, and there were reasons for optimism now that Sandefer had completely healed from a severe ankle sprain. Sandefer had languished on the bench in '56, as the injury never seemed to improve. It was truly the saddest season of his life. At five-ten, 160 pounds, Sandefer was known for his speed, but he ran with power between the tackles and would replace Tommy McDonald as the passing halfback. His return to health had been perfectly timed.

The Sooners were lucky to open the season against Pittsburgh, a team that had lost several starters to graduation. Sandefer started the ball rolling early in the game with a halfback pass to end Joe Rector, who twisted and leaped between two defenders for the opening touchdown of the season.

It was obvious by the second quarter that Pitt couldn't handle OU's rotation of twenty-two players. Pitt center Bill Brueckman told OU's Byron Searcy, "I sure wish you guys'd call a time-out. We don't have any left."

Rector set up the second touchdown by jolting the ball loose from quarterback Bill Kaliden, and Dennit Morris recovered at the Panthers' twenty-yard line. Thomas, his confidence and his starting job back, ran over two defenders for the touchdown; Dodd added a third with a pass to end Don Stiller, and Dickie Carpenter intercepted a deflected pass and returned it for the final touchdown, the Sooners winning 26–0 for the eleventh shutout in their last fifteen regular-season games.

The fans breathed a sigh of relief. The rebuilt Sooners had bumped *the Streak* to forty-one games.

Five starters and Wilkinson spent the better part of the following week in bed with the Asian flu. But Oklahoma could have whipped Iowa State, the next opponent, with the third stringers. The most exciting moment of the game was a snaking eighty-three-yard punt return by Sandefer, who took off down the shadowy western boundary of Owen Field and followed the picket fence of blockers until he reached the twenty-five-yard line, where he faked Dwight Nichols out of his jock. Amazingly, Nichols turned and pursued Sandefer and got his hands on the little halfback, but Jakie had enough energy left to wobble heavy-legged into the end zone.

The 40–14 victory over Iowa State represented the Sooners' sixtieth consecutive win in conference play.

History had been made in Oklahoma City Friday night before the Iowa State game. Racial barriers had come down. Gautt became the first Negro to enter the Skirvin Hotel through the front door. When the Sooners arrived on two buses, reporters from the all-black newspaper and radio stations were poised on the sidewalk, police surrounding them. Prentice tried to shut out the noise as he shoved through the crowd, racial taunts flying from disgruntled whites. *I wish they would all go away. I wish they would let me play ball and get my education.*

But it was not in the cards. Black activists like Clara Luper had prayed for this day. For years, she had led sit-ins at all-white restaurants and hotels across Oklahoma City. She was standing just inside the front door of the Skirvin as the Negro photographers snapped pictures and reporters hollered, "How does it *feel,* Prentice? You have made it, son."

They didn't know that Prentice was quite familiar with the opulent Skirvin with its twin brick-and-glass towers. Opened in 1911 by oilman William Skirvin, the ornate hotel had survived the Great Depression and the oil bust. Now, with the economy churning upward and the Sooners on a winning tear, the Skirvin was the grandam of Oklahoma City's luxury hotels.

Five years earlier, Prentice, without telling anyone, had walked several blocks from the Deep Deuce one afternoon to catch a glimpse of one of his heroes; he had a handful of idols at the time. The first was Jackie Robinson, the man who broke major league baseball's color barrier with the Brooklyn Dodgers, and the second was Marion Motley, the large and powerful Cleveland Brown fullback.

The third was a boy with curly brown hair.

Waiting for the Sooners, Prentice leaned against a wall across the street from the hotel. Entering through the front door was never an option. It was said that a black man had never set foot on the Skirvin's marble floors. Negro employees took their meals in the kitchen and used the back door.

Prentice saw two Greyhound buses pull up and park at the front curb. He was awestruck at the sight of the Oklahoma Sooners, dressed in coats and ties. Most wore flattops. Their faces, all white, were chiseled and determined. He knew that his hero would have a rock-hard jaw and move with a swagger. Prentice nervously approached him on the sidewalk and said, "Billy, sir, might I please have your autograph?"

Many in the sporting press believed that Billy Vessels would win the Heisman Trophy that season of 1952. Billy shook his head as he signed the little notebook.

"How old are you?" he said.

"Fourteen."

"God almighty. You look like you oughta be playin' for us."

"I hope to someday, sir. I really do." Prentice could barely feel the sidewalk as he ran all the way home.

Memories of that encounter filled Prentice's head that September night in '57 as he restlessly tossed and turned and tried to sleep in a bed situated inside a hotel that had never in forty-six years boarded a black man. He awoke at least ten times throughout the night. In his nightmares, he saw flashbulbs popping. He heard Negro reporters hurling questions as he tried to walk to the team bus the next morning. The world would *not* go away.

A week later, down in Fort Worth, it got worse. The Sooners were scheduled to play Texas and to bunk the night before the game thirty miles from the drunken pregame brawls on the streets of downtown Dallas. For years, the Sooners had found peace and comfort at the Worth Hotel in downtown Fort Worth.

As the bus pulled up to the hotel, OU business manager Ken Farris took a seat next to Prentice and handed him an envelope that contained thirty dollars: "Prentice, I have some bad news. Texas laws don't allow Negroes to stay in all-white hotels."

Prentice would walk through the front door with his teammates, then casually stroll out the back door of the hotel that was used by black maids, busboys, and dishwashers. A taxi was waiting, and it would take him to the Presidential Hotel in a black neighborhood, where he would spend the night quite alone and quite depressed. It seemed that every time he became adjusted to his white teammates, someone snatched them away.

The next morning, the proprietors of the Worth Hotel were fair enough to allow Prentice to eat breakfast with the team, but his table was set in a small adjoining room. Players became suspicious and started asking questions. "German Jim" Lawrence, a tackle from Sayre, stood to address his teammates as they took their seats on the team bus. Lawrence had participated in the restaurant boycott in Tulsa when the Chicken Corner refused to serve Prentice.

"Guys, Prentice Gautt is *our* teammate," Lawrence said, his eyes filling with tears. "Last night, he didn't get to stay at our hotel because he's colored. Goddammit, that's a shame. Football teams are supposed to stick together."

The Sooners were still buzzing when Wilkinson assembled them minutes before kickoff at the Cotton Bowl: "Win this one for Prentice Gautt." He didn't need to say another word. The Sooners almost ran over the coaches, and everyone else for that matter, as they roared down the long tunnel toward the playing field, the plight of Prentice Gautt now on their minds.

The Longhorns had a brand-new coach named Darrell Royal, who knew the powers of Wilkinson's pregame speech making. That is why he was bent over and throwing up behind the Longhorns' bench as the Sooners rumbled onto the field to the blare of "Boomer Sooner." For years, Royal had struggled to extricate his heart from Wilkinson, his home state, and the mighty Oklahoma football tradition. Now he felt hollow as he spied the Great White Father standing in the sunlight on the other side of the field.

After losing forty-five–zip in the previous season, the orange bloods had decided to keep their gambling money in their pockets. Texas was coming off a 1–9 season and now groveled in the Southwest Conference gutter. But it was not surprising to Wilkinson that Texas got the jump on the Sooners and led 7–0 following a halfback pass from Walter Fondren to Monte Lee. Thanks to the addition of Royal, Wilkinson knew the Longhorns would have fire in their bellies.

Dodd led the Sooners sixty yards in the second quarter with a fine mixture of running plays but no passes. Following Harris's cue, he called the quick dive for Thomas, and the lanky halfback burst between his blockers for the three-yard touchdown. An eighty-yard drive in the third quarter provided further proof that the passing game was dead. Wilkinson had scaled down the Split-T offense. Dodd moved the Sooners to the one-yard line, where Sandefer followed blocks by Ken Northcutt, Byron Searcy, and Hog Harrison into the end zone.

Through the years, the Sooners had become known as one of the toughest and most resilient teams in the country. End Steve Jennings made a crushing tackle near midfield and felt a pop in the middle finger of his right hand. His eyes studied the hand that was now missing a finger. He turned to Joe Rector: "Joe, I cut my finger off." The boys searched the grass for a bloody digit. Then Jennings discovered that the finger had snapped backward and was lying against the back of his hand. Trainer Ken Rawlinson sprinted onto the field and grimaced as he straightened the compound fracture. He wrapped all four fingers in tape, and Jennings, in spite of pleas from the trainer, stayed on the field and did not miss a single play.

Sandefer set up the final score with an interception that he returned nineteen yards to the Texas twenty-one. Minutes later, Dodd scored on the quarterback sneak, and the Sooners had a 21–7 victory.

Once again, though, the Sooners failed to impress the sportswriters, falling to number two in the Associated Press poll. Led by the coaching of Bear Bryant and the running of John David Crow, Texas A&M climbed to number one.

More distressing news was to follow. The two-time defending national champions, now boasting a forty-three-game winning streak, were evicted from their hotel.

After ten years of hosting the Sooners the night before home games, the Skirvin manager called Wilkinson and said, "That little nigger of yours really stirred the pot. Every nigger in Oklahoma wants to stay here now." The Sooners moved to the Biltmore in Oklahoma City. Naturally, Wilkinson fretted over one of his superstitions. The Sooners had lost only three games at home during their time at the Skirvin. Those worries melted when OU lashed Kansas, the whipping boy of the Big Seven, 34–12. The Sooners were quickly voted back to number one.

The Buffs were next. Since the tie in 1952, Colorado had played the Sooners straight down to the wire in three of the next four encounters. They were loaded with talent—Bob Stransky, John Wooten, and Boyd Dowler were cinches for All-American honors. The Sooners should have been on their toes with the Buffaloes coming to Norman. They were not.

Colorado pulled ahead 13–7 as the fourth quarter started, Stransky pitching the touchdown pass to Dowler, who was now being scouted as a wide receiver and punter for the NFL. Silence fell over Memorial Stadium as the crowd of 61,624, the largest to ever witness a Big Seven contest, squirmed.

Thomas's thirty-yard kickoff return set up the Sooners' offense at midfield, but they soon faced fourth-and-one. It was Dodd's call. He optioned right and kept the ball for an eleven-yard gain. The Sooners mowed down the Buffs, and from the eight-yard line Dodd pitched around left end to Thomas, then blocked for him. Dennit Morris provided another land-clearing block, and Thomas scored standing up.

Relief should have belonged to the Sooners. But anything could happen in this era when kicking was hardly an art. Dodd was set to kick, Jakie to hold. It was a perfect snap, and Jakie spun the laces and put it down perfectly—about two inches in front of the tee. Dodd swung his foot and then had to recoil. He punched at the ball a second time and it fluttered over the crossbar by inches. Writing for the *Topeka Capital-Journal*, Dick Snider summarized the game quite well: "Oklahoma, a football elephant hanging over the brink of defeat with its tail wrapped around a daisy, pulled from behind in the final period here Saturday to edge amazing Colorado 14–13." The Streak was still alive.

Victory number forty-six was delivered the next week on a sloppy field in Manhattan against the Kansas Jayhawks. The Sooners won 13–0, thanks to Steve Jennings's fumble recovery that set up a touchdown. Win number forty-seven came much easier as the Sooners trounced Missouri 39–14.

But the pollsters hadn't forgiven Oklahoma for its close call against Colorado; Texas A&M held onto the top spot for the third time in four weeks. Fearing that his players were no longer motivated, Wilkinson called a team meeting on the fourth floor of the Jeff House. He told them the greatest comeback story he had ever heard—the story of Billy Vessels.

• • •

The ten-year-old boy walked through moonlit darkness down the winding two-laner that connected Hominy to his hometown of

Cleveland. This was the rough country of eastern Oklahoma, the old Cherokee territory, where the only vegetation to take root and grow copiously was the pine trees and the stout cedars.

Billy was stopped in his tracks by two bright yellow dots in the distance. He expected a wave of fear to rush over his body, but it never came. His heart ticked a bit faster but registered no terror. So he started walking again.

Thanks to a full Cherokee moon, Billy could see the outline of the large creature. He moved slowly, quietly, without breathing. The figure sauntered toward him, but the boy didn't retreat. From the moment he spotted the reflective eyes, Billy knew what he was about to encounter—a large timber wolf. The predators were prevalent around Cleveland, Hominy, and Osage, where the human population was scattered, but livestock was bountiful. The Indians had practically worshiped the gray wolf for its cunning and survival instinct. But the white man targeted, hunted, harassed, and killed wolves more aggressively than any other animal in America. They were loathed for feasting on cows, horses, goats, sheep, chickens, and pets. Native Americans were keenly aware that wolves rarely attacked humans. But the white pioneers were frightened of the animals that grew to be six feet in length, three feet in height, and weigh 175 pounds.

Billy watched the outline of the long shadow move toward him and gauged the wolf to be at least five feet long. He held his breath and kept walking, straight down the middle of the asphalt highway. Their eyes studied each other as they quietly passed. Several moments later, as Billy started to breathe again, the boy said to himself, *I wasn't afraid. And I'm never gonna be scared again.*

As with every square inch of Oklahoma, Cleveland, once a boomtown, started to suffer in the thirties as the farms and ranches went bankrupt and oil prices plummeted to rock bottom. The town, just west of Tulsa, had become overly dependent on oil. The land was just too hard to grow cotton on a consistent basis, and with the crash in oil prices hundreds were out of work all over the county. The local refinery was almost forced to shut down. But dreams die hard among the strong-willed. Folks from the blue-collar sector were the first to be squeezed, and they were soon living on precious little.

Frank Vessels was a handyman who found himself unemployed, so he retreated into the deep woods, where he worked for the moonshiners. Some say that he drank his profits. His wife, Veo, labored long hours to keep the tiny secondhand store going on Main Street, where she sold hand-me-down clothes and eggs.

Veo birthed five children—three boys and two girls. The oldest son, Jack, was in trouble with the law by the second grade. He was the first in the family to be dubbed Sticky Fingers. Billy was the fastest kid on the streets of Cleveland and one of the toughest. Donnie, the youngest of the Vessels boys, struggled in school. Billie Jean and Mary Francis were the apples of their mother's eye, but they, too, wore hand-me-down clothes.

The family grew more desperate with each passing week. As Frank fell behind on the bills, he spent more time with the moonshiners. Meanwhile, Veo was selling the old clothes for pennies or trading them for scraps of food.

"We just can't keep on feedin' five kids on these here pennies," Frank told his wife. "Somethin's gotta give."

One evening, the couple took Billy to the Melba Theatre on Broadway, where they were admitted for fifteen cents. The couple knew that Billy was the strongest of their three sons, both mentally and physically. Billy possessed astounding people skills. He knew how to talk to adults, and his tongue operated as swiftly as his feet. Citizens of Cleveland admired everything about the kid and believed he would someday lead the Cleveland High Tigers to a state championship, then take off to Oklahoma A&M to star for the Aggies. Billy was large for his age, with a hard, square jaw and hands that seemed like those of a grown man.

It had been a couple of years since his parents had taken him to the picture show, and Billy found it a rare treat to be sitting between them. Halfway through the show, Veo turned to her son and said, "Billy, your daddy and I are going to get some popcorn. You stay here till we get back."

Billy couldn't figure why his mother would kiss him on the forehead. Thirty minutes later, though, he was struck by a horrible thought. He ran up the aisle and burst through the door leading into the small lobby.

"Where's my mom and dad?" he shouted to Mrs. Willis, the lady at the candy counter.

"Oh, they're long gone. I just figured that you'd gone home with 'em, Billy."

Billy felt as if his heart had been torn out. He knew that times were tough, but he never figured his parents would abandon him. The message was clear as a bell: his parents could no longer afford him. Billy began to cry.

"Billy, you can stay at my house tonight," the woman said.

But Billy was gone in seconds, sprinting up Broadway, tears streaming down his face. There came a knock on the door at 505 North C Street around ten o'clock. Bud Newcun knew from the look in the youngster's eyes what had happened.

"Come on in, Billy," he said. "Are you hungry? We got an extra bed for you. Don't worry. You can stay with us as long as you like."

For the next several months, Billy bunked at the Newcuns'. Living with his family was now out of the question. They sank deeper into poverty with each passing day and you could never count on consistent meals. Jack was in and out of jail, and the sheriff knocked on the front door almost once a day. So when Billy wasn't sleeping at the Newcuns' house, he stayed the night at the homes of Louis Beyers, the town's leading attorney, or Albert Chance Adams, the president of the Cleveland National Bank. Merle Eddington, the owner of Oklahoma Tire and Supply, also provided a bed and sustenance.

The Palace Drugstore, owned by Bud Newcun, was Billy's first stop each day after school. He would smile when he saw Bud standing in front of the drugstore on Broadway, because the man was quite generous with his ice-cream cones.

"OK," Bud would say. "You've got two minutes to run around the block."

Billy would sprint from Broadway over to Delaware to Jordan and then south on Division, which led back to Broadway. He always covered the distance in about two minutes and was timed by a huge clock in the front window of the drugstore. Bud once caught him cutting through the alley, and that was the only time that he lost out on the ice cream.

Bud Newcun was laid-back and quiet, and he possessed a big heart. He never bothered anyone and the town adored him. He loved Billy because the boy was special, and everybody in Cleveland knew it. To see the fire in his eyes, and to hear the passion in his voice inspired an entire community to lend a helping hand. Of course, this was the kind of town where people listened and paid attention to important matters, such as the care and nurturing of children. To folks from the big city, Cleveland might have seemed like the end of the earth. But it was a town built on rural idealism. Clevelanders also knew that Billy would grow up one day and carry their hopes and dreams all the way to the state championship.

Four men cared for Billy as if he were their son. Between them, they had seven daughters and only one boy. Jay Beyers had contracted polio as a young child and would never play football. The four men began a crusade to make sure Billy reached his potential and that every door of opportunity was opened.

After years of fighting off poverty, Frank Vessels decided to move the family to Oklahoma City, where there was more work. Naturally, Billy chose to stay in Cleveland, where he could depend on room and board and plenty of friends.

Frank boarded up most of the windows of the run-down two-story house on Johnson Street. Out of curiosity, Billy decided to stay there one night after the family left town. Cooking breakfast one cold morning, he burned the old house to the ground, the fire claiming his most prized possession—his number 22 Cleveland Tiger jersey.

The next Friday night, wearing a jersey much smaller than the original, Billy broke loose on a long run and, after about fifty yards, couldn't breathe. So he started ripping and tearing at the fabric as he ran until he could fill his lungs with air again.

In a game against Fairfax, playing with a cast on his broken wrist, he carried the ball five times and scored five touchdowns on runs of ninety-seven, ninety-three, ninety, seventy-six, and three yards.

The boy grew to be six-foot and two hundred pounds, and he was the fastest sprinter in Oklahoma. He struggled with schoolwork, but thanks to some loving attention, his grades improved.

From the age of ten, Billy had hitchhiked back and forth from Cleveland to Stillwater, a distance of fifty miles, to see the Aggies play football and basketball, and most folks thought he was destined to play football someday for Oklahoma A&M.

But when Billy paid a recruiting visit to Norman, everyone sensed his fire. He, in turn, sensed the Sooners' purpose. He knew he was meant to play for the Oklahoma Sooners.

• • •

After finishing his story, Wilkinson gazed about the room.

"We learned from Billy Vessels that you should never give up. Even when you think problems cannot be solved, you should never give up. Here was a boy, once homeless, who won the Heisman Trophy.

"I sense that most of you are fatigued from the pressures of the winning streak. I feel the same way at times. But if we will battle, as Billy Vessels once battled, we will keep winning."

At that moment, a chartered flight was taking off from Chicago's O'Hare Airport. The Notre Dame Fighting Irish, the last team to defeat the Sooners, were coming to Oklahoma.

19

OKLAHOMA RAIN

All week, Bud Wilkinson had felt a set of eyes tracking him, but wrote it off to paranoia, yet another side effect of *the Streak*.

Johnny Lee Foreman, a tall boy with a brush cut, had arrived at the Jeff House four days before the Notre Dame game in mid-November toting a large suitcase. He shook hands with several of the OU players, telling them he was preparing to transfer to OU from Coffeyville Junior College. He would be suiting up for the Sooners next season and wanted to get a feel for the campus, check out the chicks, learn his way around the jock dorm, watch some practice. The junior college season was over.

Johnny Lee looked every bit the part of a football player, walked like one, and talked a big game. Later that day, several players saw him tossing a football around campus. They could tell he had a strong arm.

It was widely known that Wilkinson added wrinkles to the offense on Tuesday. Practices were always closed to the public, but the only person guarding the place was an old Jewish man named Morris Tennenbaum, who stationed himself at the locker room door. Mostly, he told jokes and handed out sticks of gum.

Wilkinson preferred to conduct his practices in privacy and occasionally drafted campus security to shoo away the curious. But it would have been impossible to spy-proof OU practices. The practice site was visible for hundreds of yards across the flat campus. This day, Tennenbaum was the lone watchdog, and he was half-asleep.

Wilkinson had avoided a potential spying episode the week of the 1956 Notre Dame game by introducing his new offense—the pro set with two wide receivers—months earlier during preseason drills, when only the players and staff were around. He didn't even mention the pro set again to the players for two months, until the day before the game in South Bend. To the dismay of the Irish, the Oklahoma offense rolled up and down the field in the sophisticated passing set, winning 40–0. Never before had Wilkinson taken leave from the Split-T, the heart and soul of his winning formula.

This Tuesday, with the winning streak at forty-seven games and Notre Dame up next, Wilkinson introduced two new plays to the offense. Both were passes in the flat to fullback Dennit Morris, rarely used as a receiver. Morris was a powerful straight-ahead blocker and runner, but one who lacked the versatility and speed of Billy Pricer. He looked odd in the backfield wearing the number 51, issued to him three years earlier when he broke in as a center. Quick strikes to Morris were certain to catch the Irish off guard.

The Sooners also worked on the pro set just in case they fell behind the Irish and needed to pass. But it appeared, at least on the surface, that they were sticking with the Split-T. The only radical departures from the normal Xs and Os were the passes drawn up for Morris.

Johnny Foreman, who leaned against a tree about fifty yards from the practice fields, enjoyed watching the synchronization of the Sooner offense. He had eaten lunch that Tuesday at the Jeff House cafeteria, and the players wondered why he was asking so many doggone questions. By the time he left two days later on Thursday, he knew more about the Sooners than anyone else on campus, making sure to tell everyone good-bye, remembering each name.

"I'll be back," he said. "Really lookin' forward to playin' some ball with y'all next fall."

The new issue of *Sports Illustrated* arrived at the OU campus Friday morning and a thousand copies were sold in less than an hour. On the cover were the 1957 Oklahoma Sooners, many of them standing on the sideline, cheering on their teammates. Most prominent in the photograph were Clendon Thomas and Don Stiller. The headline read: "Why Oklahoma Is Unbeatable." When Wilkinson read those words, he rolled his eyes and headed straight for the vibrating chair.

Friday night, the chartered jet from Chicago set down in Norman with little fanfare, and the Fighting Irish were bused to Chickasha, some forty miles southwest of Norman, much farther from the action than any other OU opponent had ever chosen to stay. Chickasha (rhymes with *hay*) was a small all-white crossroads town on the edge of the south plains. Other than Native Americans, not many people of color made their way to Chickasha unless it was time to pick cotton. Hispanics migrated into the area in September and October but normally were gone by the first of November.

Several young Hispanic girls carrying fresh-cut flowers approached the Notre Dame players Saturday morning, hours before kickoff, as they walked to the hotel's dining room for breakfast. "Did you know that Oklahomans hate Catholics?" the girls said. "They treat us like dirt. They really hate you, too." The Irish players stopped and listened attentively.

Nick Pietrosante stood to speak during the pregame meal and the room fell silent. He called himself Nick the Greek God, and at six-one, 220 pounds, he was one of the toughest players in college football. He was a cross between Jerry Tubbs and Billy Pricer, but instead of being laid-back and humble, he was loud and often belligerent.

"I guess you guys know by now we're in the land of Catholic haters," he said. "These rednecks hate everybody—Negroes, Jews, Mexicans, and Catholics. They gave us shit last last year about being Catholic. I say let's whip their asses."

The players marched toward the buses with their chins and chests thrust forward. The Hispanic girls followed closely on their heels. "Please beat the Sooners. They hate us! Please, beat them for the Catholics of Oklahoma!"

When the players read what had been scrawled on the windows of the team bus in red lipstick—"Go Home Catholics!" and "F—— the Pope"—they were really pissed.

About an hour later, as the Irish arrived at Memorial Stadium, they found more fighting words were posted on the locker-room wall: "Yankees Go Home!"

As they dressed for the game, Pietrosante fueled the fire. "Kick some redneck butt today!" he yelled. "Let's kill these rednecks!"

In the 1950s, Catholics faced widespread prejudice in the southern half of the United States. In Oklahoma, Catholics often found themselves on the short end of business deals—that is, if anyone would do business with them. Living in the heart of the Bible Belt, 90 percent of Oklahomans attended the Baptist Church. Catholics were generally not trusted.

Still, the presence of the Hispanic girls at the Notre Dame hotel was puzzling. Had someone sent them there for the purpose of motivating the Irish players? Less than 1 percent of the state's population was Hispanic in 1957, and the citizens of Chickasha and Grady County were about as white as a picket fence after the cotton had been harvested and the Hispanics left town. Oklahoma was hardly a melting pot. The state had suffered serious losses to migration, especially in the 1930s, but few people had migrated *into* the state.

As the Irish strutted onto the field for pregame warm-ups, the crowd booed. Most fans had heard the stories of the Notre Dame players breaking through the OU calisthentic lines in South Bend the previous year in a blatant attempt to intimidate the Sooners. Several letters demanding retaliation had been written to Wilkinson, but that was not his style.

By noon, patches of sunlight were streaking through the low gray haze. The south wind had kicked up, and so had the humidity. Weather forecasters had predicted precipitation throughout the day, unaware that it never rained on the Great White Father. Umbrellas were left at home.

The game would be broadcast nationwide by NBC, with Lindsey Nelson doing the play-by-play and Red Grange handling the color, and, again, the game would be televised in "living color." Owen Field normally faded to the color of a corn tortilla by November. So workers had spent two days painting the brown grass grass spinach green for the benefit of the millions watching on TV. Players who rolled around on the ground during pregame warm-ups came up with green splotches. An hour before kickoff, Memorial Stadium was bursting at the seams with the largest crowed in the history of OU football—63,134.

There were many reasons to write off Notre Dame, out of the Top Twenty for two full seasons. Once the kingpins of college football, the Fighting Irish were at the nadir of the roller coaster, thanks to murderous schedules and a reduction in scholarships. It was the first time, and the last, that football would be deemphasized in South Bend. Father Hesburgh, the new president of the university, had underestimated the clout of the monied men when he started slashing scholarships. Now he was trying to negotiate a U-turn.

For decades, Notre Dame football had been an entertaining fusion of fact, legend, and lore. At times, it had transcended the boundaries of sport. But these were not the Irish of the Rockne-Leahy years. Coach Terry Brennan now walked a tightwire without the benefit of a net. The Irish had compiled a 17–3 record his first two seasons but were 6–10 since. The coach had approached Father Hesburgh before the team left for Norman.

"Father, if I beat Oklahoma, I get one more year, right?"

Hesburgh pondered the proposition and said, "You beat Oklahoma and *you deserve* one more year."

Oddsmakers had installed Oklahoma as an eighteen-point favorite, and it was one of the rare times of the last five decades that the Fighting Irish of Notre Dame were both the hungry and the sizable underdog. Believing the Irish had virtually no chance of winning, Father Hesburgh had remained in South Bend.

•   •   •

As kickoff approached, the pressure of the forty-seven-game winning streak rested squarely on the shoulders of quarterback Carl Dodd, now sitting in an awkward position in the Sooners' locker room, his head between his knees, his heart in his throat. No one loved the Sooners more than Dodd. No kid had ever pursued this dream of playing for the Sooners more fervently than this son of a poor sharecropper from Little Axe.

In the four calendar years of the winning streak, Gene Dan Calame had won ten games, Jimmy Harris thirty, and Dodd was working on number eight.

Carl was ten years old in 1946 when he was hired for the job of a lifetime—picking up empty Coke bottles during time-outs and halftimes of the OU games. When he wasn't dashing beneath the stands, he sat on the edge of Owen Field and watched his heroes whiz past in a crimson blur. He was so close to the action that he could smell the sweat-stained uniforms, hear the steel-tipped cleats ripping the grass.

He saw Darrell Royal's punts rocket above the rim of the stadium. He saw Myrle Greathouse blast ballcarriers. He saw Billy Vessels run, Max Boydston catch. He saw the Great White Father pace the sideline. He laughed when Buddy Burris lost his false teeth.

In 1953, when Carl was too old for litter patrol, he discovered yet another free ride into Memorial Stadium. He and a close friend climbed a stadium fence on Friday night and found a soft place to sleep inside a metal bin filled with red seat cushions. Carl was lucky that his high school sweetheart had a part-time job as a press-box waitress. During the game, she slid open a window of the press box and dropped sandwiches about fifteen feet into the hands of the broke and hungry boys.

That day, September 21, 1953, was the day that broke every Oklahoman's heart. The hated boys from Notre Dame, the defending national champions, had thundered into Norman for the opening game of the season at a time when OU was rebuilding. The Sooners had seven new starters, and Buddy Leake was doing something he had never done before—lining up as the starting quarterback.

Though the odds were stacked against them, the Sooners had been a study in resiliency. Merrill Green returned a punt sixty yards to cut the lead to 28–21 in the fourth quarter, and the offense was still scratching and clawing at the Notre Dame seventeen when the final gun sounded. Carl Dodd leaned against a wall high in the stadium and cried. "By god, I'll get even with them Notre Dame sonsabitches," he said to his buddy.

That was the final defeat before the monumental winning streak.

• • •

Wilkinson sensed that his players were approaching this one as just another day at the office. The pregame emotion had been no different than if Kansas were warming up at the other end of the field.

Now, minutes before kickoff, Wilkinson paced the sideline. The Great White Father had never appeared more lost in thought. A year earlier, he was a man of confidence as Jimmy Harris and the Sooners prepared to step onto the field at South Bend. Now, he stood with head bowed, thinking. Even the fans in the upper decks could sense his foreboding mood.

What he saw in the first few plays did boost spirits. Moving the ball consistently on the ground, the Sooners had already reached the Notre Dame thirty-nine. Dodd carried around right end and gained nineteen yards. Dennit Morris gained three up the middle, and

Jakie Sandefer lost three yards on the option pitch. On third down, Clendon Thomas barreled around right end, all the way to the Irish thirteen.

Now it was fourth down, time for the surprise pass. As Morris cut sharply toward the left sideline, Notre Dame linebacker John Ecuyer smothered him a full second before the pass arrived, and the ball fluttered to the ground. Though it was a clear case of pass interference, no flags fell. That, however, didn't worry Wilkinson nearly as much as the cold, hard reality that Notre Dame had anticipated the new play.

"They've been readin' our mail," Gomer Jones said to his boss.

Taking over on downs, Notre Dame ran three plays and was forced to punt.

Midway in the first quarter, the Sooners had yet another scoring opportunity when alternate linebacker David Rolle recovered a fumble at the Notre Dame thirty-three. But the second-string offense went backward; quarterback David Baker was sacked for five yards, Jimmy Carpenter threw wildly on the halfback pass, and Baker was sacked again. Oklahoma punted.

But another opportunity presented itself minutes later. Following a short punt, the Sooners took possession at the Notre Dame forty-one, and Joe Rector gained five yards on a screen pass. Dodd picked up four yards on two straight carries, and Clendon Thomas broke two tackles all the way to the twenty-three-yard line.

On third down, Pietrosante drove guard Bill Krisher far into the backfield and slammed into Dodd before he could hand off. The ball squirted backward, bouncing all the way to the forty-eight, where Pietrosante recovered it.

The big fullback shook his fist at the Sooners and yelled, "Hey, rednecks, how do you like us Catholics now?"

Buddy Oujesky, the only Catholic on the OU squad, couldn't believe his ears. "That's a bunch of bullshit," Oujesky shot back. "Half our guys don't even know what a Catholic is."

Pietrosante was a bit surprised when he saw Prentice Gautt trot onto the field and line up as a halfback with OU's alternate team. The Irish players were not aware that in this part of America, once known as the Confederacy, Gautt was the first Negro to suit up for a major college team.

After watching the Sooners waste three scoring chances, Notre Dame was determined to crack the scoreboard first. Behind the running of Pietrosante and right halfback Dick Lynch, the Irish moved to the Oklahoma three-yard line, where they set up first-and-goal. Pietrosante tried left guard and was sledgehammered by Hog Harrison. The same play to the right resulted in Harrison flattening Pietrosante again. Then Dick Lynch plowed within inches of the goal on third down.

The Sooners, lining up in an eight-man line, were waiting on Pietrosante when Lynch took the hand-off at right guard and slammed into a human wall. Byron Searcy, Morris, and Harrison dropped Lynch a foot short of the goal line. More than sixty-three thousand voices rose to the heavens. Notre Dame had run six plays inside the OU ten-yard line without scoring.

Against the alternates, just minutes before halftime, the Irish again drove inside the ten-yard line. On first-and-goal from the six, Pietrosante was stopped for no gain, and the Irish decided that enough was enough. Quarterback Bob Williams rolled right and passed straight into the arms of Sooner defensive back David Baker at the back of the end zone. The Sooners had been saved again.

The first half had been a standoff, the teams combining for fewer than a hundred total yards. Disconcerting to Wilkinson was that the Sooners had practically nowhere to run, either around end or between the tackles. Ironically, the Irish were using the "Oklahoma Defense"—five linemen, two linebackers, and four defensive backs. They often planted nine men within three yards of the line of scrimmage, knowing the Sooners couldn't pass.

Dodd was depressed at halftime.

"Coach, they know our plays," he said. "It's like they're in our huddle."

The Great White Father was keenly aware that the decisions he made at halftime would be the most important of his coaching life. But first he had to chew out big Bill Krisher, who had been knocked around for two quarters by a guard about twenty pounds lighter.

"That jersey you are wearing speaks volumes about our tradition here at Oklahoma," he said. "You do *not* deserve to wear that jersey. Take it off."

Krisher was near tears when Wilkinson finally backed off.

In the second half, the Sooners needed to shift offensive gears. But the harsh reality was that Wilkinson had failed to install a clutch and, with the graduation of Jimmy Harris, the Sooners' offense had but one speed. They would live or die with the running game and pray that the offensive line might finally move those big Yankees out of the way.

Though Dodd and Baker were fine runners, neither could execute the option with the swift efficiency of Harris. Dodd could not make the blind pitch and, in fact, often shoveled the ball from between his legs with two hands. The Irish were tipped off well in advance if he was pitching or keeping.

"Gentlemen, you have won forty-seven straight games," Wilkinson told the players. "But lose today, and people will talk about this one the rest of your lives. I promise you."

Wilkinson's singular hope was that the Notre Dame offense would keep plodding along. Oklahoma's defense had played well in the first half, gang-tackling Pietrosante and shutting him down most of the time. Quarterback Bob Williams certainly wasn't going to beat the Sooners with his rag arm.

Over in the Notre Dame locker room, Terry Brennan was having trouble controlling the Fighting Irish. His players were so anxious to play the second half that they wouldn't sit down for chalk talk. They now chanted, "Beat the Rednecks! Beat the Rednecks!"

Clouds boiling up from Texas were growing darker by the minute. Rain seemed imminent. When sunlight did slash through the low clouds, it was gone in seconds. Sooner fans had been muted in the gathering gloom. Though the game was a scoreless deadlock, it seemed that Oklahoma really trailed. Yet to be introduced to college football was the two-point conversion. If the game happened to end in a 7–7 tie, *the Streak* would die.

The fans snapped back to life when the Sooners bolted from the locker room and shot across the field as the band struck up "Boomer Sooner." Lindsey Nelson was telling the TV audience, "This will be the biggest half of football in the history of Oklahoma football." Wilkinson was telling himself that OU had to score first.

Opportunity knocked again in the third quarter in a strange manner. Notre Dame was backed up to its goal when, on first down, the Irish served up a surprise called the quick kick. The art of the quick kick was to punch it over the defense, hoping the ball might roll an extra twenty, thirty yards. But safety Bobby Boyd saw it coming. Pietrosante took two steps backward to give himself room for the leg swing, and Boyd reacted. He sped into reverse and fielded the kick at the forty and could have easily returned it to the twenty-five, possibly farther. But a flag now lay on the ground back at the line of scrimmage. The Sooners had been drawn offsides by Pietrosante's retreat, and the play was wiped out. The Irish moved the ball another twenty yards before punting, and it rolled dead at the Sooner forty-five. In a game where every yard counted, the loss of thirty yards of field position was devastating.

Early in the fourth quarter, Clendon Thomas punted for the ninth time that day, and it rolled through the end zone. Notre Dame was now eighty yards from the end zone with 13:49 to play, and the odds of an Irish touchdown seemed as remote as a man flying to the moon.

The Irish decided to do it the old-fashioned way. Every play was run between the tackles: Lynch for seven, Lynch for nine, Lynch for one, Pietrosante for seven, Lynch for three, Pietrosante for three, Pietrosante for six, Pietrosante for seven. Soon the Irish were inside Oklahoma territory, and the crowd implored Wilkinson to do *something*. He did. He pulled the starters when the Irish reached the Oklahoma thirty-two. Krisher, who seemed to be wearing roller skates, was rolled backward almost five yards on each play. Notre Dame was dominating the line of scrimmage.

The lone departure from the running game was a jump pass of ten yards from Williams to Joe Royer that moved the Irish to the eighteen. After Pietrosante battled six more yards through the middle, the Irish had a second down at the Oklahoma twelve.

Lynch reached for the hand-off on the next play on the crossbuck and he could see the hole opening like a two-lane highway. His eyes were riveted on the end zone. But Lynch got one step ahead of himself and failed to secure the football. It bounced off his chest and lay on the ground for what seemed an eternity to fans. Sooner linebacker David Rolle hovered over the ball, but Williams was the quicker of the two and smothered it. The Irish were saved.

On third-and-eight from the sixteen, the Sooners didn't see the draw coming. Lynch split the defense for eight yards and a first down. Then Pietrosante broke three tackles for five more yards. Lynch was snuffed at the line of scrimmage on second down, and Williams carried for no gain around right end.

The Irish now faced fourth-and-goal from the three. The roar of the crowd was deafening. Williams knew his teammates couldn't hear the signals over the din and asked the officials for help. The fans responded by cranking the decibel level about ten notches higher.

The Sooners were in an eight-man line and it was the job of each lineman to drive low and stop anything through the middle. Sandefer was the right halfback, Harrison the middle linebacker, and Dodd the left halfback. It was their job to contain any running play to the outside and defend the pass.

As the crowd grew louder and the game was delayed, Sooner players turned and asked for quiet. The fans in the north end zone responded, and Grange told the national TV audience, "That is one of the greatest shows of sportsmanship that I have ever seen."

Williams stepped into the huddle. On the previous play, he had spotted a flaw in the Oklahoma defense. Dodd was cheating to the inside. Instead of lining up outside the end, he was over the tackle and now about a yard deep in the end zone.

"This is it," he told the Irish, then looked at Dick Lynch. "Dick, I want you to haul-ass around end. Keep your eye on the ball. There is no fake. Nick, you lead the convoy. Dick, just get outside, dammit, and I'll get you the ball."

The day had been a strange mixture of wind, low clouds, and flashes of bright sunlight. As the Notre Dame players broke the huddle and trotted to the line, storm clouds settled over the stadium. Fans in the south end zone could barely make out what was happening through the darkness at the other end of the field.

The play Williams had called wasn't in the Notre Dame playbook. On the snap, Lynch tore out around end and Willams heaved the long pitch. Pietrosante brushed end Don Stiller out of the way and rolled Dodd with a cross-body block. But Lynch needed no help. With Dodd almost five yards out of position, Lynch could have walked into the end zone. He ran anyway, his feet sprouting wings.

The Irish players leaped and threw their fists into the air as the stadium grew quiet. The drive had covered eighty yards and consumed nineteen plays and almost ten minutes. After Monty Stickles kicked the extra point with 3:50 remaining, the Irish led 7–0. Pietronsante grabbed the football and ran toward the west stands, pointing to the stunned fans. "This is for all the Catholics of Oklahoma!"

Then the Sooner players spotted a familiar face standing in street clothes next to the Notre Dame bench, celebrating with the Irish players. It was Johnny Lee Foreman, the dirty little spy. Dodd saw Foreman jumping and shouting. Between sobs, Dodd muttered, "I knew that little sonofabitch was up to something no good last week."

With almost four minutes on the clock, Wilkinson's decision was to stick with the game plan and the Split-T offense. Dodd returned the kickoff to the OU thirty-seven, and the Sooners gained a quick seven yards on two rushing plays. But on fourth down, Dodd badly overthrew Joe Rector down the right sideline and the Irish had the ball.

After two running plays, the Irish inexplicably turned to the pass. Two Williams bombs were incomplete in the end zone, and the Sooners took over on downs just sixty yards from the end zone. It was time to gamble.

Sophomore quarterback Bennett Watts, listed on the depth chart as a halfback, had never taken a collegiate snap. But it was Wilkinson's opinion that Watts had the best passing arm on the team. So he entered the game with two new halfbacks, Brewster Hobby and Johnny "the Gnat" Pellow.

Clendon Thomas, who had been replaced, stood on the sideline sporting an expression of disbelief.

"The old man just gave up," he told Sandefer.

Watts pitched to Hobby, who heaved a deep pass well short of Pellow. Then Watts zinged an eleven-yard strike to Pellow, and the Sooners were in Notre Dame territory. A deep pass down the right sideline was aimed for Rector but closer to three Notre Dame defenders, who converged on the ball. It was tipped backward and Pellow snagged it, falling out-of-bounds at the twenty-three. A minute remained, but there was still hope for a tie. Watts now had the hot hand, but Wilkinson decided to give Bill Sturm the final shot. He promptly threw an interception to Williams in the end zone.

The Notre Dame quarterback then took a knee on back-to-back plays, and *the Streak* died a painful death.

As the players trudged off the field, public-address announcer

Jack Ogle said, "Why don't y'all stand up and give these boys a big hand." Not a soul had left the stadium. In unison, 63,134 fans stood and cheered for several minutes. Then they sat down. Nobody moved. Staring straight ahead, they were unable to comprehend what had happened. They prayed the players would come back to finish the game. Not an ignition key was turned. Not a word was uttered. The wind died and the day drew still and it began to rain.

As he walked to the locker room, Gomer Jones learned that the Sooners had been possibly infiltrated by a spy. He passed the information along to Wilkinson, who responded with his typical shrug. Wilkinson rarely belabored such matters, especially during the season. An investigation would merely act as a distraction for the Sooners as they prepared for their next game. Besides, Wilkinson believed that the Sooners had been outsmarted, outgunned, and outplayed by the Notre Dame Fighting Irish.

In the locker room, Wilkinson looked into their eyes. Carl Dodd sat with his head stuck between his knees, and he bawled like a newborn calf. Wilkinson walked over and put his right hand on the boy's shoulder pads. But he could think of nothing to say.

The Great White Father walked to the middle of the room that was funeral silent. He removed his hat and stared at the floor for several seconds. Then he raised his head and said, "Men, the only people who never lose are the ones who never play the game." He composed himself and continued. "You men were very much a part of this winning streak. Always remember that. It ended here. But that is nothing to be ashamed of."

Then he turned and walked through the door and into the cold Oklahoma rain.

Players sobbed as they stood in the shower, the warm water pouring over aching bodies. "Look, guys," Bill Krisher loudly said. "You can't win them all."

Jerry Thompson was almost six inches shorter than Krisher but built like a bull, with a thick neck and wide chest. The punch he threw caught Krisher on the right jaw, knocking him flat on the wet floor.

"In Oklahoma, we want to win them *all*," Thompson said as his teammates tried to restrain him.

Later, as the players sauntered back to the Jeff House, in need of a hot meal and a cold beer, they witnessed a scene that actually inspired laughter. An intoxicated priest had turned over a forty-five-gallon trash can and was now dancing on it while singing the Notre Dame fight song. Naturally, a crowd had gathered.

Down in Dallas, a young linebacker for the Arkansas Razorbacks slid into his seat on his team's chartered airplane and dug into the *Sports Illustrated* story about the Sooners. Arkansas had lost 27–22 that afternoon to SMU at the Cotton Bowl. A raspy voice came over the loudspeaker as the players settled into their seats. "Guys," the captain said, "you are not going to believe this. Notre Dame seven. Oklahoma nothing." Barry Switzer dropped the magazine.

The forty-seven-game winning streak had consumed the better part of five seasons and lasted 1,491 days. It was doubtful that another major college team would ever break that record.

Thirty minutes passed before the Memorial Stadium stands began to clear, and the dark streets of Norman were soon filled with the brokenhearted. Oklahomans had survived the drought, the Depression, floods, tornadoes, black blizzards, and John Steinbeck. They had freed themselves from the tentacles of poverty and destitution. No place in America had produced a more resilient people. Thanks to the revival of OU football, pride had always been the victor on the fall afternoons at Owen Field when the Sooners played. No other state could claim a greater love for its football team. The winning streak was dead, but the people's spirit would live on.

Oklahoma was like no other place in the world. In many cases, folks with the fastest horses had gained the best land. More than a million citizens migrated from the state in the 1930s. Oil slowly boosted the economy. The musical *Oklahoma!* inspired nationwide respect. Bud Wilkinson and the Oklahoma Sooners restored the swagger. And on this day, November 16, 1957, the state celebrated its fiftieth birthday.

The drought and the Dust Bowl had motivated the Oklahoma regents, for the sake of morale, to rebuild the football program. They hired Wilkinson as their savior. He, in turn, brought rain to the dusty frontier. Now, as he strode through that rain for the first time on a Sooner game day, the circle had become complete.

The man in the gray flannel suit began the long trek home by himself. Down Lindsey Street, on a street corner not far from the stadium, students began to gather outside of the Lambda Chi house. More than a hundred stood there when the bus filled with the rowdy Irish stopped at the intersection. Notre Dame players poked their heads through the open windows and yelled, "Happy Homecoming, y'all!" and "Catholics are god!" They saluted with the single finger, and Nick Pietrosante bellowed, "So long, rednecks!"

Head down, hat pulled down low against the rain, Wilkinson walked along the sidewalk past the Lambda Chi house moments later. The students began to clap and cheer. Wilkinson never looked up, never heard their voices. He had traveled above the storm, his mind now focused on the Nebraska Cornhuskers, up next on the Oklahoma schedule.

20

BEYOND THE STREAK

October 14, 1958

After the heartbreaking defeat to Notre Dame, the Sooners reeled off five straight victories, including an impressive 48–21 win over Duke in the January 1, 1958, Orange Bowl.

Oklahoma would have been vying for its fifty-fourth straight victory against Texas in early October of '58 if not for the huge upset from the previous season. When Texas and Oklahoma played, though, no hype was necessary. Fans of both teams were bred and born to hate each other, and this would be the biggest game on the schedule regardless of the stakes.

The Sooners had won the last six games against Texas, and now the betting bankroll was a little lean on the south side of the Red River. But Texans had reasons to dig deeper. Darrell Royal, in his second season as the head coach, had rescued the once-proud program from the dregs of the Southwest Conference, compiling a 3–0 record and pushing the 'Horns to the brink of the Top Twenty once more.

Though Notre Dame had stolen their thunder, the Sooners were the same efficient team that had roared through college football for the last dozen years, since Wilkinson arrived in Norman. Overall, the '58 team might have been better than the one that finished the previous season with a 10–1 record. Bobby Boyd had gained his footing as the starting quarterback, and Wilkinson was pleased with his progress. Wilkinson's only wish was that Bobby would give Prentice Gautt the ball a little more often. The captains for the '58 teams were Hog Harrison and Joe Rector.

It was a gray, breezy day at the Cotton Bowl with 75,504 fans wearing either crimson or burnt orange, still recovering from the Big Party the previous night down on Commerce Street.

Wilkinson didn't need to study films to know that the pendulum had already begun to swing at Texas. The Longhorns were destined to share the SWC championship that season with Arkansas and TCU. Royal was one of the most ambitious men Wilkinson had ever met and reminded Bud of himself. No longer would the Texas game represent an automatic win on the Sooners' schedule.

The National Rules Committee, of which Wilkinson was a member, had legalized the two-point conversion the previous off-season. Though Royal objected to the rule, he quickly embraced it after 'Horn halfback Rene Ramirez threw a touchdown pass to George Blanch in the first quarter. Fullback Don Allen dived off right guard for the two-pointer, and Texas led 8–0.

In the third quarter, Boyd tossed a touchdown pass to halfback Dickie Carpenter, but the Sooners failed on the two-point try and trailed 8–6.

Texas had the ball at their twenty-four in the fourth quarter when OU nose tackle Jerry Thompson blew through the line and nailed fullback Mike Dowdle as he was taking the hand-off. The ball squirted straight up and OU tackle Jim Davis caught it, lumbering twenty yards into the end zone. Boyd passed to Jerry Tillery for the two-point conversion and the Sooners led 14–8 with less than seven minutes to play.

The seventy-five-yard drive that ensued was to foreshadow the brilliant play of the Longhorns during the Royal era. Texas tore through the Sooners in thirteen plays, scoring the tying touchdown on a quick pass from quarterback Bobby Lackey to Bob Bryant with three minutes to play. Lackey kicked the extra point and Royal had his greatest win to date, 15–14.

Oklahoma president Dr. George L. Cross trekked to the 'Horns' locker room after the game to congratulate Royal, the Sooners' All-American quarterback and punter in 1949. But Cross couldn't find him among the revelers. So he stepped out back and found the coach throwing up on the sidewalk.

Bending over, Royal saw two feet approaching. He raised up and said, "Dr. Cross, it's sure hard on your stomach and your nerves beating your lifelong hero."

September 21, 1959

Since the first week of the 1953 season, the Oklahoma Sooners had lost but two games by a total of eight points, winning fifty-nine of their last sixty-one. They now seemed poised for yet another national championship run in spite of the graduation of several great players, including All-American center Hog Harrison. A major reason for Wilkinson's unmatched success in the '50 was the lineage of All-American centers—Tom Catlin, Kurt Burris, Jerry Tubbs, and Harrison.

A major change in conference rules permitted the Sooners to participate in their second straight Orange Bowl, and they whipped the Syracuse Orangemen 21–6. The Most Valuable Player was Prentice Gautt, who became the first Negro player to score a touchdown in the Orange Bowl, dashing forty-two yards down the left sideline, taking advantage of a thundering cross-body block from end Joe Rector at the goal. Quarterback Bob Cornell, after being promoted late from third string to starter, also received kudos for his Orange Bowl performance.

Now on tap for the start the '59 season was an intriguing matchup—

up-and-coming Northwestern, led by coach Ara Parseghian, against the decade's best college football team. Though the Wildcats had defeated Ohio State and Michigan the previous season, the Sooners, ranked number five in the preseason polls, were an early fourteen-point favorite. Northwestern was not yet in Oklahoma's class, though the Wildcats boasted two All-Americans, running back Ron Burton and center James Andreotti. Just two seasons earlier, the Wildcats had failed to win a game, inspiring suggestions that Northwestern should drop big-time football and depart the Big Ten.

The Sooners normally arrived for out-of-town games on Friday, but for this game they arrived in Chicago Thursday morning, two days before the contest, and were bused straight to Evanston for an afternoon workout.

After the practice, the players showered, dressed, and were bused back to downtown Chicago for a special night at the Chez Paree, an exclusive dinner theater that attracted popular entertainers, along with celebrities and monied people from all over the country. It was also famous for drawing members of the Mafia, and, at the time, Sam Giancana was at the height of power in the Chicago mob.

Oddly, members of the regular OU coaching staff were absent, along with a few others, including Prentice Gautt, who felt certain he would not be served. But most of the players were in attendance. Graduate assistant coach Jimmy Harris, who had taken a year off from the NFL to complete his geology degree, made the trip.

As they were seated, a young, attractive woman made her way around the tables, asking the name and the position of each player, taking down notes. Minutes later, the players were served onion soup, and it wasn't long before several of the Sooners were dashing to the rest room. They crowded into stalls or vomited into the sinks. The floor was soon coated with fluid an inch thick.

As their stomachs settled, many of the players hurried outside to hail taxicabs back to the hotel. But most of them went straight to

Louise Weiss Memorial Hospital in Evanston. Bobby Boyd was so ill that he lay prostrate on the ground outside of the Chez Paree. As they waited for taxis, several of the players stood in the grassy median and heaved. Halfback Jimmy Carpenter was so ill that he leaned out of the taxicab and threw up and might have fallen head-first into the street if teammate Brewster Hobby had not taken ahold of the back of his belt.

Backup quarterback Bob Page suffered a circulatory collapse at the hospital and went into shock. Several of the players had their stomachs pumped.

Meanwhile, back at the team hotel, Bud Wilkinson received an anonymous call in his room.

"Has there been a train or a bus wreck?" the caller asked.

"No. Why?"

"Because the betting line's dropping like a rock. I figured half your team got killed."

Harold Keith, the sports information director, received a similar phone call from Fred Russell, the sports editor of the *Nashville Banner,* who also wrote a college football preview for the *Saturday Evening Post.* Russell's newspaper ran the point spread in the Friday editions. A local bookmaker supplied the information, and he called back Thursday evening to report that the Oklahoma line was dramatically dropping. By the time the Sooners were transported to the hospital, the point spread had plummeted from fourteen points to seven, and it would continue to fall until kickoff.

All but Page were released from the hospital Friday morning and, as might be expected, the pregame practice was a total washout. Wilkinson was informed about the radical shift in the betting line and that gamblers might have organized the food poisoning but typically refused to make an issue of it.

The FBI contacted Wilkinson Friday evening and began to interview several of the people who had dined at Chez Paree, including

Harris. Each of the infected players turned out to be either a first stringer or a member of the alternates, and most were running backs or quarterbacks. There was a clear attempt to afflict the Sooners who might have the greatest impact on Saturday's game. The FBI informed the Sooners that the onion soup had been spiced with a flavored morphine.

"They intended to make you guys sick," the agent told Harris. "But I doubt they intended to make you that sick at first. They might have put too much morphine in the soup."

Saturday, the Sooners were whipped even before kickoff.

"I feel like I got a bad case of the flu," Hobby told Wilkinson. Boyd barely had the strength to pull on his uniform. Several players had lost more than ten pounds and were less than half-strength.

On a warm and humid afternoon at Dyche Stadium, the Sooners fumbled twelve times and lost five, allowing Northwestern to launch drives from the OU eight, nine, twenty-three, and thirty-seven. Watching the game from the press box, Harris turned to assistant coach Eddie Crowder and said, "That's not the same team we brought to Chicago. Hell, they're moving in slow motion." A driving rainstorm in the second half didn't help matters as the Split-T offense bogged down, and the Sooners lost 45–13.

In the ensuing weeks, the Chicago Police Department showed little interest in the case. On the night of the poisoning, seven Sooners, along with Harris, had had their stomachs pumped. The FBI asked that those samples be released by the hospital for use in their investigation. But those samples mysteriously disappeared.

Two weeks later in Los Angeles, Occidental College canceled a game when their players displayed signs of food poisoning the night before.

Wilkinson, in spite of being given several chances, never blamed the loss on the food poisoning. Naturally, this was the question on everyone's lips: Was Northwestern really four touchdowns better than the Sooners? The Wildcats finished the season with a 6–3 record and out of the Top Twenty. Oklahoma crushed Colorado a week after the Chicago trip 42–12 and finished with a 7–3 record. By the end of the season, they were ranked number fifteen in the wire service polls. According to the results of an entire season, it appeared that OU had the superior team.

January 11, 1964

"Why should I become a head coach?" Gomer Jones asked Wilkinson. "I already got an ulcer."

The question was posed the day that Wilkinson decided to step down as the head coach of the Oklahoma Sooners. Several factors had entered into Bud's decision. For one, he had tired of recruiting. He was spending more and more time playing golf, socializing, and traveling with Clyde Davis, the head of the Halliburton Air Force.

Thanks to another round of NCAA probation in 1960, the Sooners were no longer a national power. Wilkinson had suffered through his first and only losing season in '60, going 3–6–1, and the Sooners finished 5–5 the following season. Some speculated that Wilkinson lost control of the team in the late fifties when he failed to crack down on the likes of Wahoo McDaniel. Then more trouble arrived on the OU campus in the form of one Joe Don Looney.

Looney was an All-American in '62 and one of the most gifted athletes ever to play for the Sooners, but in real life he was a walking contradiction. He detested authority and often missed practice. Wilkinson dismissed him after the '63 Texas game, a resounding 28–7 loss to the 'Horns en route to their first national championship under Darrell Royal.

Oklahoma had a respectable 8–2 record in '63 and entered the Texas game in early October as the number-one team in the land.

But it turned out to be a season of sadness for Wilkinson. Six weeks after the Texas loss, the Sooners were in Lincoln, Nebraska, on November 22 when they returned to the hotel following a pregame workout to learn that John F. Kennedy had been assassinated. For three years, Wilkinson had led the President's Council on Youth Fitness and, in spite of his political differences with Kennedy, held a great fondness for the man.

Naturally, Wilkinson wanted to see the Nebraska game either postponed or canceled. It was played against his wishes, and friends believed this was the final push toward the exit. The Sooners lost 29–20.

But the largest contributing factor to Wilkinson's retirement from coaching was the death of Sen. Robert S. Kerr on January 1, 1963. The U.S. Senate seat was vacant and there would be a special election in '64. The Great White Father was ready to run.

He resigned the coaching position on January 11, 1964, but held onto the title of athletic director, believing it might hasten the promotion of Gomer Jones to head coach. It did not. In fact, it was reported in the *Daily Oklahoman* that some of the regents were "fed up" with Wilkinson's political maneuvering and vacillation in spite of the fact that he had compiled a record of 139-27-4 and a winning percentage of 84 percent.

So Wilkinson called a press conference a week later to announce his resignation and spent most of the time eschewing the coaching virtues of Jones. He practically demanded that Gomer be named head coach. The board, in spite of serious reservations, relented and named Jones the head coach and athletic director a few days later.

In truth, Jones wanted to be the athletic director but not head coach. He thought the job was merely another ulcer waiting to happen. The board of regents, however, flatly stated that he could not have one without the other. Over the next two seasons, he would tell his assistant coaches on numerous occasions, "I don't want to be the head coach. I never wanted to be the head coach in the first place." It showed. In two years, he compiled a 9-11-1 record. The final blow was delivered in the '65 season finale, a 17–16 loss to hated Oklahoma State, formerly known as Oklahoma A&M. Gomer was fired as coach the next day but managed to hold onto the title of athletic director.

November 3, 1964

Wilkinson and campaign coordinator Dick Snider stood in the kitchen of Bud's house in Norman that morning, sipping milk punches, a mixture of scotch and milk. The roof had collapsed the previous night as Wilkinson lost the U.S. Senate race by some twenty-one thousand votes to Fred Harris. It was a defeat that Wilkinson didn't see coming in spite of the clear warnings.

As they consumed one milk punch after another, Snider tried to convince Wilkinson not to give up on politics. Harris, after all, would hold the temporary seat for two years, and there would be another election in the fall of 1966. But the former coach was having nothing to do with this pep talk.

"They had their chance to elect me and now it is time to move on," he said.

Wilkinson's campaign mistakes were extensive. He shifted party allegiances from Democrat to Republican in a state that supported Democrats like no other. He never hired a "campaign manager," preferring that he and Snider run the operation like a two-headed monster. He changed his official name from Charles Burnham to Bud Wilkinson, which turned off some voters. He spent too much time at the country clubs and inside bank boardrooms and not enough time at diners and truck stops with the common people.

Whenever Snider, or anyone else for that matter, mentioned that the election was slipping away, Wilkinson would say, "Oh ye of little faith. When they see my name on the ballot, they will vote for me."

On the morning after the election, Wilkinson was emotionally crushed. He had given Oklahomans the best football years of their life. He expected the favor to be returned. Instead, he felt like packing up and leaving the state.

September 4, 1978

For the first time in fifteen years, Wilkinson paced the sideline of a football game. It was a warm and windy day in Chicago, and he stood on the edge of Soldier Field, quite a distance from the heartland of Oklahoma. The new coach of the St. Louis Cardinals was wearing his lucky red tie.

Wilkinson's decision to reenter coaching had shocked the sports world and raised eyebrows. It seemed that everyone doubted him. On the day he was hired, columnist Tom Barnidge wrote in the *St. Louis Post-Dispatch:* "Insanity Prevails!"

Months earlier, Wilkinson had predicted to a St. Louis booster club that the Cardinals would win the Super Bowl that season, a bold remark met with resounding laughter. The Cardinals had never won a postseason game dating to their days as the Chicago Cardinals of the 1940s.

Reasons abounded for Bud's Brigadoon-like reappearance. An insurance venture had turned sour when the IRS failed to rule in his favor for additional government supplemental pension programs. So, for the moment, he had time on his hands.

Two years earlier, he had divorced Mary Wilkinson, his wife of thirty-seven years, in order to marry a woman thirty-three years his junior. Bud was sixty-one and Donna O'Donnohue twenty-eight on the day they married in 1977. They had met in East Lansing, Michigan, when Wilkinson was still broadcasting college football games. He had launched a successful career as a football analyst with ABC not long after his coaching career ended in 1964.

Former Michigan State coach Duffy Daugherty, a longtime friend and business associate of Wilkinson, had introduced the couple. A year later, when he informed Daugherty of his intentions to divorce Mary and marry Donna, the big, red-faced coach blustered, "Have you lost your frigging mind?"

A similar sentiment existed back in Oklahoma City when Bud and his new bride moved into an apartment not far from his old neighborhood. Close friends refused to socialize with them. Clyde Davis, once his best friend, turned his back on Wilkinson.

So the offer from St. Louis owner Billy Bidwill in March of 1978 provided a fresh start in a new town. Wilkinson jumped at the opportunity, not knowing that Bidwill was a lonely and eccentric man who inspired little admiration from anyone in the NFL. The Cardinals were in a familiar downward spiral.

St. Louis opened the '78 season with a 17–10 loss to Chicago and proceeded to go 0–8. The Cardinals did win six games in the second half of the season and finished with a 6–10 record, but Wilkinson was fighting with a short stick. He failed to create a rapport with the players or the front office. The NFL with its intricate passing strategies was a far cry from the Split-T offense. Then, in summer preseason camp of '79, the Cardinals were dealt an emotional blow when tight end J. V. Cain collapsed and died on the practice field.

The '79 season quickly fell apart after a heartbreaking 22–21 loss to the Cowboys on opening day, and the Cardinals were 3–10 when Bidwill dropped the ax in late November. The man who had won 84 percent of his games at Oklahoma and had compiled a forty-seven-game winning streak walked away from the NFL with a 9–20 record.

September 15, 1986

No one could blame Barry Switzer for feeling overconfident. The Sooners had won their third national title under his tutelage, and their sixth overall, the previous season.

During a team meeting, the OU coach turned off the lights and said, "Men, we are going to watch a little film. But you won't recognize these guys."

The coach fired up a reel of the 1956 Sooners.

"I want you guys to see just how slow these guys were back in the fifties," he said.

Not a word was spoken as they watched the old Sooners in total awe. Switzer turned toward the projector and said, "That thing must be running fast. Those guys couldn't possibly be that *fast.*"

They were.

September 13, 1991

The man *The New York Times* called "the most handsome in college football," a man whose greatest fear was the aging process, suffered congestive heart failure in 1986. By the time he reached the lectern in Oklahoma City for his final testimonial dinner, the face was distorted and the eyes dimmer.

More than five hundred Oklahomans came to worship him one last time. His former coaches and players extolled his greatness. Curt Gowdy served as the master of ceremonies, and among the guest speakers were Jim Simpson and Chris Schenkel, his former TV cronies.

Billy Vessels remembered winning the Heisman Trophy in '52 in spite of being a poor boy from Cleveland, Oklahoma. He turned toward Wilkinson with microphone in hand and said, "Coach, I remember we were on our way to New York City and I had never made a speech before. And my teammates will tell you that I was not an English major. We were flying over a snowstorm in Indiana and I said, 'Coach Wilkinson, I have never made a speech and I am scared.' He said, 'Billy, I'm going to give you a very simple solution to that. As long as you believe in what you are saying, the audience will not care about your delivery.' Coach Wilkinson, that message has stayed with me all of my life. Thank you for being my friend."

Prentice Gautt, who broke the color barrier at Oklahoma in 1957, delivered one of the most touching tributes.

"Coach Wilkinson, we sure went through some tough times together," he said. "Let me say that you were responsible for opening the door and letting me be a part of the Oklahoma football legacy. Coach, you didn't need me. You didn't need the negative letters and the hate mail. Many people said that allowing me to play football at the University of Oklahoma was the beginning of the downfall. But you opened a lot of doors by doing so. I thank you. From the bottom of my heart, I thank you."

Wilkinson smiled and seemed to drink in the adulation as he stepped to the lectern. But he barely resembled the man they had come to love and respect. A large portrait of him from the fifties hung directly behind the dais. His face now juxtaposed against that smiling and vibrant expression drove home the reality of four decades gone by.

Naturally, Wilkinson delivered *the* message that had once transformed the Sooners into greatness. It was the message his former players desperately wanted to hear one last time. It is called "The Will to Prepare":

"The will to prepare is the juncture of where it all happens. It is about the player who can get out of bed at six-fifteen in the morning when he is sore and he is stiff and he does not want to practice. But he goes to practice. And he gears up and does his best totally in every drill of that practice. The will to prepare is what develops the discipline and the know-how that transforms itself on game day into the will to win. More importantly, preparation engenders the confidence that enables the will to win."

On February 9, 1994, Bud Wilkinson took his last breath, dead at the age of seventy-seven. His wife, Donna, and son Jay were at his side.

On Valentine's Day, Darrell Royal stood before a packed congregation at the Christ Church Cathedral in St. Louis and could barely speak or look at the casket as he delivered the eulogy.

Among the hundreds in attendance were several of Wilkinson's former OU players. The pallbearers included Eddie Crowder, Billy Vessels, Prentice Gautt, and Pete Elliott, a former assistant coach.

Royal cleared his throat and tried to temper his emotions. "Coach Wilkinson, one thing I think I never told you is that you were like a father to me. But I think you were like a father to all the boys."

Royal had to steady himself before he could continue.

"Coach, on this day I consider myself doubly lucky. I don't know if I ever told you this. But I used a lot of your ideas over the years. I probably used them in my own personality so you wouldn't recognize them. But those ideas were yours. A lot of the players I coached have gone on to coach. And many times, they thought they were carrying out my ideas. Actually, they came from you, Coach Wilkinson."

The legacy lives on.

Jimmy Harris was passed over for All-American honors in spite of his undefeated record at Oklahoma for the three straight seasons in the mid-fifties. But in 1990, thirty-four years after his final game at OU, *Sports Illustrated* released its top fifty college quarterbacks of all time. Harris weighed in at number eleven. Not bad considering that Dan Marino was number thirty, Joe Montana thirty-one, John Elway thirty-three, and Roger Staubach thirty-seven. Steve Young occupied the number one ranking.

In a personal letter to Harris in 1987, Bud Wilkinson wrote, "The contributions that you made to our team were unsurpassed. When interviewed, I always try to avoid the question, 'Who is the best player you coached?' If the reporter persists, I always say someone you have not heard too much about. He played both ways. He started thirty-three games. We won all thirty-three. The man is Jim Harris."

Harris played four seasons as a defensive back with the Philadelphia Eagles, Los Angeles Rams and Dallas Cowboys. He became a petroleum geologist in the early 1960s and has been drilling all over the South and Southwest the last forty years. In one stretch, he hit thirty straight oil wells in northern Louisiana. The president of Midrock Oil Exploration, his offices are in Shreveport. He has no plans of retirement and said, "The competitive strain will not go away."

Jerry Tubbs was one of two original members of the Dallas Cowboys to span twenty-nine seasons with the club. The other was Tom Landry. Tubbs was the Cowboys original middle linebacker, playing for eight seasons and serving as a player-coach in 1966 and '67. During ten seasons as a player, Tubbs was considered one of the hardest hitters in the NFL. He became a full-time coach in '68 and tutored four All-Pro linebackers—Lee Roy Jordan, Bob Breunig, Chuck Howley and Thomas Henderson. He coached in five Super Bowls, winning two rings.

Before the Cowboys, Tubbs played briefly for the Chicago Cardinals, who made him their number one draft choice in '57, and San Francisco 49ers. He was inducted into the College Football Hall of Fame in 1996. Now in retirement from football, Tubbs spends each day working a large ranch near McKinney, Texas, where he tends to 180 head of cattle.

Clendon Thomas played eleven years in the National Football League as a defensive back with the Rams and Steelers. He made the Pro Bowl once. One of the biggest defensive backs in the league, he was shifted to defensive end for a game against the Browns in 1963. Thomas moved back to Oklahoma City in 1970s and started Chemical Product Corporation that was sold two years ago.

Tommy McDonald was a six-time Pro Bowl selection, playing seven seasons with the Eagles, one with the Cowboys, two with the Los Angeles Rams and one each with the Atlanta Falcons and the Cleveland Browns. He was known for never wearing a facemask. During a four-year stretch with the Eagles (1958–62) he caught fifty-six touchdown passes in sixty-three games, including the game-winner from Norm Van Brocklin in the 1960 championship game against the Green Bay Packers. The Eagles won 17–13.

On being inducted into the Pro Football Hall of Fame in 1998, he danced on the steps of the Canton shrine. McDonald recently retired from McDonald Enterprise, which produced sports oil paintings and photos. He lives in King of Prussia, Pennsylvania.

Dr. Prentice Gautt, after leading the Sooners in rushing in 1958 and '59, spent eight seasons as a running back with the St. Louis Cardinals. He served one year as an assistant coach with the Missouri Tigers before becoming a counselor in the athletic department. In 1968, he decided to pursue his doctorate in psychology.

"There was so much that I wanted to analyze about my life that psychology seemed the natural place to be," he said. On April 1, 1979, he became an assistant commissioner of the Big Eight Conference and currently serves as an associate commissioner of the Big Twelve, working from his office in Lawrence, Kansas. In 1998, the athletic academic center at OU was renamed the Prentice Gautt Academic Center in his honor.

Billy Pricer, another OU player who never lost a game, played in what is still considered the greatest NFL game—the 1958 championship game between Baltimore and New York, won by the Colts in overtime on a touchdown by Alan Ameche. The Colts were 33–17 during Pricer's tenure. He was forced to retire in 1961 due to a damaged knee. He died of diabetes not along after the fortieth reunion of the Colts-Giants game in 1998.

Happy-go-lucky Edmon Gray was the first member of the 47-game winning club to die in 1976. He was working in the oil business in Odessa, Texas, en route to work one morning, when his sports car was broadsided by a tanker truck. He played in the CFL for three years after graduating from OU.

Billy Vessels was through with professional football by the age of twenty-six, having played two seasons for Edmonton of the CFL and one with the Baltimore Colts. He was bothered by a knee injury and failed to see eye-to-eye with Colts coach Weeb Ewbank, who moved him to defense full-time. But he never regretted his decision to leave football, and rarely played on his name recognition, even after he was inducted into the College Football Hall of Fame in 1974.

For more than three decades, Vessels was the chief assistant to Robert Mackle, the president of Deltona Corporation, a huge real estate development firm in South Florida. He became close to the rich and the famous. Two days before John F. Kennedy was assassinated, he rode on Air Force One with the President, a close friend.

In 1968, Vessels negotiated the release of Mackle's kidnapped daughter, Barbara Mackle, when she was buried alive for eighty-three hours in Georgia. He was responsible for delivering the ransom money that saved the girl. A book and a movie entitled "Eighty-Three Hours Until Dawn" later depicted the event.

Kurt Burris was a number one draft choice of the Cleveland Browns in 1956, but never reached contract terms with Paul Brown. He played five seasons for three different teams in the Canadian Football League. While playing for the Edmonton Eskimos, he launched a career in oil exploration that would last the rest of his life. He later opened Burris Drilling in Denver. He was working in his garage at home in Billings, Montana, in the summer of 1999 when he collapsed and died of a heart attack. He was inducted into the College Football Hall of Fame in December of 2000, his brother, Bob, accepting on his behalf.

Bob Burris launched a coaching career soon after his graduation from Oklahoma at Northeastern University. He also coached three seasons at Oklahoma State. He coached high school football for sixteen years in Oklahoma and Texas. His Oklahoma stops included Paul's Valley and Ardmore, and he coached south of the Red River at Midland Lee, Port Arthur Jefferson, and Big Spring. He continues to work in the drilling fluids business in Oklahoma City.

Buddy Burris played guard and tackle for the Green Bay Packers from 1949 through the '54 season. He worked for several years in the oilfield for Dowell Well Chemical as a field engineer and later in the Tinker Air Force procurement office. He is retired and living in Norman, but often has to dodge some barbs. As a predictor for the *Daily Oklahoman*, he picked Florida State to beat Oklahoma in the 2001 Orange Bowl.

Max Boydston was the number one draft choice of the Chicago Cardinals in 1955 and played four seasons in the Windy City. He played a total of twelve pro seasons, including stints with the Oakland Raiders, Dallas Texans, and the Canadian Football League. He also scouted for the Texans. As a high school football coach in Texas, he made stops at Sherman, Grapevine, and R. L. Turner in Carrollton. He died in 1997 of a heart ailment. The O Varsity Club at the University of Oklahoma sponsors a scholarship in his name.

John Herman Bell was lucky that he had a brother-in-law like Max Boydston when he started looking for work in Texas shortly after his football career ended at Oklahoma. Boydston introduced him to several coaches and Bell landed a job at Smiley High School, north of Houston. Three years later, he started working part-time as a salesman for a custom homes builder and it wasn't long before he became a sales manager and one of the area's leading producers. Bell retired from Green Homes in 1997, but soon became bored. He now works for Home Depot in the kitchen and bath department and estimates that he walks tens miles a day. He and Shirley Boydston Bell live in The Woodlands.

Port Robertson retired from the university in 1971 and it literally took eight men to replace him. He continues to attend OU social functions and all of the home games. At age eighty-four, he can still remember the full name of each of his former players. He can also recite without notes the number of stadium steps they still owe him. The ex-players still hold a deep affection for the former czar of discipline.

Jakie Sandefer, like his father, plunged headfirst into the oil business from the day he graduated from Oklahoma in 1959. He was a stripper operator in both Breckenridge and Abilene. He moved to Houston in 1980 and invested more than $500 million from 1981 to '91 in the drilling of both oil and gas before selling the company. He is semi-retired and living in Houston, but still dabbles in the oil business, along with following the Sooners and playing golf in Palm Springs.

Gene Calame worked for forty years for Globe Life and Accident Insurance Company in Oklahoma City and held the title of executive vice president, secretary, and general counsel. He retired in

1999. Today he is a tennis nut and a rosarian. He grows more than sixty different kinds of roses in his backyard.

Carl Dodd is an owner, breeder, and trainer of horses on his ranch in Milsap, Texas, about thirty miles west of Fort Worth. The highlight of his career was winning the All-American futurity, the most prestigious race for quarter horses, with Mito Rise in 1971. He continues to train and run horses at racetracks all over Texas. One of his most recent successes has been Uturn Laverne, a thoroughbred mare.

Gomer Jones was fired after two seasons as the Sooners head coach, but held onto the title of athletic director until he died in New York in 1971 while riding a subway to Madison Square Garden for the NIT basketball tournament.

Billy Carr Harris graduated from Oklahoma Law School in 1961 and has been practicing general civil law in Shawnee for the last forty years.

Johnny "the Gnat" Pellow has been a physical therapist in Oklahoma City since 1961. Among some of his more celebrated clients are Dick Butkus and Joe Namath. He has no plans to retire.

Charlie Rountree, the party animal, took a knee from drinking at age forty. He has been in the life insurance business since 1961, and also works in long-term care coverage. He is one of the country's leading authorities on World War II in Europe and participated in the promotion of the national D Day Memorial that was dedicated on June 6, 2001, in Bedford, Virginia. His mother, Kitty Rountree, died in 1974, and Doc Rountree passed on in 1982. In the sixties, Kitty became the first female president of the OU alumni association.

BIBLIOGRAPHY

Banks, Jimmy. *The Darrell Royal Story.* Shoal Creek, 1973.

Clark, Brent. *Sooner Century.* Quality Sports Publications, 1995.

Cross, Dr. George L. *Presidents Can't Punt.* University of Oklahoma Press, 1977.

Delsohn, Steve. *Talking Irish.* Avon, 1998.

Faulk, Odie and Laurie. *The Life of Lloyd Noble.* Oklahoma Heritage Association, 1995.

Gibson, Arrell M. *The Oklahoma Story.* University of Oklahoma Press, 1978.

Greene, A. C., and Jake Sandefer. *It's Been Fun.* Hardin-Simmons, 1986.

Halberstam, David. *The Fifties.* Villard, 1993.

Hamons, Lucille. *Mother of the Mother Roads.* 1998.

Harris, Jack. *A Passion for Victory.* Taylor, 1990.

Jones, Mike. *Dance with Who Brung Ya.* Masters Press, 1998.

Keith, Harold. *Forty-seven Straight.* University of Oklahoma Press, 1984.

King, Gary T. *An Autumn Remembered.* Red Earth, 1986.

Luper, Clara. *Behold the Walls.* Jim Wire, 1979.

McCallum, John D. *Big Eight Football.* Charles Scribner's Sons, 1979.

Morgan, Anne Hodges. *Robert Kerr: The Senate Years.* University of Oklahoma Press, 1977.

Morgan, Anne and H. Wayne. *New Views of the Forty-sixth State.* University of Oklahoma Press, 1982.

Steinbeck, John. *The Grapes of Wrath.* Viking, 1939.

Teague, Tom. *Searching for 66.* Samizdat House, 1991.

Weeks, Jim. *The Sooners.* Strode, 1978.

Wilk, Max. *The Story of Oklahoma!* Grove, 1993.

Wilkinson, Jay. *Bud Wilkinson: An Intimate Portrait of an American Legend.* Sagamore, 1992.

Worster, Donald. *Dust Bowl.* Oxford University Press, 1979.